THE
# PURSUIT
### OF HOLINESS

The *Pursuit of Holiness*
# BIBLE STUDY

THE
# PRACTICE
### OF GODLINESS

## Jerry Bridges

## NAVPRESS

Bringing Truth to Life
P.O. Box 35001, Colorado Springs, Colorado 80935

## OUR GUARANTEE TO YOU

We believe so strongly in the message of our books that
we are making this quality guarantee to you. If for any reason you are disappointed with the content of this book,
return the title page to us with your name and address and
we will refund to you the list price of the book. To help us
serve you better, please briefly describe why you were disappointed. Mail your refund request to: NavPress, P.O.
Box 35002, Colorado Springs, CO 80935.

The Navigators is an international Christian organization. Our mission is to reach, disciple, and equip people to know Christ and to make Him known through successive
generations. We envision multitudes of diverse people in the United States and every
other nation who have a passionate love for Christ, live a lifestyle of sharing Christ's
love, and multiply spiritual laborers among those without Christ.

NavPress is the publishing ministry of The Navigators. NavPress publications help
believers learn biblical truth and apply what they learn to their lives and ministries.
Our mission is to stimulate spiritual formation among our readers.

Some of the anecdotal illustrations in this book are true to life and are included with
the permission of the persons involved. All other illustrations are composites of real
situations, and any resemblance to people living or dead is coincidental.

*The Pursuit of Holiness:* Unless otherwise identified, all Scripture quotations in this
publication are taken from the *HOLY BIBLE: NEW INTERNATIONAL VERSION®* (NIV®).
Copyright © 1973, 1978, 1984 by International Bible Society. Used by permission of
Zondervan Publishing House. All rights reserved. Other versions include: the *New
American Standard Bible* (NASB), © The Lockman Foundation 1960, 1962, 1963, 1968,
1971, 1972, 1973, 1975, 1977; *The New Testament in Modern English* (PH), J. B.
Phillips Translator, © J. B. Phillips 1958, 1960, 1972, used by permission of Macmillan
Publishing Company; and the *King James Version* (KJV).

*The Practice of Godliness:* Unless otherwise identified, all Scripture quotations in this
publication are taken from the *HOLY BIBLE: NEW INTERNATIONAL VERSION®* (NIV®).
Copyright © 1973, 1978, 1984 by International Bible Society. Used by permission of
Zondervan Publishing House. All rights reserved. Other versions include: the *New
American Standard Bible* (NASB), © The Lockman Foundation 1960, 1962, 1963, 1968,
1971, 1972, 1973, 1975, 1977; the *Good News Bible Today's English Version* (TEV),
copyright © American Bible Society 1966, 1971, 1976; the *Amplified New Testament*
(AMP), © The Lockman Foundation 1954, 1958; and the *King James Version* (KJV).

Printed in Canada

4 5 6 7 8 9 10 / 05 04

FOR A FREE CATALOG OF
NAVPRESS BOOKS & BIBLE STUDIES,
CALL 1-800-366-7788 (USA)
OR 1-416-499-4615 (CANADA)

# THE
# PURSUIT
# OF HOLINESS

# Contents

*To*
*Lorne C. Sanny*
*whose life has,*
*for more than twenty years,*
*served as an example*
*in my own pursuit*
*of holiness*

# Foreword

Jerry Bridges, the Vice President for Corporate Affairs of The Navigators, who previously served this fruitful enterprise in field ministries in Missouri, Colorado, and Holland before becoming responsible for the administration of its legal and financial affairs, has given the world one of the most incisive, appealing, and conscience-stirring treatises on scriptural holiness ever written. Without doubt, the Lord has enabled His servant to prepare a volume that will have a far-reaching impact upon the lives of countless numbers who read it.

The dominant theme of this heart-moving study is the need for increasing pursuit by believers for the holiness of life which God, whose holiness is ever gratefully remembered, can alone make possible. *Pursuit* is the key word which the author, whose personal pursuit has been long and strong, constantly repeats.

In the *Declaration of Independence*, Thomas Jefferson declared that one of the inherent and unalienable rights of men is "the pursuit of happiness." Professing Christians must be brought to realize that the preeminent desire and demand of God for us is that of the continual pursuit of holiness of life, and the reflection of His own holiness. "Be ye holy, for I am holy."

Well over 100 years ago, William Blake urged his readers to "put off holiness, and put on intellect." But divorced from divine holiness, intellect is like a ship without a captain, and doomed to disaster. In our quest for holiness the prayer must ever rise from the heart,

> "Take my intellect and use
> Every power as Thou shalt choose."

This is why we must warmly commend this compelling coverage of practical holiness, in which the author fully shows that the whole of life must be permeated with the holiness a thrice-holy God can impart.

Dr. Herbert Lockyer, Sr.

# Preface

A farmer plows his field, sows the seed, and fertilizes and cultivates—all the while knowing that in the final analysis he is utterly dependent on forces outside of himself. He knows he cannot cause the seed to germinate, nor can he produce the rain and sunshine for growing and harvesting the crop. For a successful harvest, he is dependent on these things from God.

Yet the farmer knows that unless he diligently pursues his responsibilities to plow, plant, fertilize, and cultivate, he cannot expect a harvest at the end of the season. In a sense he is in a partnership with God, and he will reap its benefits only when he has fulfilled his own responsibilities.

Farming is a joint venture between God and the farmer. The farmer cannot do what God must do, and God will not do what the farmer should do.

We can say just as accurately that the pursuit of holiness is a joint venture between God and the Christian. No one can attain any degree of holiness without God working in his life, but just as surely no one will attain it without effort on his own part. God has made it possible for us to walk in holiness. But He has given to us the responsibility of doing the walking; He does not do that for us.

We Christians greatly enjoy talking about the provision of God, how Christ defeated sin on the cross and gave us His Holy Spirit to empower us to victory over sin. But we do not as readily talk about our own responsibility to walk in holiness. Two primary reasons can be given for this.

First, we are simply reluctant to face up to our responsibility. We prefer to leave that to God. We pray for victory when we know we should be acting in obedience.

The second reason is that we do not understand the proper distinction between God's provision and our own responsibility for holiness. I struggled for a number of years with the question, "What am I to do myself, and what am I to rely on God to do?" Only as I came to see what the Bible teaches on this question, and then faced up to my own responsibility, did I see any progress in the "pursuit of holiness."

The title for this book comes from the biblical command, "Pursue holiness, for without holiness no one will see the Lord" (Hebrews 12:14, author's paraphrase). The word *pursue* suggests two thoughts: first, that diligence and effort are required; and second, that it is a lifelong task. These two thoughts form a dual theme throughout this book. While seeking to set forth clearly and accurately God's provision for our holiness, I have deliberately stressed our responsibility, feeling that this is an emphasis sorely needed among Christians today. At the same time I have sought to emphasize that holiness is a process, something we never completely attain in this life. Rather, as we begin to conform to the will of God in one area of life, He reveals to us our need in another area. That is why we will always be pursuing—as opposed to attaining—holiness in this life.

In addition to my own personal Bible study on the subject of holiness, I have profited greatly from the writings of the Puritans—and those who followed in their school of thought—on the subject of holiness. On numerous occasions I have quoted directly from them and have so indicated in the appropriate footnotes. In other instances their phraseology has crept into my own manner of expression. This is particularly true of the writings of John Owen and of Dr. D. Martyn Lloyd-Jones of London, both of whose writings on this subject have been of invaluable personal blessing.

I do not profess to know all about this subject, nor can I claim all that much personal progress. Many times while writing this book I have had to first make application to my own life. But what I have discovered has been of invaluable help to me in my own pursuit of holiness, and I trust will be of help to all who read it.

To explore more fully the scriptural principles of holiness, which I studied in writing this book, I encourage the reader to work through *A Bible Study on the Pursuit of Holiness*, which is published by NavPress as a companion to this book.

Finally, I want to express my thanks to Mrs. Peggy Sharp and Miss Linda Dicks, who patiently typed and retyped the various drafts of the manuscript.

CHAPTER

# Holiness
# Is for You

~

*For sin shall not be
your master,
because you are not
under law,
but under grace.*

~

ROMANS 6:14

The shrill ring of the telephone shattered the stillness of the beautiful, crisp Colorado morning. On the other end was one of those utterly impossible individuals God seems to have sprinkled around here on earth to test the grace and patience of His children.

He was in top form that morning—arrogant, impatient, demanding. I hung up the phone seething inside with anger, resentment, and perhaps even hatred. Grabbing my jacket, I walked out into the cold air to try to regain my composure. The quietness of my soul, so carefully cultivated in my "quiet time" with God that morning, had been ripped into shreds and replaced with a volatile, steaming emotional volcano.

As my emotions subsided, my anger turned to utter discouragement. It was only 8:30 in the morning and my day was ruined. Not only was I discouraged, I was confused. Only two hours before, I had read Paul's emphatic declaration, "For sin shall not be your master, because you are not under law, but under grace." But despite this nice-sounding promise of victory over sin, there I was locked in the vise-like grip of anger and resentment.

"Does the Bible really have any answers for real life?" I asked myself that morning. With all my heart I desired to live an obedient, holy life; yet there I was utterly defeated by one phone call.

Perhaps this incident has a familiar ring to you. The circumstances probably differed, but your reaction was similar. Perhaps your problem was anger with your children, or a temper at work, or an immoral habit you can't overcome, or maybe several "besetting sins" that dog you day in and day out.

Whatever your particular sin problem (or problems), the Bible does have the answer for you. There is hope. You and I can walk in obedience to God's Word and live a life of holiness. In fact, as we will see in the next chapter, God expects every Christian to live a holy life. But holiness is not only expected; it is the promised birthright of every Christian. Paul's statement is true. Sin shall not be our master.

The concept of holiness may seem a bit archaic to our current generation. To some minds the very word *holiness* brings images of bunned hair, long skirts, and black stockings. To others the idea is associated with a repugnant "holier than thou" attitude. Yet holiness is very much a scriptural idea. The word *holy* in various forms occurs more than 600 times in the Bible. One entire book, Leviticus, is devoted to the subject, and the idea of holiness is woven elsewhere throughout the fabric of Scripture. More important, God specifically commands us to be holy (see Leviticus 11:44).

The idea of exactly how to be holy has suffered from many false concepts. In some circles, holiness is equated with a series of specific prohibitions — usually in such areas as smoking, drinking, and dancing. The list of prohibitions varies depending on the group. When we follow this approach to holiness, we are in danger of becoming like the Pharisees with their endless lists of trivial do's and don'ts, and their self-righteous attitude. For others, holiness means a particular style of dress and mannerisms. And for still others, it means unattainable perfection, an idea that fosters either delusion or discouragement about one's sin.

All of these ideas, while accurate to some degree,

miss the true concept. To be holy is to be morally blameless.[1] It is to be separated from sin and, therefore, consecrated to God. The word signifies "separation to God, and the conduct befitting those so separated."[2]

Perhaps the best way of understanding the concept of holiness is to note how writers of the New Testament used the word. In 1 Thessalonians 4:3-7, Paul used the term in contrast to a life of immorality and impurity. Peter used it in contrast to living according to the evil desires we had when we lived outside of Christ (1 Peter 1:14-16). John contrasted one who is holy with those who do wrong and are vile (Revelation 22:11). To live a holy life, then, is to live a life in conformity to the moral precepts of the Bible and in contrast to the sinful ways of the world. It is to live a life characterized by the "[putting] off of your old self, which is being corrupted by its deceitful desires . . . and [putting] on the new self, created to be like God in true righteousness and holiness" (Ephesians 4:22,24).

If holiness, then, is so basic to the Christian life, why do we not experience it more in daily living? Why do so many Christians feel constantly defeated in their struggle with sin? Why does the Church of Jesus Christ so often seem to be more conformed to the world around it than to God?

At the risk of oversimplification, the answers to these questions can be grouped into three basic problem areas.

Our first problem is that *our attitude toward sin is more self-centered than God-centered*. We are more concerned about our own "victory" over sin than we are about the fact that our sins grieve the heart of God. We cannot tolerate failure in our struggle with sin chiefly because we are success-oriented, not because we know it is offensive to God.

W. S. Plumer said, "We never see sin aright until we see it as against God. . . . All sin is against God in this sense: that it is His law that is broken, His authority that is despised, His government that is set at naught. . . . Pharaoh and Balaam, Saul and Judas each said, 'I have sinned'; but the returning prodigal said, 'I have sinned *against heaven* and before thee'; and David said, 'Against Thee, Thee only have I sinned.'"[3]

God wants us to walk in *obedience*—not victory. Obedience is oriented toward God; victory is oriented toward self. This may seem to be merely splitting hairs over semantics, but there is a subtle, self-centered attitude at the root of many of our difficulties with sin. Until we face this attitude and deal with it we will not consistently walk in holiness.

This is not to say God doesn't want us to experience victory, but rather to emphasize that victory is a byproduct of obedience. As we concentrate on living an obedient, holy life, we will certainly experience the joy of victory over sin.

Our second problem is that *we have misunderstood "living by faith"* (Galatians 2:20) to mean that no effort at holiness is required on our part. In fact, sometimes we have even suggested that any effort on our part is "of the flesh."

The words of J. C. Ryle, Bishop of Liverpool from 1880 to 1900, are instructive to us on this point: "Is it wise to proclaim in so bald, naked, and unqualified a way as many do, that the holiness of converted people is by faith only, and not at all by personal exertion? Is it according to the proportion of God's Word? I doubt it. That faith in Christ is the root of all holiness . . . no well-instructed Christian will ever think of denying. But surely the Scriptures teach us that in following holiness the true Christian needs personal exertion and work as well as faith."[4]

We must face the fact that we have a personal responsibility for our walk of holiness. One Sunday our pastor in his sermon said words to this effect: "You can put away that habit that has mastered you if you truly desire to do so." Because he was referring to a particular habit which was no problem to me, I quickly agreed with him in my mind. But then the Holy Spirit said to me, "And you can put away the sinful habits that plague you if you will accept your personal responsibility for them." Acknowledging that I did have this responsibility turned out to be a milestone for me in my own pursuit of holiness.

Our third problem is that *we do not take some sin seriously*. We have mentally categorized sins into that which is unacceptable and that which may be tolerated a bit. An incident that occurred just as this book was nearing completion illustrates this problem. Our office was using a mobile home as temporary office space, pending the delayed completion of new facilities. Because our property is not zoned for mobile homes, we were required to obtain a variance permit to occupy the trailer. The permit had to be renewed several times. The last permit renewal expired just as the new facilities were completed, but before we had time to move out in an orderly manner. This precipitated a crisis for the department occupying the trailer.

At a meeting where this problem was discussed,

the question was asked, "What difference would it make if we didn't move that department for a few days?" Well, what difference would it make? After all, the trailer was tucked in behind some hills where no one would see it. And legally we didn't have to move the trailer; just vacate it. So what difference would it make if we overstayed our permit a few days? Isn't insistence on obeying the letter of the law nit-picking legalism?

But the Scripture says it is "the little foxes that ruin the vineyards" (Song of Songs 2:15). It is compromise on the little issues that leads to greater downfalls. And who is to say that a little ignoring of civil law is not a serious sin in the sight of God?

In commenting on some of the more minute Old Testament dietary laws God gave to the children of Israel, Andrew Bonar said, "It is not the importance of the thing, but the majesty of the Lawgiver, that is to be the standard of obedience. . . . Some, indeed, might reckon such minute and arbitrary rules as these as trifling. But the principle involved in obedience or disobedience was none other than the same principle which was tried in Eden at the foot of the forbidden tree. It is really this: Is the Lord to be obeyed in *all* things whatsoever He commands? Is He a holy Lawgiver? Are His creatures bound to give implicit assent to His will?"[5]

Are we willing to call sin "sin" not because it is big or little, but because God's law forbids it? We cannot categorize sin if we are to live a life of holiness. God will not let us get away with that kind of attitude.

These three problems will be addressed in greater detail in subsequent chapters of this book.

But before moving on, take time to settle these issues in your heart, right now. Will you begin to look at sin as an offense against a holy God, instead of as a personal defeat only? Will you begin to take personal responsibility for your sin, realizing that as you do, you must depend on the grace of God? And will you decide to obey God in all areas of life, however insignificant the issue may be?

As we move on, we will first consider the holiness of God. This is where holiness begins—not with ourselves, but with God. It is only as we see His holiness, His absolute purity and moral hatred of sin, that we will be gripped by the awfulness of sin against the Holy God. To be gripped by that fact is the first step in our pursuit of holiness.

---

NOTES

1. *Strong's Exhaustive Concordance of the Bible* (New York: Abingdon Press, 1890), page 7 of the "Greek Dictionary of the New Testament."
2. W. E. Vine, *An Expository Dictionary of New Testament Words* (1940; single volume edition, London: Oliphants, Ltd., 1957), pages 225-226.
3. William S. Plumer, *Psalms* (1867; reprint edition, Edinburgh: The Banner of Truth Trust, 1975), page 557.
4. J. C. Ryle, *Holiness* (1952 edition, London: James Clarke & Co.), page viii.
5. Andrew Bonar, *A Commentary on Leviticus* (1846; reprint edition, Edinburgh: The Banner of Truth Trust, 1972), page 218.

CHAPTER

# The Holiness
# of God

*But just as he who called you
is holy, so be holy in all you do;
for it is written: "Be holy,
because I am holy."*

1 PETER 1:15–16

God has called every Christian to a holy life. There are no exceptions to this call. It is not a call only to pastors, missionaries, and a few dedicated Sunday school teachers. Every Christian of every nation, whether rich or poor, learned or unlearned, influential or totally unknown, is called to be holy. The Christian plumber and the Christian banker, the unsung homemaker and the powerful head of state are all alike called to be holy.

This call to a holy life is based on the fact that God Himself is holy. Because God is holy, He requires that we be holy. Many Christians have what we might call a "cultural holiness." They adapt to the character and behavior pattern of Christians around them. As the Christian culture around them is more or less holy, so these Christians are more or less holy. But God has not called us to be like those around us. He has called us to be like Himself. Holiness is nothing less than conformity to the character of God.[1]

As used in Scripture, holiness describes both the majesty of God and the purity and moral perfection of His nature. Holiness is one of His attributes;[2] that is, holiness is an essential part of the nature of God. His holiness is as necessary as His existence, or as necessary, for example, as His wisdom or omniscience. Just as He cannot but *know* what is right, so He cannot but *do* what is right.

We ourselves do not always know what is right, what is just and fair. At times we agonize over decisions having moral overtones. "What is the right thing to do?" we ask. God, of course, never faces this predicament. His perfect knowledge precludes any uncertainty on what is right and wrong.

But sometimes, even when we know what is right there is a reluctance on our part to do it. The right action may involve sacrifice, or a blow to our pride (for example, when we know we should confess a sin to someone), or some other obstacle. But here again, this is never true with God. God never vacillates. He always does what is just and right without the slightest hesitation. It is impossible in the very nature of God for Him to do otherwise.

God's holiness then is perfect freedom from all evil. We say a garment is clean when it is free from any spot, or gold is pure when all dross has been refined from it. In this manner we can think of the holiness of God as the absolute absence of any evil in Him. John said, "God is light; in him there is no darkness at all" (1 John 1:5). Light and darkness, when used this way in Scripture, have moral significance. John is telling us that God is absolutely free from any moral evil and that He is Himself the essence of moral purity.

The holiness of God also includes His perfect conformity to His own divine character. That is, all of His thoughts and actions are consistent with His holy character. By contrast, consider our own lives. Over time, as we mature in the Christian life, we develop a certain degree of Christian character. We grow in such areas as truthfulness, purity, and humility. But we do not always act consistently with our character. We tell a lie or allow ourselves to get trapped into a series of impure thoughts. Then we are dismayed with ourselves for these actions because they are inconsistent with our character. This never happens to God. He always acts consistently with His holy character. And it is this standard of holiness that God has called us to when He says, "Be holy, because I am holy."

The absolute holiness of God should be of great comfort and assurance to us. If God is perfectly holy, then we can be confident that His actions toward us are always perfect and just. We are often tempted to question God's actions and complain that He is unfair in His treatment of us. This is the devil's lie, the same thing he did to Eve. He essentially told her, "God is being unfair to you" (Genesis 3:4-5). But it is impossible in the very nature of God that He should ever be unfair. Because He is holy, all His actions are holy.

We must accept by faith the fact that God is holy, even when trying circumstances make it appear otherwise. To complain against God is in effect to deny His holiness and to say He is not fair. In the seventeenth century Stephen Charnock said, "It is less injury to Him to deny His being, than to deny the purity of it; the one makes Him no God, the other a deformed, unlovely, and a detestable God . . . he that saith God is not holy speaks much worse than he that saith there is no God at all."[3]

I still vividly recall how God first dealt with me over twenty-five years ago about complaining against Him. In response to His will, I had settled in San Diego, California, and had begun to look for a job. When several weeks went by without success, I mentally began to accuse God. "After all, I gave up my plans to do His will and now He has let me down." God graciously directed my attention to Job 34:18-19: "Is he not the One who says to kings, 'You are worthless,' and to nobles, 'You are wicked,' who shows no partiality to princes and does not favor the rich over the poor, for they are all the work of his hands?" As soon as I read that passage I immediately fell to my knees confessing to Him my terrible sin of complaining and questioning His holiness. God mercifully forgave and the next day I received two job offers.

Acknowledging His holiness is one of the ways we are to praise God. According to John's vision of heaven described in Revelation 4, the four living creatures around God's throne never stop saying, "Holy, holy, holy is the Lord God Almighty, who was, and is, and is to come" (Revelation 4:8). The seraphim in Isaiah's vision of God's glory also uttered this threefold ascription of God's holiness (Isaiah 6:3). When Moses was praising God for the deliverance of the Israelites from Pharaoh's army, he also sang of God's holiness:

> Who among the gods is like you, O Lord?
> Who is like you—majestic in holiness,
> awesome in glory, working wonders?
> (Exodus 15:11)

God is often called in Scripture by such names as the Holy One, or the Holy One of Israel.[4] Holy, according to Stephen Charnock,[5] is used more often as a prefix to His name than any other attribute. Holiness is God's crown. Imagine for a moment that God possessed omnipotence (infinite power), omniscience (perfect and complete knowledge), and omnipresence (everywhere present), but without perfect holiness. Such a one could no longer be described as God. Holiness is the perfection of all His other attributes: His power is holy power, His mercy is holy mercy, His wisdom is holy wisdom. It is His holiness more than any other attribute that makes Him worthy of our praise.

But God demands more than that we acknowledge His holiness. He says to us, "Be holy, because I am holy." God rightfully demands perfect holiness in all of His moral creatures. It cannot be otherwise. He cannot possibly ignore or approve of any evil committed. He cannot for one moment relax His perfect standard of holiness. Rather He must say, as He does say, "So be holy in *all* you do." The Prophet Habakkuk declared, "Your eyes are too pure to look on evil; you cannot tolerate wrong" (Habakkuk 1:13). Because God is holy, He can never excuse or overlook any sin we commit, however small it may be.

Sometimes we try to justify to God some action which our own conscience calls into question. But if we truly grasp the significance of God's perfect holiness, both in Himself and in His demands of us, we will readily see we can never justify before Him even the slightest deviation from His perfect will. God does not accept the excuse, "Well, that's just the way I am," or even the more hopeful statement, "Well, I'm still growing in that area of my life."

No, God's holiness does not make allowance for minor flaws or shortcomings in our personal character. Well might we Christians, though justified solely through the righteousness of Christ, ponder carefully the words of the writer to the Hebrews: "Make every effort . . . to be holy; without holiness no one will see the Lord" (Hebrews 12:14).

Because God is holy, He cannot ever tempt us to sin. "When tempted, no one should say, 'God is tempting me.' For God cannot be tempted by evil, nor does he tempt anyone" (James 1:13). Probably none of us ever imagines that God is actively soliciting us to do evil, but we may feel that God has put us in a situation where we have no choice.

King Saul felt this way in his first major campaign against the Philistines (1 Samuel 13). Before going into battle Saul was to wait seven days for the Prophet Samuel to come and offer a burnt offering and ask the favor of the Lord. Saul waited the seven days for Samuel. When he didn't come, Saul became anxious and took it on himself to offer the burnt offering. Saul felt he had no alternative. The people were fearful and had begun to scatter; the Philistines were assembling for battle; Samuel was overdue. Something had to be done! God had put him in a place where he had no choice, it seemed, but to disobey God's explicit instructions.

But because Saul disobeyed God's express will, he lost his kingdom (1 Samuel 13:13-14). What about us? Do we sometimes feel we have no choice but to shade the truth a little, or commit just a slightly dishonest act? When we feel this way, we are in effect saying that God is tempting us to sin, that He has put us in a position where we have no alternative.

People under authority are particularly vulnerable to this temptation. Supervisors often put pressure on those below them to commit dishonest or unethical acts. As a young officer in the Navy I faced this temptation. For a few pounds of coffee to the right people, our ship could get "free" all kinds of valuable equipment we needed to do our job. "And after all," so the reasoning went, "it all belongs to the Navy." I finally had to stand up to my commanding officer and, in jeopardy to my Navy career, tell him I could have no part of that.

Because God is holy, He hates sin. Hate is such a strong word we dislike using it. We reprove our children for saying they hate someone. Yet when it comes to God's attitude toward sin, only a strong word such as hate conveys an adequate depth of meaning. Speaking of various sins in Israel, God says, "For all these things are what I hate" (Zechariah 8:17, NASB). Hatred is a legitimate emotion when it comes to sin. In fact, the more we ourselves grow in holiness, the more we hate sin. David said, "I gain understanding from your precepts; therefore I hate every wrong path" (Psalm 119:104). Now if that is true of a man, think of God. As we grow in holiness, we grow in hatred of sin; and God, being infinitely holy, has an infinite hatred of sin.

We often say, "God hates the sin but loves the sinner." This is blessedly true, but too often we quickly rush over the first half of this statement to get to the second. We cannot escape the fact that God hates our sins. We may trifle with our sins or excuse them, but God hates them.

Therefore every time we sin, we are doing something God hates. He hates our lustful thoughts, our pride and jealousy, our outbursts of temper, and our rationalization that the end justifies the means. We need to be gripped by the fact that God hates all these things. We become so accustomed to our sins we sometimes lapse into a state of peaceful coexistence with them, but God never ceases to hate them.

We need to cultivate in our own hearts the same hatred of sin God has. Hatred of sin as sin, not just as something disquieting or defeating to ourselves, but as displeasing to God, lies at the root of all true holiness. We must cultivate the attitude of Joseph, who said when he was tempted, "How then could I do such a wicked thing and sin against God?" (Genesis 39:9).

God hates sin wherever He finds it, in saint and sinner alike. He does not hate sin in one person and overlook it in another. He judges each man's works impartially (1 Peter 1:17). In fact, biblical evidence indicates that God may judge the sins of His saints more severely than those of the world. David was a man after God's own heart (Acts 13:22), yet after his sin against Uriah, he was told, "Now therefore, the sword will never depart from your house" (2 Samuel 12:10). Moses, for one act of unbelief, was excluded from the land of Canaan despite many years of faithful service. Jonah, for his disobedience, was cast into a horrible prison in the stomach of a giant fish for three days and nights, that he might learn not to run from the command of God.

In the deceitfulness of our hearts, we sometimes play with temptation by entertaining the thought that we can always confess and later ask forgiveness. Such thinking is exceedingly dangerous. God's judgment is without partiality. He never overlooks our sin. He never decides not to bother, since the sin is only a small one. No, God hates sin intensely whenever and wherever He finds it.

Frequent contemplation on the holiness of God and His consequent hatred of sin is a strong deterrent against trifling with sin. We are told to live our lives on earth as strangers in reverence and fear (1 Peter 1:17). Granted, the love of God to us through Jesus Christ should be our primary motivation to holiness. But a motivation prompted by God's hatred of sin and His consequent judgment on it is no less biblical.

The holiness of God is an exceedingly high standard, a perfect standard. But it is nevertheless one that He holds us to. He cannot do less. While it is true that He accepts us solely through the merit of Christ, God's standard for our character, our attitudes, affections, and actions is, "Be holy, because I am holy." We must take this seriously if we are to grow in holiness.

---

NOTES

1. Holiness "is characteristically Godlikeness" (G. B. Stevens, in *Hastings Bible Dictionary*, as quoted by W. E. Vine in *An Expository Dictionary of New Testament Words* [1940; single volume edition, London: Oliphants, Ltd., 1957], page 227). Charles Hodge, writing on the phrase in Romans 6:19, *righteousness unto holiness*, said, "The proximate result of obedience to God is inward conformity to the Divine image" (*Commentary on the Epistle to the Romans* [1886; reprint edition, Grand Rapids, Michigan: Wm. B. Eerdmans Publishing Co., 1955], page 209). A. W. Pink said, "Holiness . . . consists of that internal change or renovation of our souls whereby our minds, affections and wills are brought into harmony with God" (*The Doctrine of Sanctification* [Swengel, Pennsylvania: Bible Truth Depot, 1955], page 25).
2. Attributes as applied to God refer to His essential qualities, and are inferred from Scriptures describing God. His attribute of holiness is taken from such passages as Exodus 15:11, Leviticus 19:2, Psalm 89:35, Isaiah 57:15, and 1 Peter 1:15-16.
3. Stephen Charnock, *The Existence and Attributes of God* (reprint edition, Evansville, Indiana: Sovereign Grace Book Club, 1958), page 449.
4. For examples see Psalm 89:18, Isaiah 40:25 and 43:14, Hosea 11:9, Habakkuk 3:3, Jeremiah 51:5, and Ezekiel 39:7.
5. Charnock, *Existence and Attributes*, page 448.

# Holiness Is Not an Option

*Make every effort
to live in peace with all men
and to be holy;
without holiness no one
will see the Lord.*

HEBREWS 12:14

Just what do these words, "without holiness no one will see the Lord" actually mean? Does our salvation in the final analysis depend to some degree on our attaining some level of personal holiness?

On this question the Scripture is clear on two points. First, the best Christians can never in themselves merit salvation through their personal holiness. Our righteous deeds are like filthy garments in the light of God's holy law (Isaiah 64:6). Our best works are stained and polluted with imperfection and sin. As one of the saints of several centuries ago put it, "Even our tears of repentance need to be washed in the blood of the lamb."

Second, Scripture repeatedly refers to the obedience and righteousness of Christ on our behalf. "For just as through the disobedience of the one man the many were made sinners, so also through the obedience of the one man the many will be made righteous" (Romans 5:19). "For Christ died for sins once for all, the righteous for the unrighteous, to bring you to God" (1 Peter 3:18). These two passages teach a twofold aspect of Christ's work on our behalf. They are often referred to as His active and His passive obedience.

Active obedience means Christ's sinless life here on earth, His perfect obedience and absolute holiness. This perfect life is credited to those who trust in Him for their salvation. His passive obedience refers to His death on the cross through which He fully paid the penalty for our sins and placated the wrath of God toward us. In Hebrews 10:5-9 we read that Christ came to do the will of the Father. Then the writer said, "And by that will, *we have been made holy* through the sacrifice of the body of Jesus

Christ once for all" (Hebrews 10:10). So we see that our holiness before God depends entirely on the work of Jesus Christ for us, by God's will.

Does Hebrews 12:14 refer then to this holiness which we have in Christ? No, for at this point the writer speaks of a holiness which we are to strive after; we are to "make every effort . . . to be holy." And without this holiness, the writer says, no one will see the Lord.

Scripture speaks of both a holiness which we have in Christ before God, and a holiness which we are to strive after. These two aspects of holiness complement one another, for our salvation is a salvation to holiness: "For God did not call us to be impure, but to live a holy life" (1 Thessalonians 4:7). To the Corinthians Paul wrote: "To the church of God in Corinth, to those sanctified in Christ Jesus and called *to be holy*" (1 Corinthians 1:2). The word *sanctified* here means "made holy." That is, we are through Christ *made* holy in our standing before God, and *called* to be holy in our daily lives.

So the writer of Hebrews is telling us to take seriously the necessity of personal, practical holiness. When the Holy Spirit comes into our lives at our salvation, He comes to make us holy in practice. If there is not, then, at least a yearning in our hearts to live a holy life pleasing to God, we need to seriously question whether our faith in Christ is genuine.

It is true that this desire for holiness may be only a spark at the beginning. But that spark should grow till it becomes a flame—a desire to live a life wholly pleasing to God. True salvation brings with it a desire to be made holy. When God saves us through Christ, He not only saves us from the penalty of sin,

33

but also from its dominion. Bishop Ryle said, "I doubt, indeed, whether we have any warrant for saying that a man can possibly be converted without being consecrated to God. More consecrated he doubtless can be, and will be as his grace increases; but if he was not consecrated to God in the very day that he was converted and born again, I do not know what conversion means."[1]

The whole purpose of our salvation is that we be "holy and blameless in his sight" (Ephesians 1:4). To continue to live in sin as a Christian is to go contrary to God's very purpose for our salvation. One of the writers of three centuries ago put it like this: "What a strange kind of salvation do they desire that care not for holiness. . . . They would be saved by Christ and yet be out of Christ in a fleshly state. . . . They would have their sins forgiven, not that they may walk with God in love, in time to come, but that they may practice their enmity against Him without any fear of punishment."[2]

Holiness, then, is not necessary as a *condition* of salvation—that would be salvation by works—but as a *part* of salvation that is received by faith in Christ. The angel said to Joseph, "You are to give him the name Jesus [which means 'Jehovah is salvation'], because he will save his people from their sins" (Matthew 1:21).

Therefore, we may say that no one can trust in Jesus Christ for true salvation unless he trusts in Him for holiness. This does not mean the desire for holiness must be a conscious desire at the time a person comes to Christ, but rather it means that the Holy Spirit who creates within us saving faith also creates within us the desire for holiness. He simply does not create one without the other.

Paul said, "For the grace of God that brings salvation has appeared to all men. It teaches us to say 'No' to ungodliness and worldly passions, and to live self-controlled, upright and godly lives in this present age" (Titus 2:11-12). The same grace that brings salvation teaches us to renounce ungodly living. We cannot receive half of God's grace. If we have experienced it at all, we will experience not only forgiveness of our sins but also freedom from sin's dominion.

This is the point James is making in his hard-to-understand passage on faith and works (James 2:14-26). He is simply telling us that a "faith" that does not result in works—in a holy life, in other words—is not a living faith but a dead one, no better than that which the demons possess.

God's nature demands holiness in the life of a Christian. When He calls us to salvation, He calls us to fellowship with Himself and His Son Jesus Christ (1 John 1:3). But God is light; in Him is no darkness at all (1 John 1:5). How then can we have fellowship with Him if we continue to walk in darkness?

Holiness then is required for *fellowship with God*. David asked the question, "LORD, who may dwell in your sanctuary? Who may live on your holy hill?" (Psalm 15:1). That is to say, "Lord, who may live in fellowship with You?" The answer given in the next four verses may be summarized as "he who leads a holy life."

Prayer is a vital part of our fellowship with God; yet the Psalmist said, "If I had cherished sin in my heart, the Lord would not have listened" (Psalm 66:18). To regard wickedness is to cherish some sin, to love it to the extent that I am not willing to part with it. I know it is there, yet I justify it in some way like the child who says, "Well, he hit me first." When we are holding on to some sin, we are not pursuing holiness and we cannot have fellowship with God.

God does not require a perfect, sinless life to have fellowship with Him, but He does require that we be serious about holiness, that we grieve over sin in our lives instead of justifying it, and that we earnestly pursue holiness as a way of life.

Holiness is also required for *our own well-being*. Scripture says, "The Lord disciplines those he loves, and he punishes everyone he accepts as a son" (Hebrews 12:6). This statement presupposes our need of discipline, for God is not capricious in administering it. He disciplines us because we need discipline.

To persist in disobedience is to increase our necessity for discipline. Some of the Corinthian Christians persisted in disobedience to the point where God had to take their lives (1 Corinthians 11:30).

David described the discipline of the Lord this way: "When I kept silent, my bones wasted away through my groaning all day long. For day and night your hand was heavy upon me; my strength was sapped as in the heat of summer" (Psalm 32:3-4).

When God speaks to us about some sin, we need to heed and take action. To fail to deal with that sin is to risk incurring His hand of discipline. One icy morning as I was turning into the driveway of The Navigators headquarters where I work, my car skidded out of control into a corner fence post. Someone else in a similar predicament had already bent the post, and I only increased the angle. I said nothing to the property manager, despite several gentle proddings from God. Two weeks later I had another slight accident. After over fifteen years of accident-free driving, I knew God was trying to get my attention, so I called up the property manager, reported my first accident, and offered to pay for a new fence post. As Peter said, "Live your lives as strangers here in reverent fear" (1 Peter 1:17). God is serious about holiness in the lives of His people, and He will discipline us to attain it.

Holiness is also necessary for *effective service to God*. Paul wrote to Timothy, "If a man cleanses himself from [ignoble purposes], he will be an instrument for noble purposes, made holy, useful to the Master and prepared to do any good work" (2 Timothy 2:21). Holiness and usefulness are linked together. We cannot bring our service to God in an unclean vessel.

The One who makes our service effective and who empowers us for service is the Holy Spirit. Note well that He is called the *Holy* Spirit, or the Spirit of Holiness. When we indulge our sinful natures and dwell in unholiness, the Spirit of God is grieved (Ephesians 4:30) and will not prosper our service. These are not times when we fall into temptation and immediately seek God's forgiveness and cleansing, but lives that are characterized by unholy living.

Holiness also is necessary for our *assurance of salvation*—not at the moment of salvation, but over the course of our lives. True faith will always show itself by its fruits. "Therefore, if anyone is in Christ, he is a new creation" (2 Corinthians 5:17).

I recall a young man, a fairly new Christian, whose father was visiting him. He had not seen his father for several years and not since he had become a Christian. He was eager to share his newfound faith with his dad, and we prayed together that he might be an effective witness to his father.

Several days later I asked him how it had gone with his witness. He told me his dad had claimed to have trusted Christ as his Savior when he "went forward" at age ten in an evangelistic meeting. I asked the young man, "In all the years you were growing up, did you ever see any evidence that your father was a Christian?" His answer was "No." What reason have we to put confidence in that man's salvation? He was almost sixty and had never once given his son any evidence that he was a Christian.

The only safe evidence that we are in Christ is a holy life. John said everyone who has within him the hope of eternal life purifies himself just as Christ is pure (1 John 3:3). Paul said, "Those who are led by the Spirit of God are sons of God" (Romans 8:14). If we know nothing of holiness, we may flatter ourselves that we are Christians but we do not have the Holy Spirit dwelling within us.

Everyone, then, who professes to be a Christian should ask himself, "Is there evidence of practical holiness in my life? Do I desire and strive after holiness? Do I grieve over my lack of it and earnestly seek the help of God to be holy?"

It is not those who profess to know Christ who will enter heaven, but those whose lives are holy. Even those who do "great Christian works" will not enter heaven unless they also do the will of God. Jesus said,

"Not everyone who says to me, 'Lord, Lord,' will enter the kingdom of heaven, but only he who does the will of my Father who is in heaven.

"Many will say to me on that day, 'Lord, Lord, did we not prophesy in your name, and in your name drive out demons, and perform many miracles?' Then I will tell them plainly, 'I never knew you. Away from me, you evildoers!'" (Matthew 7:21-23)

---

NOTES
1. J. C. Ryle, *Holiness*, page xv.
2. Walter Marshall; 1692, quoted in A. W. Pink, *The Doctrine of Sanctification* (Swengel, Pennsylvania: Bible Truth Depot, 1955), page 29.

# The Holiness of Christ

~

*God made him*
*who had no sin*
*to be sin for us,*
*so that in him*
*we might become*
*the righteousness of God.*

~

2 CORINTHIANS 5:21

Before speaking further of holiness in ourselves, it is well that we also consider the holiness of Christ. We need this first of all *to be firmly grounded in our security in Christ*. As we study more fully the implications of "Be holy because I am holy," we will see more of our own sinfulness. We will see the wickedness and deceitfulness of our hearts, and how far we miss the mark of God's perfect holiness. As this happens, the true Christian will in his heart flee for refuge in Christ. It is important therefore that we understand the righteousness of Christ, and the fact that His righteousness is credited to us.

On numerous occasions the Scriptures testify that Jesus during His time on earth lived a perfectly holy life. He is described as "without sin" (Hebrews 4:15); as One who "committed no sin" (1 Peter 2:22); and as "him who had no sin" (2 Corinthians 5:21). The Apostle John stated, "In him is no sin" (1 John 3:5). The Old Testament describes Him prophetically as "the righteous servant" (Isaiah 53:11), and as One who "loved righteousness and hated wickedness" (Psalm 45:7). These statements, taken from six different writers of Scripture, show that the sinlessness of Jesus Christ is the universal teaching of the Bible.

Even more compelling, however, is Jesus' own testimony concerning Himself. On one occasion He looked the Pharisees squarely in the eye and asked, "Can any of you prove me guilty of sin?" (John 8:46). As someone has observed, it was not their failure to answer His question that is so significant, but the fact He dared to ask it. Here was Jesus in direct confrontation with people who hated Him. He had just told them they were of their father the devil, and that they wanted to carry out his desires. Surely if any people had a reason to point out to Him some careless act of His or some flaw of His character, they would. Furthermore, Jesus asked this question in the presence of His disciples, who lived with Him continuously and had ample opportunity to observe any inconsistencies. Yet Jesus dared to ask the question because He knew there was only one answer. He was without sin.

But the holiness of Jesus was more than simply the absence of actual sin. It was also a perfect conformity to the will of His Father. He stated that He came down from heaven "not to do my will but to do the will of him who sent me" (John 6:38). On another occasion, He said, "My food is to do the will of him who sent me" (John 4:34). Perhaps His highest testimony to His positive holiness was His statement, "I always do what pleases him" (John 8:29).

Such a positive declaration must include not only His actions but also His attitudes and motives. It is possible for us to do the right action from a wrong motive, but this does not please God. Holiness has to do with more than mere acts. Our motives must be holy, that is, arising from a desire to do something simply because it is the will of God. Our thoughts should be holy, since they are known to God even before they are formed in our minds. Jesus Christ perfectly met these standards, and He did it for us. He was born into this world subject to the law of God that He might fulfill it on our behalf (Galatians 4:4-5).

Whenever we seriously contemplate the holiness of God, our natural reaction is to say with Isaiah,

43

"Woe is me, for I am ruined! Because I am a man of unclean lips, and I live among a people of unclean lips, and my eyes have seen the King, the Lord Almighty" (Isaiah 6:5).

A serious view of the holiness of God—His own moral perfection and infinite hatred of sin—will leave us, as it did Isaiah, seeing with utter dismay our own lack of holiness. His moral purity serves to magnify our impurity.

Therefore, it is important that we receive the same assurance that Isaiah received: "See . . . your guilt is taken away and your sin atoned for" (Isaiah 6:7). It is not only at the initial point of salvation that we need this assurance. In fact, the more we grow in holiness, the more we need assurance that the perfect righteousness of Christ is credited to us. This is true because a part of growing in holiness is the Holy Spirit's making us aware of our need of holiness. As we see this need, it is well for us to always keep in mind the righteousness of Jesus Christ on our behalf, and the fact that "God made him who had no sin to be sin for us, so that in him we might become the righteousness of God" (2 Corinthians 5:21).

The truth of our acceptance by God through the righteousness of Christ may seem so elementary that you wonder why it is stressed here. It is because we need to dwell on it to thwart the attacks of Satan. The Holy Spirit makes us more aware of our lack of holiness to stimulate us to deeper yearning and striving for holiness. But Satan will attempt to use the Holy Spirit's work to discourage us.

One of Satan's attacks is to try to convince you that you are not a genuine Christian after all. He will say something like, "A true Christian wouldn't think the evil thoughts you've been thinking today." Now it may be that six months ago Satan would not have come to you with such a suggestion because you were not troubled about your thoughts. But now that the Holy Spirit has begun to reveal how sinful your thoughts of lust and resentment and pride really are, you may begin to have doubts about your salvation.

A number of years ago, God was allowing me to go through some deep inner struggles to teach me something of the sinfulness of my heart. During this time I was leading a weekly Bible study at a military base about an hour's drive from where I lived. Every Monday night as I left the fellowship of that Bible study and started my lonely drive home, Satan would begin to attack me: "How can anyone who is having the struggles you are having be a Christian?" he would ask. I began to fight him by resorting to an old Gospel hymn, which begins,

"Just as I am, without one plea,
But that Thy blood was shed for me,
And that Thou bidst me come to Thee;
O Lamb of God, I come."

I would sing through that hymn, and by the time I finished I would be praising God for His salvation given freely to me through Jesus Christ.

You, too, if you diligently pursue holiness, must often flee to the Rock of your salvation. You flee there, not to be saved again, but to confirm in your heart that you are saved through His righteousness alone. You begin to identify with Paul when he said, "Here is a trustworthy saying that deserves full acceptance: Christ Jesus came into the world to save sinners—of whom I am the worst" (1 Timothy 1:15). It is at this point that Christ's holy life lived on your behalf becomes so important to you.

A second reason we need to consider the holiness of Christ is because *His life is meant to be an example of holiness for us*. Peter told us that Christ left an example for us to follow in His steps (1 Peter 2:21). Peter spoke particularly of Christ's suffering without retaliation, but in the following verse he said also that Christ committed no sin. Paul urged us to be imitators of God (Ephesians 5:1), and also said "Follow my example, as I follow the example of Christ" (1 Corinthians 11:1).

Clearly then, the sinless holy life of Jesus Christ is meant to be an example for us. Consider then His statement, "I always do what pleases Him." Do we dare take that as our personal goal in life? Are we truly willing to scrutinize all our activities, all our goals and plans, and all of our impulsive actions in the light of this statement: "I am doing this to please God"?

If we ask that question honestly, we will begin to squirm a bit. We know we do some things, good things in themselves, to gain admiration for ourselves rather than glory for God. We do other things strictly for our own pleasure, without any regard for the glory of God.

What is my reaction when the neighborhood bully pesters my little boy? Usually my initial reaction comes from a spirit of retaliation till the Holy Spirit reminds me of the example of Jesus. How do we view those who do not show love for us? Do we see them as persons for whom Christ died or as persons who make our lives difficult?

I recall an unpleasant business encounter once with a person who later became a Christian through another's witness. When I learned of this, I was deeply chagrined to reflect on the fact that I had never once thought of him as a person for whom Christ died, but only as someone with whom I had an unpleasant experience. We need to learn to follow the example of Christ, who was moved with compassion for sinners and who could pray for them even as they nailed Him to the cross on Calvary.

In the words of nineteenth-century Scottish theologian John Brown, "Holiness does not consist in mystic speculations, enthusiastic fervours, or uncommanded austerities; it consists in thinking as God thinks, and willing as God wills."[1] Neither does holiness mean, as is so often thought, adhering to a list of "do's and don'ts," mostly don'ts. When Christ came into the world, He said, "I have come to do your will, O God" (Hebrews 10:7). This is the example we are to follow. In all of our thoughts, all of our actions, in every part of our character, the ruling principle that motivates and guides us should be the desire to follow Christ in doing the will of the Father. This is the high road we must follow in the pursuit of holiness.

---

NOTE
1. John Brown, *Expository Discourses on 1 Peter* (1848; reprint edition, Edinburgh: The Banner of Truth Trust, Volume 1), page 106.

CHAPTER

# A Change of Kingdoms

~

*For we know that our old self was crucified with him so that the body of sin might be rendered powerless, that we should no longer be slaves to sin because anyone who has died has been freed from sin.*

~

ROMANS 6:6–7, NASB

Many Christians have a basic desire to live a holy life, but have come to believe they simply cannot do it. They have struggled for years with particular sins or deficiencies of character. While not living in gross sin, they have more or less given up ever attaining a life of holiness and have settled down to a life of moral mediocrity with which neither they nor God are pleased. The promise of Romans 6:6-7 seems impossibly beyond them. The strong commands of Scripture to live a consistently holy life only frustrate them.

Many have sought to live a holy life by their own willpower; others have sought it solely by faith. Many have agonized in prayer over particular sins, seemingly without success. Scores of books have been written to help us discover the "secret" of the "victorious life."

In our search for answers to our sin problems, a troublesome question arises: "What should I look to God for and what am I responsible for myself?" Many are confused at this point. When we first start to live the Christian life, we confidently assume we will simply discover from the Bible what God wants us to do and start doing it. We fail to reckon with our tendency to cling to our old sinful ways.

After experiencing a great deal of failure with our sinful nature, we are told that we have been trying to live the Christian life in the energy of the flesh. We need to "stop trying and start trusting," or to "let go and let God." We are told that if we just turn our sin problem over to Christ and rest in His finished work on Calvary, He will then live His life in us and we will experience a life of victory over sin.

Having experienced failure and frustration with our sin problem, we are delighted to be told that God has already done it all and that we only need to rest in Christ's finished work. After struggling with our sins to the point of despair, this new idea is like a life preserver to a drowning man, almost like hearing the Gospel for the first time.

But after a while, if we are truly honest with ourselves, we discover we are still experiencing defeat at the hands of our sinful natures. The victory seemingly promised us still eludes us. We still struggle with pride, jealousy, materialism, impatience, and lust. We still eat too much, waste our time, criticize each other, shade the truth just a little, and indulge in a dozen other sins, all the time hating ourselves for doing them.

Then we wonder what is wrong. "Why can't I," we ask ourselves, "experience the victory described in all the books that others seem to have experienced?" We begin to feel that something is uniquely wrong with us, that somehow our sinful natures must be worse than others. Then we begin to despair.

Years ago a fellow Christian warned me that Satan would try to confuse us on the issue of what God has done for us and what we must do ourselves. I have come to see the insight he had in making that statement. Lack of understanding on that issue has led to great confusion in our pursuit of holiness. It is very important that we make this distinction; for God has indeed made provision for us to live a holy life, but He also has given us definite responsibilities.

Let us first look at God's provision for us.

In the Bible we read, "Therefore, do not let sin

reign in your mortal body so that you obey its evil desires" (Romans 6:12). The first thing we should notice in this passage is that the pursuit of holiness—this not allowing sin to reign in our mortal bodies—is something *we* have to do. Paul's statement is one of exhortation. He addressed himself to our wills. He said, "Do not let sin reign," implying that this is something for which we ourselves are responsible. The experience of holiness is not a gift we receive like justification, but something which we are clearly exhorted to work at.

The second thing to note from Paul's exhortation is that it is based on what he had just said. Note the connecting word *therefore*. Clearly he meant to say something like, "In view of what I have just said, do not let sin reign in your mortal body." To state it another way, we are to pursue holiness because certain facts are true.

What are these facts?

Let us take a look at Romans 6. In answer to the question "Shall we go on sinning so that grace may increase?" Paul said, "We died to sin; how can we live in it any longer?" (verses 1-2). Then Paul developed that idea (verses 3-11). It is evident that the word *therefore* (verse 12) refers back to this fact that we died to sin. Because we died to sin, we are not to let it reign in our mortal bodies.

If we are to obey the exhortation of verse 12, it is vital that we understand what Paul means by the expression *we died to sin*. As we read this passage, the first thing we observe is that our dying to sin is the result of our union with Christ (verses 2-11). Because He died to sin, we died to sin. Therefore, it is apparent that our dying to sin is not something we do, but something Christ has done, the value of which accrues to all who are united with Him.

The second observation we can make is that our dying to sin is a fact whether we realize it or not. Because Christ died to sin, all who are united with Him died to sin. Our dying to sin is not something we do, or something we make come true in our experience by reckoning it to be so. Some have misunderstood this point. We have gotten the idea that to have died to sin means to somehow be removed from sin's ability to touch us. However, to experience this in our daily lives we are told we must *reckon* ourselves dead to sin (verse 11, KJV). We are further told that if we are not experiencing victory over our besetting sins, it is because we are not reckoning on the fact that we died to sin.

We are indeed to reckon—or to count or consider—ourselves dead to sin, but our reckoning does not make it true, even in our experience. Verses 11 and 12 must be taken together. Because we are dead to sin through our union with Christ, we are not to let sin reign in our mortal bodies. Our daily experience with regard to sin is determined—not by our reckoning, but by our will—by whether we allow sin to reign in our bodies. But our will must be influenced by the fact that we died to sin.

What then does Paul mean by his expression *died to sin*? He means we died to the dominion of sin, or to the reign of sin. Before we trusted in Jesus Christ for our salvation we were in the kingdom of Satan and sin. We "followed the ways of this world and of the ruler of the kingdom of the air [the devil]" (Ephesians 2:2). We were under the power of Satan (Acts 26:18) and the dominion of darkness (Colossians 1:13). Paul said we were slaves of sin (Romans 6:17). We were born into this kingdom of sin, slavery, and death. Every person who has ever lived since Adam, except for the incarnate Son of God, has been born a slave in the kingdom of sin and Satan.

But through our union with Christ we have died to this realm of sin. We have been set free from sin (Romans 6:18), rescued from the dominion of darkness (Colossians 1:13), and turned from the power of Satan to God (Acts 26:18). Before our salvation we were in bondage to sin, under the reign and rule of sin. Regardless of how decent and moral we were, we lived in the kingdom of sin. But now through our union with Christ in His death to sin, we have been delivered out of the realm of sin and placed in the kingdom and realm of righteousness.[1]

Professor John Murray, in commenting on the clause *we died to sin*, said, "If we view sin as a realm or sphere, then the believer no longer lives in that realm or sphere. And just as it is true with reference to life in the sphere of this world that the person who has died 'passed away, and lo, he was not: yea, I sought him, but he could not be found' (Psalm 37:36), so it is with the sphere of sin; the believer is no longer there because he has died to sin. . . . The believer died to sin once and he has been translated to another realm."[2]

It is because we were in this realm of sin, under its reign and rule, that we began to sin from infancy. Because we were slaves we acted like slaves. We developed sinful habits and a sinful character. Even if we were what the world considers "good," we lived for ourselves, not for God. Our attitude toward Christ was expressed by the words of His enemies: "We

54

don't want this man to be our king" (Luke 19:14).

But if we have been delivered from this realm, why do we still sin? Though God has delivered us from the reign of sin, our sinful natures still reside within us. Even though sin's dominion and rule are broken, the remaining sin that dwells in believers exerts a tremendous power, constantly working toward evil.

An illustration from warfare can help us see how this is true. In a particular nation two competing factions were fighting for control of the country. Eventually, with the help of an outside army, one faction won the war and assumed control of the nation's government. But the losing side did not stop fighting. They simply changed their tactics to guerrilla warfare and continued to fight. In fact, they were so successful that the country supplying the outside help could not withdraw its troops.

So it is with the Christian. Satan has been defeated and the reign of sin overthrown. But our sinful natures resort to a sort of guerrilla warfare to lead us into sin. This results in the struggle between the Spirit and our sinful natures which Paul wrote about: "For the sinful nature desires what is contrary to the Spirit, and the Spirit what is contrary to the sinful nature. They are in conflict with each other, so that you do not do what you want" (Galatians 5:17).

Further, because we are born as sinners, we have from birth developed habits of sin. As Jay Adams says, "We were born sinners, but it took practice to develop our particular styles of sinning. The old life was disciplined [trained] toward ungodliness."[3] We all tend to act according to these sinful habits that have been engraved in us from long practice.

Suppose, for example, I had a lame leg and as a result developed a limp. If through surgery my lameness is cured, I would still tend to limp out of habit. Or do you suppose that when slaves were freed by President Lincoln's Emancipation Proclamation, they immediately began to think as free men? Undoubtedly they still tended to act as slaves because they had developed habit patterns of slavery.

In a similar manner, Christians tend to sin out of habit. It is our habit to look out for ourselves instead of others, to retaliate when injured in some way, and to indulge the appetites of our bodies. It is our habit to live for ourselves and not for God. When we become Christians, we do not drop all this overnight. In fact, we will spend the rest of our lives putting off these habits and putting on habits of holiness.

Not only have we been slaves to sin, but we still live in a world populated by slaves of sin. The conventional values around us reflect this slavery, and the world tries to conform us to its own sinful mold.

Therefore, though sin no longer reigns in us, it will constantly try to get at us. Though we have been delivered from the kingdom of sin and its rule, we have not been delivered from its attacks. As Dr. Martin Lloyd-Jones says in his exposition of Romans 6, though sin cannot reign in us, that is, in our essential personality, it can, if left unchecked, reign in our mortal bodies.[4] It will turn the natural instincts of our bodies into lust. It will turn our natural appetites into indulgence, our need for clothing and shelter into materialism, and our normal sexual interest into immorality.

That is why Paul exhorted us to be on our guard so that we will not let sin reign in our bodies. Before our salvation, before our death to the reign of sin, such an exhortation would have been futile. You cannot say to a slave, "Live as a free man," but you can say that to someone delivered from slavery. Now that we are in fact dead to sin—to its rule and reign—we are to count on that as being true. We are to keep before us this fact that we are no longer slaves. We can now stand up to sin and say no to it. Before we had no choice; now we have one. When we sin as Christians, we do not sin as slaves, but as individuals with the freedom of choice. We sin because we choose to sin.

To summarize then, we have been set free from the reign and rule of sin, the kingdom of unrighteousness. Our deliverance is through our union with Christ in His death. When Christ entered this world He voluntarily entered the realm of sin, though He never sinned. When He died, He died to this realm of sin (Romans 6:10), and through our union with Him we died to this realm also. We are to count on this fact that we are dead to sin's rule, that we can stand up to it and say no. Therefore we are to guard our bodies so that sin does not reign in us.

So we see that God has made provision for our holiness. Through Christ He has delivered us from sin's reign so that we now can resist sin. But the responsibility for resisting is ours. God does not do that for us. To confuse the *potential* for resisting (which God provided) with the *responsibility* for resisting (which is ours) is to court disaster in our pursuit of holiness.

NOTES
1. I am indebted to Dr. D. Martyn Lloyd Jones for his helpful exposition of the term "died to sin" in chapter 2 of his book *Romans: An Exposition of Chapter 6 — The New Man* (Edinburgh: The Banner of Truth Trust, 1972).
2. John Murray, *The Epistle to the Romans, The New International Commentary on the New Testament* (Grand Rapids, Michigan: Wm. B. Eerdmans Publishing Co., 1968), page 213. Used by permission.
3. From *Godliness Through Discipline* by Jay E. Adams, page 6. Reprinted 1973 by Baker Book House and used by permission.
4. Lloyd-Jones, *Romans: An Exposition of Chapter 6*, pages 152-153.

CHAPTER

6

# The Battle for Holiness

*So I find this law at work:
When I want to do good,
evil is right there with me.*

ROMANS 7:21

Through our union with Christ in His death we are delivered from the dominion of sin. But we still find sin struggling to gain mastery over us, as Paul depicted so vividly: "When I want to do good, evil is right there with me" (Romans 7:21). We may not like the fact that we have this lifelong struggle with sin, but the more we realize and accept it, the better equipped we will be to deal with it. The more we discover about the strength of indwelling sin, the less we feel its effects. To the extent that we discover this law of sin within ourselves, we will abhor and fight against it.

But though believers still have this indwelling propensity to sin, the Holy Spirit maintains within us a prevailing desire for holiness (1 John 3:9). The believer struggles with the sin God enables him to see in himself. This is the picture we see in Romans 7:21, and it distinguishes believers from unbelievers who lie serenely content in their darkness.

Interpretations of Romans 7:14-25 fall into three basic groups. It is not the purpose of this book to discuss those interpretations or to decide in favor of one of them. Whatever our interpretation of Romans 7, all Christians acknowledge the universal application of Paul's statement, "When I want to do good, evil is right there with me."

As indicated in the previous chapter, indwelling sin remains in us even though it has been dethroned. And though it has been overthrown and weakened, its nature has not changed. Sin is still hostile to God and cannot submit to His law (Romans 8:7). Thus we have an implacable enemy of righteousness right in our own hearts. What diligence and watchfulness is required of us when this enemy in our souls is ready to oppose every effort to do good!

If we are to wage a successful war against this enemy within, it is important that we know something of its nature and tactics. First of all, the Scripture indicates that *the seat of indwelling sin is the heart*. "For from within, out of men's hearts, come evil thoughts, sexual immorality, theft, murder, adultery, greed, malice, deceit, lewdness, envy, slander, arrogance, and folly. All these evils come from inside and make a man 'unclean'" (Mark 7:21-23; see also Genesis 6:5 and Luke 6:45).

*Heart* in Scripture is used in various ways. Sometimes it means our reason or understanding, sometimes our affections and emotions, and sometimes our will. Generally it denotes the whole soul of man and all its faculties, not individually, but as they all work together in doing good or evil. The mind as it reasons, discerns, and judges; the emotions as they like or dislike; the conscience as it determines and warns; and the will as it chooses or refuses—are all together called the heart.[1]

The Bible tells us that the heart is deceitful and unsearchable to any but God alone (Jeremiah 17:9-10). Even as believers we do not know our own hearts (1 Corinthians 4:3-5). None of us can discern fully the hidden motives, the secret intrigues, the windings and turnings of his heart. And in this unsearchable heart dwells the law of sin. Much of sin's strength lies in this, that we fight with an enemy we cannot fully search out.

The heart is also deceitful. It excuses, rationalizes, and justifies our actions. It blinds us to entire areas of sin in our lives. It causes us to deal with sin using only halfway measures, or to think that mental assent to the Word of God is the same as obedience (James 1:22).

Knowing that indwelling sin occupies a heart that is deceitful and unsearchable should make us extremely wary. We need to ask God daily to search our hearts for sin that we cannot or will not see. This was David's prayer: "Search me, O God, and know my heart; test me and know my anxious thoughts. See if there is any offensive way in me, and lead me in the way everlasting" (Psalm 139:23-24). God's primary means of searching our hearts this way is through His Word, as we read it under the power of the Holy Spirit. "The word of God is living and active. Sharper than any double-edged sword, it penetrates even to dividing soul and spirit, joints and marrow; it judges the thoughts and attitudes of the heart" (Hebrews 4:12). As we pray for God to search our hearts, we must continually expose ourselves to the searching of His Word.

We must be careful to let the Holy Spirit do this searching. If we try to search our own hearts, we are apt to fall into one or both of two traps. The first is the trap of morbid introspection. Introspection can easily become the tool of Satan, who is called the "accuser" (Revelation 12:10). One of his chief weapons is discouragement. He knows that if he can make us discouraged and dispirited, we will not fight the battle for holiness.

The second trap is that of missing the real issues in our lives. The deceitfulness of Satan and of our own hearts will lead us to focus on secondary issues. I recall a young man who came to talk to me about a sin problem in his life over which he had no control.

But though this problem loomed overwhelmingly in his mind, there were other areas of need in his life to which he was blind. The sin he saw was hurting only himself, but the problems he didn't see were hurting others every day. Only the Holy Spirit can enable us to see such areas to which we are blind.

The seat of indwelling sin, then, is our deceitful, unsearchable heart. A second thing we should realize is that *indwelling sin works largely through our desires*. Ever since his fall in the Garden of Eden, man has listened to his desires more than his reason. Desire has come to be the strongest faculty of man's heart.[2] The next time you face one of your typical temptations, watch for the struggle between your desires and your reason. If you give in to temptation, it will be because desire has overcome reason in the struggle to influence your will. The world recognizes this and makes appeals to our desires through what the writer of Hebrews calls the pleasures of sin (Hebrews 11:25).

Not all desire is evil, of course. Paul speaks of his desire to know Christ (Philippians 3:10), of his desire for the salvation of his fellow Jews (Romans 10:1), and the desire that his spiritual children grow to maturity (Galatians 4:19).

We are speaking here, however, about the evil desires that lead us into sin. James said we are tempted when we are dragged away and enticed by our own evil desires (James 1:14). If we are to win this battle for holiness, we must recognize that the basic problem lies within us. It is our own evil desires that lead us into temptation. We may think we merely respond to outward temptations that are presented to us. But the truth is, our evil desires are constantly searching out temptations to satisfy their insatiable lusts. Consider the particular temptations to which you are especially vulnerable, and note how often you find yourself searching out occasions to satisfy those evil desires.

Even when we are engaged in one way or another with the battle against a particular sin, our evil desire or indwelling sin will lead us into playing with that very sin. Sometimes while confessing a sin we find ourselves starting once again to dwell on the evil thoughts associated with that sin, and we may be tempted again.

There are also, of course, many occasions when we encounter temptation unexpectedly. When this happens our evil desires are ready and prompt to receive and embrace them. Just as fire burns any combustible material presented to it, so our own evil desires immediately respond to temptation. John Owen said that sin carries on its war by entangling our affections (what I have here called desires) and drawing them away. Hence, said Owen, denying sin must be chiefly directed on the affections. We must make sure our desires are directed toward glorifying God, he said, and not satisfying the lusts of our bodies.[3]

The third thing we must understand about indwelling sin is that *it tends to deceive our understanding or reasoning*. Our reason, enlightened by the Holy Spirit through the Word of God, stands in the way of sin gaining mastery over us through our desires. Therefore Satan's great strategy is to deceive our minds. Paul spoke of the "deceitful desires" of the old self (Ephesians 4:22). He said that we were at one time "deceived and enslaved by all kinds of passions and pleasures" (Titus 3:3). These passages speak of our old life, but we must realize that this deceit still wages war against us, though it no longer has mastery over us.

Deceit of the mind is carried on by degrees, little by little. We are first drawn away from watchfulness, then from obedience. We become like Ephraim, of whom God said, "Foreigners sap his strength, but he does not realize it. His hair is sprinkled with gray, but he does not notice" (Hosea 7:9). We are drawn away from watchfulness by overconfidence. We come to believe we are beyond a particular temptation. We look at someone else's fall and say, "I would never do that." But Paul warned us, "If you think you are standing firm, be careful that you don't fall" (1 Corinthians 10:12). Even when helping a fallen brother, we are to watch ourselves lest we also be tempted (Galatians 6:1).

We are often drawn away from obedience by the abuse of grace. Jude speaks of certain men "who change the grace of our God into a license for immorality" (Jude 4). We abuse grace when we think we can sin and then receive forgiveness by claiming 1 John 1:9. We abuse grace when, after sinning, we dwell on the compassion and mercy of God to the exclusion of His holiness and hatred of sin.

We are drawn away from obedience when we begin to question what God says in His Word. This was Satan's first tactic with Eve (Genesis 3:1-5). Just as he said to Eve, "You surely shall not die!" so he says to us, "It is just a little thing!" or "God will not judge that sin."

So we see that though sin no longer has dominion over us, it wages its guerrilla warfare against us. If left unchecked, it will defeat us. Our recourse against this warfare is to deal swiftly and firmly with the first motions of indwelling sin. If temptation finds any lodging place in the soul, it will use that to lead us into sin. "When the sentence for a crime is not quickly carried out, the hearts of the people are filled with schemes to do wrong" (Ecclesiastes 8:11).

Furthermore, we must never consider that our fight against sin is at an end. The heart is unsearchable, our evil desires are insatiable, and our reason is constantly in danger of being deceived. Well did Jesus say, "Watch and pray so that you will not fall into temptation" (Matthew 26:41). And Solomon warned us, "Above all else, guard your heart, for it is the wellspring of life" (Proverbs 4:23).

---

NOTES
1. Adapted from the definition of the heart by the Puritan John Owen in his treatise *Indwelling Sin* (1656) as it appears in *Temptation and Sin* (reprint edition, Evansville, Indiana: Sovereign Grace Book Club, 1958), page 170.
2. This idea is taken from comments on James 1:14 by the Puritan James Manton in *An Exposition on the Epistle of James* (1693; reprint edition, Sovereign Grace Publishers, 1962), page 93.
3. Owen, *Temptation and Sin*, page 199.

CHAPTER

# Help in the Daily Battle

~

*In the same way
count yourselves dead to sin
but alive to God
in Christ Jesus.*

~

ROMANS 6:11

In chapter 5 we saw how God has delivered us from the realm and reign of sin through union with Christ in His death. We were slaves to sin and in slavery we committed sins. We developed sinful habits regardless of how "good" we were. But Jesus Christ came into this sinful world and took our place on Calvary. He died to sin and through our union with Him we died to sin also. Now we are freed from sin's reign; we are no longer its slaves. We are to count on this fact and resist sin so that it does not reign in our mortal bodies.

In chapter 6 we saw how sin still lives within us, waging its "guerrilla warfare" through evil desires and deceiving our minds. It may well seem that whatever hope for holiness was held out in chapter 5 was effectively taken away in chapter 6. "What good does it do," you may ask, "to be told that the war with sin was won by Christ in His death on the cross if I am still harassed and often defeated by sin in my heart?"

To experience practical, everyday holiness, we must accept the fact that God in His infinite wisdom has seen fit to allow this daily battle with indwelling sin. But God does not leave us to do battle alone. Just as He delivered us from the overall reign of sin, so He has made ample provision for us to win the daily skirmishes against sin.

This brings us to the second point in Romans 6:11 which we are to count on and keep before us. We are not only dead to sin, as we saw in chapter 5; we also are alive to God. We have not only been delivered from the dominion of darkness; we also have been brought into the kingdom of Christ. Paul said we have become slaves of righteousness (Romans 6:18). God does not leave us suspended in a state of neutrality. He delivers us from sin's reign into the reign of His Son.

What is the significance of being alive unto God? How does it help us in our pursuit of holiness? For one thing, it means *we are united with Christ in all His power*. It is certainly true we cannot live a holy life in our own strength. Christianity is not a do-it-yourself thing.

Notice the attitude of the Apostle Paul in Philippians 4:11-13. He is talking about how he has learned to be content whatever the circumstances, whether plenty or want, whether well-fed or hungry. He says he can respond this way through Christ, who gives him strength. How does this apply to holiness? Our reactions to circumstances are a part of our walk of holiness. Holiness is not a series of do's and don'ts, but conformity to the character of God and obedience to the will of God. Accepting with contentment whatever circumstances God allows for me is very much a part of a holy walk.

But notice that Paul said he could respond in contentment because Christ gave the strength to do so. We see this again where Paul said he prayed that the Colossians would be "strengthened with all power according to his glorious might so that you may have great endurance and patience" (Colossians 1:11). Where do endurance and patience come from? They come as we are strengthened with God's power.

Consider again another prayer Paul described in his letter to the Ephesians. He said he was praying for them "that out of his glorious riches he may strengthen you with *power* through his Spirit in your inner being" (Ephesians 3:16). He concluded the prayer by acknowledging that God "is able to do immeasurably more than all we ask or imagine, according to his *power* that is at work within us" (3:20).

This is the first implication we should grasp of being "alive unto God." We are united with the One who is at work in us to strengthen us with His mighty power. We have all known the awful sense of hopelessness caused by sin's power. We have resolved scores of times never to give in again to a particular temptation, and yet we do. Then Satan comes to us and says, "You might as well give up. You can never overcome that sin." It is true that in ourselves we cannot. But we are alive to God, united to Him who will strengthen us. By reckoning on this fact—counting it to be true—we will experience the strength we need to fight that temptation.

Only as we reckon on these twin facts—that I am dead to sin and its reign over me and that I am alive to God, united to Him who strengthens me—can I keep sin from reigning in my mortal body.

Dr. Martyn Lloyd-Jones says, "To realize this takes away from us that old sense of hopelessness which we have all known and felt because of the terrible power of sin. . . . How does it work? It works in this way: I lose my sense of hopelessness because I can say to myself that not only am I no longer under the dominion of sin, but I am under the dominion of another power that nothing can frustrate. However weak I may be, it is the power of God that is working in me."[1]

This is not theoretical teaching, something to be placed on the library shelves of our minds and admired, but of no practical value in the battle for holiness. To count on the fact that we are dead to sin and alive to God is something we must do actively.

To do it we must *form the habit* of continually realizing that we are dead to sin and alive to God. Practically speaking, we do this when by faith in God's Word we resist sin's advances and temptations. We count on the fact that we are alive to God when by faith we look to Christ for the power we need to do the resisting. Faith, however, must always be based on fact, and Romans 6:11 is a fact for us.

A second implication of being alive to God is that *He has given us His Holy Spirit to live within us.* Actually this is not a second result, but another way of looking at our union with Christ, for His Spirit is the agent of this union. It is He who gives spiritual life and the strength to live that life (Romans 8:9-11). It is the Spirit of God who works in us that we may decide and act according to God's good purpose (Philippians 2:13).

Paul said, "God did not call us to be impure, but to live a holy life. Therefore, he who rejects this instruction does not reject man but God, who gives you his Holy Spirit" (1 Thessalonians 4:7-8). Here Paul connects the giving of the Holy Spirit with our living a holy life. He is called the Holy Spirit and He is sent primarily to make us holy—to conform us to the character of God. The connection of these two thoughts, the Holy Spirit and a holy life, is also found in other passages. For example, we are told to flee sexual immorality because our bodies are temples of the Holy Spirit (1 Corinthians 6:18-19). We are also told that we are controlled not by our sinful nature but by the Spirit, if the Spirit of God lives in us (Romans 8:9). We read, "Live by the Spirit, and you will not gratify the desires of the sinful nature" (Galatians 5:16).

Why do we have the Holy Spirit living within us to strengthen us toward holiness? It is because we are alive to God. We are now living under the reign of God, who unites us to Christ and gives us His Holy Spirit to dwell within us.[2]

The Holy Spirit strengthens us to holiness first by enabling us to see our need of holiness. He enlightens our understanding so that we begin to see God's standard of holiness. Then he causes us to become aware of our specific areas of sin. One of Satan's most powerful weapons is making us spiritually blind—unable to see our sinful character. The Bible says, "The heart is deceitful above all things and beyond cure. Who can understand it?" (Jeremiah 17:9). No one can understand it and expose it except the Holy Spirit.

Even Christians taking in the teaching of the Bible can be deceived about their own sins. We somehow feel that consent to the teaching of Scripture is equivalent to obedience. We may hear a point of application in a sermon, or perhaps discover it in our own personal Bible reading or study. We say, "Yes that is true; that is something I need to act on." But we let it drop at that point. James says when we do that, we deceive ourselves (James 1:22).

As we grow in the Christian life we face increasing danger of spiritual pride. We know the correct doctrines, the right methods and the proper do's and don'ts. But we may not see the poverty of our own spiritual character. We may not see our critical and unforgiving spirit, our habit of backbiting, or our tendency to judge others. We may become like the Laodiceans of whom our Lord said, "You say, 'I am rich; I have acquired wealth and do not need a thing.' But you do not realize that you are wretched, pitiful, poor, blind, and naked" (Revelation 3:17).

David was like this when he committed adultery

with Bathsheba and then had her husband murdered to cover his first sin (2 Samuel 12:1-13). Was he repentant and humbled over his despicable acts? Not at all. In fact, he was ready to judge another man for a far lesser crime and to condemn him to death (verse 5). How could he do this? Because he was spiritually blind. It was not till Nathan the prophet said to David, "You are the man!" that David was able to see the awful heinousness of his crime.

It is the Holy Spirit's ministry to make us see that we are poverty-stricken because of our sins. He comes to us and says, "You are the man!" Even though such a message may come from the loving, caring lips of a brother in Christ, it is the Holy Spirit who enables us to accept it and to say as David did, "I have sinned against the Lord." The Holy Spirit opens the inner recesses of our hearts and enables us to see the moral cesspools hidden there. This is where He begins His ministry of making us holy.

The natural result of seeing God's standard and our sinfulness is the awakening within us of a desire to be holy. This is also the ministry of the Holy Spirit as He works to make us holy. We are sorry for our sins with a godly sorrow that leads to repentance (2 Corinthians 7:10). We say with David, "Wash away all my iniquity, and cleanse me from my sin. . . . Cleanse me with hyssop, and I will be clean; wash me, and I will be whiter than snow" (Psalm 51:2,7).

Paul said, "For it is God who works in you to will and to act according to his good purpose" (Philippians 2:13). Before we can *act* we must *will*. To will means to desire and resolve. When the Holy Spirit shows us our sinfulness, He does not do this to lead us to despair but to lead us to holiness. He does

73

this by creating within us a hatred of our sins and a desire for holiness.

Only one who has a strong desire to be holy will ever persevere in the painfully slow and difficult task of pursuing holiness. There are too many failures. The habits of our old nature and the attacks of Satan are too strong for us to persevere unless the Holy Spirit is at work in us to create a desire for holiness.

The Holy Spirit creates this desire, not only by showing us our sins, but also by showing us God's standard of holiness. He does this through the Scriptures. As we read and study the Scriptures or hear them taught, we are captivated by the moral beauty of God's standard of holiness. Even though His standard may seem far beyond us, we recognize and respond to that which is "holy, righteous, and good" (Romans 7:12). Even though we fail so often, in our inner being we "delight in God's law" (Romans 7:22).

Here then is another distinction we must make between what God does and what we must do. If the Holy Spirit uses Scripture to show us our need and to stimulate a desire for holiness, then doesn't it follow that we must be in God's Word on a consistent basis? Should we not go to the Word, whether to hear it preached or to do our own study, with the prayer that the Holy Spirit would search our hearts for any sin in us? (Psalm 139:23-24).

After the Holy Spirit has enabled us to see our need and created within us a desire for holiness, there remains something more which He must do. He must give us the spiritual strength to live a holy life. Paul said, "Live by the Spirit, and you will not gratify the desires of the sinful nature" (Galatians 5:16). To live by the Spirit is to live both in obedience *to* and dependence *on* the Holy Spirit. There is a balance then between our wills (expressed by obedience) and our faith (expressed by our dependence). But at this point we are considering the aspect of our dependence on the Holy Spirit.

No one overcomes the corruptions of his heart except by the enabling strength of the Spirit of God. Peter said that God has given us "His very great and precious promises, so that through them you may participate in the divine nature and escape the corruption in the world" (2 Peter 1:4). Through participation in the divine nature we escape corruption—and this participation is through the indwelling Holy Spirit.

We express our dependence on the Holy Spirit for a holy life in two ways. The first is through *a humble and consistent intake of the Scripture*. If we truly desire to live in the realm of the Spirit we must continually feed our minds with His truth. It is hypocritical to pray for victory over our sins yet be careless in our intake of the Word of God.

It is possible, though, to be consistent in our intake of the Word of God without an attitude of dependence on the Holy Spirit. God says, "This is the one I esteem: he who is humble and contrite in spirit, and trembles at my word" (Isaiah 66:2). We are to come to the Word in a spirit of humility and contrition because we recognize that we are sinful, that we are often blind to our sinfulness, and that we need the enlightening power of the Holy Spirit in our hearts.

The second way we express our dependence on the Spirit is *to pray for holiness*. The Apostle Paul prayed continually for the working of God's Spirit in the lives of those to whom he was writing. He told the Ephesians that he prayed God would "strengthen you with power through his Spirit in your inner being"

(Ephesians 3:16). He prayed that God would fill the Colossians "with the knowledge of his will through all spiritual wisdom and understanding" so that they might "live a life worthy of the Lord and may please him in every way" (Colossians 1:9-10).

He wrote to the Thessalonians, "May God Himself, the God of peace, sanctify you [make you holy] through and through" (1 Thessalonians 5:23); and, "May the Lord make your love increase and overflow for each other and for everyone else. . . . May he strengthen your hearts so that you will be blameless and holy in the presence of our God" (1 Thessalonians 3:12-13). Clearly the Apostle Paul knew we depend on the Holy Spirit for holiness, and he expressed this dependence through prayer.

As a young Christian I had the idea that all I had to do to live a holy life was to find out from the Bible what God wanted me to do and go do it. Christians with maturity will smile at this naive assumption, but I see younger Christians starting off with the same air of self-confidence. We have to learn that we are dependent upon the enabling power of the Holy Spirit to attain any degree of holiness. Then, as we look to Him, we will see Him working in us—revealing our sin, creating a desire for holiness, and giving us the strength to respond to Him in obedience.

---

NOTES

1. D. Martyn Lloyd-Jones, *Romans: An Exposition of Chapter 6*, page 144.

2. It is also true that the Holy Spirit is the divine Agent who has made us alive to God (John 6:63). But we are here considering the results of being delivered from the realm of sin into the realm of God, and the indwelling of the Holy Spirit is one of the results.

# 8

# Obedience — Not Victory

~

*For if you live according to
the sinful nature, you will die;
but if by the Spirit
you put to death
the misdeeds of the body,
you will live.*

~

ROMANS 8:13

God has made provision for our holiness and He has also given us a responsibility for it. As we saw in chapters 5 and 7, God's provision for us consists in delivering us from the reign of sin, uniting us with Christ, and giving us the indwelling Holy Spirit to reveal sin, to create a desire for holiness, and to strengthen us in our pursuit of holiness. Through the power of the Holy Spirit and according to the new nature He gives, we are to put to death the misdeeds of the body (Romans 8:13).

Though it is the Spirit who enables us to put to death our corruptions, yet Paul says this is our action as well. The very same work is from one point of view the work of the Spirit, and from another the work of man.

In the previous chapter we emphasized the "by the Spirit" part of this verse. In this chapter we want to look at our responsibility—"you put to death the misdeeds of the body."

It is clear from this passage that God puts responsibility for living a holy life squarely on us. We are to do something. We are not to "stop trying and start trusting"; we are to put to death the misdeeds of the body. Over and over again in the epistles— not only Paul's, but the other apostles' as well—we are commanded to assume our responsibility for a holy walk. Paul exhorted, "Put to death, therefore, whatever belongs to your earthly nature" (Colossians 3:5). This is something we are told to do.

The writer of Hebrews said, "Therefore, since we are surrounded by such a great cloud of witnesses, let us throw off everything that hinders and the sin that so easily entangles, and let us run with perseverance the race marked out for us" (Hebrews

12:1). He says *let us* throw off the sin and *let us* run with perseverance. Clearly he expects us to assume responsibility for running the Christian race. James said, "Submit yourselves, then, to God. Resist the devil, and he will flee from you" (James 4:7). It is we who are to submit to God and resist the devil. This is our responsibility. Peter said, "Make every effort to be found spotless, blameless and at peace with him" (2 Peter 3:14). The clause *make every effort* addresses itself to our wills. It is something we must decide to do.

During a certain period in my Christian life I thought that any effort on my part to live a holy life was "of the flesh" and that "the flesh profits for nothing." I thought God would not bless any effort on my part to live the Christian life, just as He would not bless any effort on my part to become a Christian by good works. Just as I received Christ Jesus by faith, so I was to seek a holy life only by faith. Any effort on my part was just getting in God's way. I misapplied the statement, "You will not have to fight this battle. Take up your positions; stand firm and see the deliverance the Lord will give you" (2 Chronicles 20:17), to mean that I was just to turn it all over to the Lord and He would fight the sin in my life. In fact, in the margin of the Bible I was using during that period I wrote alongside the verse these words: "Illustration of walking in the Spirit."

How foolish I was. I misconstrued dependence on the Holy Spirit to mean I was to make no effort, that I had no responsibility. I mistakenly thought if I turned it all over to the Lord, He would make my choices for me and would choose obedience over disobedience. All I needed was to look to Him for holiness. But this is not God's way. He makes provision for our holiness, but He gives us the responsibility of using those provisions.

The Holy Spirit has been given to all Christians. Dr. Martyn Lloyd-Jones says,

> "The Holy Spirit is in us; He is working in us, and empowering us, giving us the ability. . . . This is the New Testament teaching—'Work out your own salvation with fear and trembling.' We have to do so. But note the accompaniment—'Because it is God that worketh in you, both to will and to do of His good pleasure'! The Holy Spirit is working in us 'both to will and to do.' It is because I am not left to myself, it is because I am not 'absolutely hopeless,' since the Spirit is in me, that I am exhorted to work out my own salvation with fear and trembling."[1]

We must rely on the Spirit in our putting to death the deeds of the body. As Lloyd-Jones observes in his exposition of Romans 8:13, it is the Holy Spirit who "differentiates Christianity from morality, from 'legalism' and false Puritanism."[2] But our reliance on the Spirit is not intended to foster an attitude of "I can't do it," but one of "I can do it through Him who strengthens me." The Christian should never complain of want of ability and power. If we sin, it is because we choose to sin, not because we lack the ability to say no to temptation.

It is time for us Christians to face up to our responsibility for holiness. Too often we say we are "defeated" by this or that sin. No, we are not defeated; we are simply disobedient! It might be well if we stopped using the terms "victory" and "defeat" to describe our progress in holiness. Rather we should use the terms "obedience" and "disobedience." When I say I am defeated by some sin, I am unconsciously slipping out from under my responsibility. I am saying something outside of me has defeated me. But when I say I am disobedient, that places the responsibility for my sin squarely on me. We may, in fact, be defeated, but the reason we are defeated is because we have chosen to disobey. We have chosen to entertain lustful thoughts, or to harbor resentment, or to shade the truth a little.

We need to brace ourselves up, and to realize that we are responsible for our thoughts, attitudes, and actions. We need to reckon on the fact that we died to sin's reign, that it no longer has any dominion over us, that God has united us with the risen Christ in all His power, and has given us the Holy Spirit to work in us. Only as we accept our responsibility and appropriate God's provisions will we make any progress in our pursuit of holiness.

---

NOTES

1. D. Martyn Lloyd-Jones, *The Sons of God—Exposition of Romans 8:5-17* (Edinburgh: The Banner of Truth Trust, 1974), page 124.
2. Lloyd-Jones, *The Sons of God*, page 136.

CHAPTER

9

# Putting Sin to Death

*Put to death,
therefore, whatever belongs
to your earthly nature:
sexual immorality, impurity,
lust, evil desires and greed,
which is idolatry.*

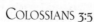

COLOSSIANS 3:5

83

The New Testament leaves no doubt that holiness is our responsibility. If we are to pursue holiness, we must take some decisive action. I once discussed a particular sin problem with a person who said, "I've been praying that God would motivate me to stop." Motivate him to stop? What this person was saying in effect was that God had not done enough. It is so easy to ask God to do something more because that postpones facing up to our own responsibility.

The action we are to take is to put to death the misdeeds of the body (Romans 8:13). Paul uses the same expression in another book: "Put to death, therefore, whatever belongs to your earthly nature" (Colossians 3:5). What does the expression *put to death* mean? The *King James Version* uses the term *mortify*. According to the dictionary, mortify means "to destroy the strength, vitality, or functioning of; to subdue or deaden."[1] To put to death the misdeeds of the body, then, is to destroy the strength and vitality of sin as it tries to reign in our bodies.

It must be clear to us that mortification, though it is something we do, cannot be carried out in our own strength. Well did the Puritan John Owen say, "Mortification from a self-strength, carried on by ways of self-invention, unto the end of a self-righteousness is the soul and substance of all false religion."[2] Mortification must be done by the strength and under the direction of the Holy Spirit.

Owen says further, "The Spirit alone is sufficient for this work. All ways and means without Him are useless. He is the great efficient. He is the One who gives life and strength to our efforts."[3]

But though mortification must be done by the

strength and under the direction of the Holy Spirit, it is nevertheless a work which we must do. Without the Holy Spirit's strength there will be no mortification, but without our working in His strength there will also be no mortification.

The crucial question then is, "How do we destroy the strength and vitality of sin?" If we are to work at this difficult task, we must first have *conviction*. We must be persuaded that a holy life of God's will for every Christian is important. We must believe that the pursuit of holiness is worth the effort and pain required to mortify the misdeeds of the body. We must be convinced that "without holiness no one will see the Lord" (Hebrews 12:14).

Not only must we develop conviction for living a holy life in general, but we must also develop convictions in specific areas of obedience.

These convictions are developed through exposure to the Word of God. Our minds have far too long been accustomed to the world's values. Even after we become Christians, the world around us constantly seeks to conform us to its value system. We are bombarded on every side by temptations to indulge our sinful natures. That is why Paul said, "Don't let the world around you squeeze you into its own mold, but let God remake you so that your whole attitude of mind is changed" (Romans 12:2, PH).

Only through God's Word are our minds remolded and our values renewed. When giving instructions for future kings of Israel, God said that a copy of His Law "shall be with him, and he shall read it all the days of his life, that he may learn to fear the Lord his God, by carefully observing all the words of this law and these statutes"

(Deuteronomy 17:19, NASB). The king was to read God's law all the days of his life to learn to fear the Lord. In that way he could learn the necessity of holiness, and how he might know God's specific will in various situations.

Jesus said, "Whoever has my commands and obeys them, he is the one who loves me" (John 14:21). Obedience is the pathway to holiness, but it is only as we *have* His commands that we can obey them. God's Word must be so strongly fixed in our minds that it becomes the dominant influence in our thoughts, our attitudes, and our actions. One of the most effective ways of influencing our minds is through memorizing Scripture. David said, "I have hidden your word in my heart that I might not sin against you" (Psalm 119:11).

To memorize Scripture effectively, you must have a plan. The plan should include a selection of well-chosen verses, a practical system for learning those verses, a systematic means of reviewing them to keep them fresh in your memory, and simple rules for continuing Scripture memory on your own.

I know from personal experience how important such a plan is. I instinctively realized the importance of God's Word for my life as a young Christian at college, but I did not know what to do about it. I memorized a few verses in a spasmodic and haphazard fashion, but they were of little profit to me. Then one day I was introduced to The Navigators' *Topical Memory System*, and began a plan of regular Scripture memorization. Twenty-eight years later, I still profit from this simple but effective plan for hiding God's Word in my heart.[4]

Of course, the goal of memorization is application of the Scripture to one's daily life. It is through the application of Scripture to specific life situations that we develop the kind of conviction to see us through the temptations that trip us up so easily.

A number of years ago my wife and I lived in Kansas City, Missouri, while I worked across the river in Kansas City, Kansas. As an employee working in Kansas, I was subject to Kansas state income tax, but as a resident of Missouri I did not have to pay the tax till the end of the year. We moved to Colorado in July of one year, and at the end of the year I realized that I owed Kansas for seven months of income tax. My first thought was to forget it; after all, the amount was fairly small and they wouldn't come all the way to Colorado to collect. But then the Holy Spirit brought to my mind a verse I had previously memorized, "Give everyone what you owe him: if you owe taxes, pay taxes" (Romans 13:7). God brought conviction to my heart that I must pay the State of Kansas the tax I owed out of obedience to God. God gave *conviction* that day regarding the payment of taxes, and this conviction has influenced and governed my actions ever since.

This is the way we develop conviction—by bringing God's Word to bear on specific situations that arise in our lives and determining God's will in that situation from the Word.

Many issues of life are clearly addressed in the Bible, and we would do well to memorize verses that speak to those issues. For example, God's will concerning honesty is plainly spelled out: "Therefore each of you must put off falsehood and speak truthfully to his neighbor. . . . He who has been stealing must steal no longer" (Ephesians 4:25,28).

His will concerning abstinence from sexual immorality also is described clearly: "It is God's will that you should be sanctified: that you should avoid sexual immorality" (1 Thessalonians 4:3). These are clearly stated issues where we should have no difficulty developing convictions as to God's will if we are willing to obey His Word.

But what about issues that are not specifically mentioned in the Scriptures—how do we determine God's will and develop conviction in those areas?

Years ago a friend gave me what he called his "Formula: How to Know Right from Wrong." The formula asks four questions based on three verses in 1 Corinthians:

- ❖ "'Everything is permissible for me'—but not everything is beneficial" (1 Corinthians 6:12). *Question 1:* Is it helpful—physically, spiritually, and mentally?
- ❖ "'Everything is permissible for me'—but I will not be mastered by anything" (1 Corinthians 6:12). *Question 2:* Does it bring me under its power?
- ❖ "Therefore, if what I eat causes my brother to fall into sin, I will never eat meat again, so that I will not cause him to fall" (1 Corinthians 8:13). *Question 3:* Does it hurt others?
- ❖ "So whether you eat or drink or whatever you do, do it all for the glory of God" (1 Corinthians 10:31). *Question 4:* Does it glorify God?

As simple as this formula may appear, it is powerful in developing conviction—if we are willing to use it. These questions can get rather searching. But they must be asked if we are to pursue holiness as a total way of life.

Let's apply these principles to some typical situations. Take the television programs you watch, for example. Are they helpful—physically, spiritually, or mentally? For some programs the answer may be yes, but for those to which you must honestly answer no, you should consider not viewing them.

What about the question, "Does it bring me under its power?" You may instantly apply that question to such habits as drinking, taking drugs, or smoking, and feel it doesn't apply to you. But again, what about the television set? Have certain programs "grabbed" you so that you just cannot miss them? If so, they have brought you under their power. For another example, I know a Christian woman who as a teenager was a national junior tennis champion. She was so caught up in tennis that it was her whole life, even though she was a Christian. When she began to consider the claims of Christian discipleship seriously, she realized tennis held a certain power over her which was keeping her from wholly following Christ. She then made a decision to hang up her tennis racket to break that power. Not till a number of years later, when the pull was totally gone, did she begin to play tennis again solely for recreational value, and with freedom of conscience.

This illustration of the tennis player emphasizes an important fact. It may not be the activity itself that determines whether something is sinful for us, but rather our response to that activity. Certainly the game of tennis is morally neutral and, under the right conditions, physically beneficial. But because this woman had made it an idol in her life, it had become sinful for her.

Let's examine the next question, "Does it hurt others?" with this same story of my tennis-playing friend. Suppose another Christian who enjoyed playing tennis purely for recreational value had insisted to this woman that there's nothing wrong with tennis. Technically that person would be correct, but he would be insisting on a view that would likely be harmful to the young woman's spiritual life. Many activities, strictly speaking, are morally neutral, but because of some immoral associations in a person's past may be detrimental to that person, at least for a time. Those of us who do not have that immoral association must be considerate of these people lest we cause them to slip back into an activity that is sinful for them.

But what about those areas in which Christians differ in their convictions as to God's will? Paul speaks to this question in Romans 14, where he takes up the problem of eating certain food. He lays down three general principles to guide us. The first is that we should not judge those whose convictions are different from ours (verses 1-4). The second principle is that whatever our convictions are, they must be "to the Lord," that is, developed out of a sense of obedience to Him (verses 5-8). The third principle is that whatever convictions we have developed as "to the Lord," we must be true to them (verse 23). If we go against our convictions, we are sinning, even though others may have perfect freedom in that particular thing.

For several years I struggled with the question of how my family and I should observe Sunday as the

Lord's Day. Early in my Christian life I was taught that Sunday was a sacred day and that its activities should be governed accordingly. I soon came to realize, however, that there is genuine disagreement among sincere Christians as to how Sunday is to be observed. Applying the principles of Romans 14 to this question, then, I must first of all not judge those who observe Sunday differently than I do. Second, whatever my own convictions, they must be out of a sincere response of obedience to how God is leading *me*. And then, having developed my own convictions, I must be careful not to violate them, regardless of what other Christians may do.

The question we must ask in a serious pursuit of holiness is this: "Am I willing to develop convictions from the Scriptures, and to live by these convictions?" This is often where the rub comes. We hesitate to face up to God's standard of holiness in a specific area of life. We know that to do so will require obedience that we are unwilling to give.

This leads us to the second quality we must develop if we are to put to death the misdeeds of the body. That quality is *commitment*. Jesus said, "Any of you who does not give up everything he has cannot be my disciple" (Luke 14:33). We must honestly face the question, "Am I willing to give up a certain practice or habit that is keeping me from holiness?" It is at this point of commitment that most of us fail. We prefer to dally with sin, to try to play with it a little without getting too deeply involved.

We have the "just one more time" syndrome. We will take just one more lustful look, eat just one more rich dessert before starting our diet, watch just one more television program before sitting down to our

Bible study. In all of this we are postponing the day of commitment, the day when we say to sin, "Enough!"

I well recall when God spoke to me about indulging my sweet tooth. It wasn't that I was overweight; it was just that I couldn't resist any dessert that came along. I was the one who always went back for seconds at the church pie socials! Then one morning right in the middle of the Christmas festivities, when all the fudge and cookies and fruitcake were so plentiful, God spoke to my heart about this problem. My initial response was, "Lord, wait till after Christmas and I will deal with it." I wasn't willing that day to make a commitment.

Solomon tells us that the eyes of man are never satisfied (Proverbs 27:20). One more lustful look or one more piece of pie never satisfies. In fact, quite the opposite takes place. Every time we say yes to temptation, we make it harder to say no the next time.

We must recognize that we have developed habit patterns of sin. We have developed the habit of shading the facts a little bit when it is to our advantage. We have developed the habit of giving in to the inertia that refuses to let us get up in the morning. These habits must be broken, but they never will till we make a basic commitment to a life of holiness without exceptions.

The Apostle John said, "My dear children, I write this to you so that you will not sin" (1 John 2:1). The whole purpose of John's letter, he says, is that we *not* sin. One day as I was studying this chapter I realized that my personal life's objective regarding holiness was less than that of John's. He was saying, in effect, "Make it your aim *not* to sin." As I thought about this, I realized that deep within my heart my real aim was not to sin *very much*. I found it difficult to say, "Yes, Lord, from here on I will make it my aim not to sin." I realized God was calling me that day to a deeper level of commitment to holiness than I had previously been willing to make.

Can you imagine a soldier going into battle with the aim of "not getting hit very much"? The very suggestion is ridiculous. His aim is not to get hit at all! Yet if we have not made a commitment to holiness without exception, we are like a soldier going into battle with the aim of not getting hit very much. We can be sure if that is our aim, we will be hit — not with bullets, but with temptation over and over again.

Jonathan Edwards, one of the great preachers of early American history, used to make resolutions. One of his was, "Resolved, never to do anything which I would be afraid to do if it were the last hour of my life."[5] Dare we twentieth-century Christians make such a resolution? Are we willing to commit ourselves to the practice of holiness without exceptions? There is no point in praying for victory over temptation if we are not willing to make a commitment to say no to it.

It is only by learning to deny temptation that we will ever put to death the misdeeds of the body. Learning this is usually a slow and painful process, fraught with much failure. Our old desires and our sinful habits are not easily dislodged. To break them requires persistence, often in the face of little success. But this is the path we must tread, painful though it may be.

NOTES
1. By permission. From *Webster's New Collegiate Dictionary* © 1977 by G. & C. Merriam Co., Publishers of the Merriam Webster Dictionaries, page 750.
2. John Owen, *Temptation and Sin*, page 7.
3. Owen, *Temptation and Sin*, page 16. Author's paraphrase.
4. The Navigators' *Topical Memory System* may be obtained from your local Christian bookstore.
5. *Jonathan Edwards—Representative Selections, with Introduction, Bibliography, and Notes*, Clarence H. Faust and Thomas H. Johnson, editors (revised edition, New York: Hill and Wang, 1962), page 38.

CHAPTER

# 10

# The Place of Personal Discipline

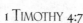

*Have nothing to do
with godless myths
and old wives' tales;
rather, train yourself
to be godly.*

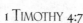

1 TIMOTHY 4:7

It is possible to establish convictions regarding a life of holiness, and even make a definite commitment to that end, yet fail to achieve the goal. Life is strewn with broken resolutions. We may determine by God's grace to stop a particular sinful habit—entertaining lustful thoughts, criticizing our Christian brother, or whatever. But alas, only too frequently we find we don't succeed. We do not achieve that progress in holiness we so intensely desire.

Jay Adams puts his finger on the problem when he says, "You may have sought and tried to obtain *instant* godliness. There is no such thing . . . We want somebody to give us three easy steps to godliness, and we'll take them next Friday and be godly. The trouble is, godliness doesn't come that way."[1]

Adams goes on to show that the way to obtain godliness is through Christian discipline.[2] But the concept of discipline is suspect in our society today. It appears counter to our emphasis on freedom in Christ, and often smacks of legalism and harshness.

Yet Paul says we are to train or discipline ourselves to be godly (1 Timothy 4:7). The figure of speech he uses comes from the physical training that Greek athletes went through. Paul also said, "Everyone who competes in the games goes into strict training" (1 Corinthians 9:25). He said this was an attitude of his life, and one that each Christian should have (1 Corinthians 9:24-27). If an athlete disciplines himself to obtain a temporal prize, he said, how much more should we Christians discipline ourselves to obtain a crown that lasts forever.

As these verses indicate, discipline is structured training. *Webster's New Collegiate Dictionary* lists as one definition of discipline, "training that corrects, molds, or perfects the mental faculties or moral character."[3] This is what we must do if we pursue holiness: We must correct, mold, and train our moral character.

Discipline toward holiness begins with the Word of God. Paul said, "All Scripture is God-breathed and is useful for teaching, rebuking, correcting and training in righteousness" (2 Timothy 3:16). The last item he mentions is *training* or *discipline* in doing righteousness. This is what the Scriptures will do for us if we use them. Jay Adams says, "It is by willing, prayerful and persistent obedience to the requirements of the Scriptures that godly patterns are developed and come to be a part of us."[4]

We read in Scripture, "You were taught . . . to put off your old self . . . to be made new in the attitude of your minds; and to put on the new self, created to be like God in true righteousness and holiness" (Ephesians 4:22-24). Where are we taught these things? Only in the Word of God. Discipline toward holiness begins then with the Scriptures—with a disciplined plan for regular intake of the Scriptures and a disciplined plan for applying them to our daily lives.

Here our cooperation with the Holy Spirit is very clear. A diagram of our interaction with the Spirit looks like this:

The Holy Spirit has already done a good part of His work by providing us with the Scriptures to discipline us. And as we learn them, He will faithfully bring them to our minds as we need them to face temptations. As we seek to apply His Word to daily situations, He will work in us to strengthen us. But we must respond to what the Holy Spirit has already done if we are to expect Him to do more.

So we see that we must discipline our lives for a regular healthy diet of the Word of God. We need a planned time each day for reading or studying the Bible. Every Christian who makes progress in holiness is a person who has disciplined his life so that he spends regular time in the Bible. There simply is no other way.

Satan will always battle us at this point. He will try to persuade us that we are too sleepy in the morning, too busy during the day, and too tired at night. It seems there is never a suitable time for the Word of God. This means we must discipline ourselves to provide this time in our daily schedules. I have found the early morning hour before breakfast to be the most profitable time for me to read the Bible and pray over areas of concern and need. That is also the only time of day when I can be consistent in my principal means of exercise—jogging. To do all this before breakfast requires that I get up at five o'clock. And since I need about seven hours of sleep each night, that means I must be in bed—lights out—by ten p.m. That is hard to do. It can only be done by disciplining my evening hours.

Some wives may not find this time before breakfast practical, especially if they have very young children or must get the rest of the family off to work or school at an early hour. In this case they may find the time immediately after breakfast to be most suitable for time alone with God. This, too, requires discipline to take time when the responsibilities of the day are demanding attention.

Whether before breakfast or after, morning or evening, the point is we must all arrange our schedules to provide for this daily intake of the Word of God.

A disciplined intake of the Word of God not only involves a planned *time*; it also involves a planned *method*. Usually we think of methods of intake as falling into four categories — *hearing* the Word taught by our pastors and teachers (Jeremiah 3:15), *reading* the Bible ourselves (Deuteronomy 17:19), *studying* the Scriptures intently (Proverbs 2:1-5), and *memorizing* key passages (Psalm 119:11). All of these methods are needed for a balanced intake of the Word. Pastors are gifted by God and trained to teach the "whole counsel of God." Reading the Scripture gives us the overall perspective of divine truth, while study of a passage or topic enables us to dig more deeply into a particular truth. Memorization helps us retain important truths so we can apply them in our lives.

But if we are to pursue holiness with discipline, we must do more than hear, read, study, or memorize Scripture. We must meditate on it. God said to Joshua, as he was assuming leadership over Israel, "Do not let this Book of the Law depart from your mouth; meditate on it day and night, so that you may be careful to do everything written in it" (Joshua 1:8). To meditate on the Scriptures is to think about them, turning them over in our minds, and applying them to our life's situations. Few of us practice meditation on the Scriptures. Somehow the idea of meditation sounds like something medieval monks did in monasteries. Yet Joshua, a very busy commander-in-chief of the army of Israel, was told to meditate on the law of God day and night.

The practice of meditation on the Word of God—simply thinking about it and its application to life—is a practice we develop through discipline. Most of us think we don't have time for this, but there are blocks of minutes during the day when we can meditate if we develop the habit.

I am something of a "bug" for the daily news and I enjoy listening to the news on the radio as I drive to and from work or elsewhere. One day I was challenged by the example of a friend to use that time to meditate on Scripture verses. Now I am surprised at how many minutes I can use to think about Scripture passages and their application to my life. You may not have the same opportunity I have to meditate as you drive, but if you prayerfully think about it, you will probably find other opportunities in your schedule.[5]

The objective of our meditation is application—obedience to the Scriptures. This too requires discipline. Obeying the Scriptures usually requires change in our patterns of life. Because we are sinful by nature, we have developed sinful patterns, which we call habits. Discipline is required to break any habit. If a boy has developed the wrong style of swinging a baseball bat, he cannot just decide to change instantly. He has developed a certain habit, and much discipline—much correction and training—is required to break that bad habit and develop a new one.

In the same way, our patterns of disobedience to God have been developed over a number of years and are not broken easily or without discipline. Discipline does not mean gritting your teeth and saying, "I'll not do that anymore." Rather, discipline means structured, planned training. Just as you need a plan for regular Bible reading or study, so you need a plan for applying the Word to your life.

As you read or study the Scriptures and meditate on them during the day, ask yourself these three questions:

1. What does this passage teach concerning God's will for a holy life?
2. How does my life measure up to that Scripture; specifically where and how do I fall short? (Be specific; don't generalize.)
3. What definite steps of action do I need to take to obey?

The most important part of this process is the specific application of the Scripture to specific life situations. We are prone to vagueness at this point because commitment to specific actions makes us uncomfortable. But we must avoid general commitments to obedience and instead aim for specific obedience in specific instances. We deceive our souls when we grow in knowledge of the truth without specifically responding to it (James 1:22). This may lead to spiritual pride (1 Corinthians 8:1).

Suppose you were meditating on 1 Corinthians 13, the great love chapter. As you think about the chapter, you realize the importance of love and you also see the practical outworkings of love: Love is patient and kind and does not envy. You ask yourself, "Am I impatient or unkind or envious toward anyone?" As you think about this, you realize you are envious toward Joe at work who seems to be getting all the breaks. You confess this sin to God, being very specific to name Joe and your sinful reaction to his good fortune. You ask God to bless him even more and to give you a spirit of contentment so that you will not continue to envy Joe, but will instead love him. You might memorize 1 Corinthians 13:4 and think about it as you see Joe at work. You even look for ways to help him. Then you do the same thing tomorrow and the next day and the next till finally you see God working a spirit of love in your heart toward Joe.

This is discipline toward holiness. You will never put to death that spirit of envy toward Joe without a definitely structured plan for doing it. That plan is what we call discipline.

You can readily see that this structured training in holiness is a lifelong process. So a necessary ingredient of discipline is *perseverance*.

Any training — physical, mental, or spiritual — is characterized at first by failure. We fail more often than we succeed. But if we persevere, we gradually see progress till we are succeeding more often than failing. This is true as we seek to put to death particular sins. At first it seems we are making no progress, so we become discouraged and think, *What's the use?! I can never overcome that sin*. That is exactly what Satan wants us to think.

It is at this point that we must exercise perseverance. We keep wanting instant success, but holiness doesn't come that way. Our sinful habits are not broken overnight. Follow-through is required to make any change in our lives, and follow-through requires perseverance.

Jonathan Edwards, who resolved never to do anything he would be afraid to do if it were the last hour of his life, also made this resolution: "Resolved, never to give over, nor in the least to slacken, my fight with my corruptions, however unsuccessful I may be."[6] At first glance these two resolutions seem somewhat contradictory. If Edwards had resolved never to do anything he shouldn't do, then why talk about never giving up the fight regardless of how *unsuccessful* he might be? Was he not sincere in making the first resolution? Yes, he was sincere, but he also knew there would be much failure, and that perseverance was required. So he first resolved to seek to live a holy life, then to persevere despite the failures he knew would come.

A verse of Scripture I often use in the face of failure with my own sins is Proverbs 24:16: "For though a righteous man falls seven times, he rises again, but the wicked are brought down by calamity." The person who is disciplining himself toward holiness falls many times, but he doesn't quit. After each failure he gets up and continues the struggle. Not so with the unrighteous. He stumbles in his sin and gives up. He has no power to overcome because he does not have the Spirit of God at work in him.

One of the chapters in the Bible we have the most trouble with is Romans 7. Christians are always trying to "get out of Romans 7 and into Romans 8." The reason we don't like Romans 7 is because it so accurately mirrors our own struggle with sin. And we don't like the idea that we have to struggle with sin. We want instant victory. We want to "walk in the Spirit and let Him win the victory." But God wants us to persevere in discipline toward holiness.

103

Some feel that such statements of Paul's as "For what I want to do I do not do, but what I hate I do" (Romans 7:15) are too strong for a Christian walking in the Spirit. But what Christian can deny that this is often his own experience? The truth is, the more we see the holiness of God and His law revealed to us in the Scripture, the more we recognize how far short we fall.

Isaiah was a prophet of God, walking in the righteousness of God's commandments. Yet on seeing the Lord God in His holiness, he was compelled to cry out, "Woe is me!" I cried. "I am ruined! For I am a man of unclean lips, and I live among a people of unclean lips, and my eyes have seen the King, the Lord Almighty" (Isaiah 6:5).

As we grow in the *knowledge* of God's holiness, even though we are also growing in the *practice* of holiness it seems the gap between our knowledge and our practice always gets wider. This is the Holy Spirit's way of drawing us to more and more holiness. This is illustrated by the following graph:

As we progress in holiness, we come to hate sin (Psalm 119:104) and to delight in God's law (Romans 7:22). We see the perfection of God's law and the rightness of all He requires of us. We agree that "his commands are not burdensome" (1 John 5:3), but are "holy, righteous, and good" (Romans 7:12). But during all this time we also see our own inner corruption and our frequent falls into sin. We cry out with Paul, "What a wretched man I am!" (Romans 7:24), and we want to give up. This we dare not do. If we would succeed in our pursuit of holiness we must persevere in spite of failure.

---

NOTES
1. Jay E. Adams, *Godliness Through Discipline*, page 3.
2. Godliness is closely akin to holiness in Scripture. *Strong's Concordance* lists holiness as a synonym for godliness. *Vine* says godliness is "that piety which is characterized by a Godward attitude, and does that which is well pleasing to Him" (*Expository Dictionary of New Testament Words*, page 162).
3. *Webster's New Collegiate Dictionary*, page 325.
4. Adams, *Godliness Through Discipline*, page 14.
5. The Navigators have materials to help you develop a Bible reading plan, start systematic Bible study, and begin a Scripture memory program. These materials are available from your local Christian bookstore.
6. Clarence H. Faust and Thomas H. Johnson, *Jonathan Edwards*, page 43.

# Holiness
# in Body

~

*No, I beat my body
and make it my slave
so that after I have preached
to others, I myself will not be
disqualified for the prize.*

~

True holiness includes control over our physical bodies and appetites. If we are to pursue holiness we must recognize that our bodies are temples of the Holy Spirit and that we are to glorify God with them.

Modern Christians, especially those in the Western world, have generally been found wanting in the area of holiness of body. Gluttony and laziness, for example, were regarded by earlier Christians as sin. Today we may look on these as weaknesses of the will but certainly not sin. We even joke about our overeating and other indulgences instead of crying out to God in confession and repentance.

Our physical bodies and natural appetites were created by God and are not sinful in themselves. Nevertheless, if left uncontrolled, we will find our bodies becoming "instruments of wickedness" rather than "instruments of righteousness" (Romans 6:13). We will be pursuing the "cravings of sinful man" (1 John 2:16) instead of holiness. If we watch ourselves closely, we can see how often we eat and drink just to gratify physical desire; how often we lie in bed in the morning simply because we don't "feel" like getting up when we should; how often we give in to immoral looks and thoughts simply to satisfy the sin-tainted sex drive within us.

Michel Quoist, in his book *The Christian Response*, says, "If your body makes all the decisions and gives all the orders, and if you obey, the physical can effectively destroy every other dimension of your personality. Your emotional life will be blunted and your spiritual life will be stifled and ultimately will become anemic."[1] Over 200 years ago Susannah Wesley wrote, "Whatever increases the strength and authority of your body over your mind—that thing is sin to you."[2]

The Apostle Paul emphasized the need to keep our natural appetites and desires under control. He spoke of his body as his adversary, as the instrument through which appetites and lusts, if left unchecked, would war against his soul (1 Corinthians 9:27). He was determined that his body with these appetites would be his slave, not his master.

Paul further urged us to present our bodies a living and holy sacrifice, acceptable to God, and to not be conformed to this world (Romans 12:1-2). Quite possibly there is no greater conformity to the world among evangelical Christians today than the way in which we, instead of presenting our bodies as holy sacrifices, pamper and indulge them in defiance of our better judgment and our Christian purpose in life.

I am not here singling out those who have a so-called "weight problem." Those of us who can eat what we please without gaining weight may be more guilty of gluttony and indulging the appetites of the body than the person who struggles—often with failure—to control his appetite for food. On the other hand, the overweight person should not excuse his failure. We should all examine ourselves as to whether we eat and drink to the glory of God, recognizing that our bodies are the temples of the Holy Spirit.

The Mormon people are noted for their abstinence from tobacco, liquor, and all beverages containing caffeine. We Christians may shrug off their abstinence as legalistic and as one more group's list of prohibitions. But we should not miss the point that their actions are a practical response to their belief that their bodies are the temple of God. For the Christian, his body truly is the temple of God. How sad, then, that a false religion should be more diligent in this area than we Christians. Let me be emphatic: I am neither approving nor disapproving the Mormons' particular list of prohibitions. But we need to ask ourselves if our consumption of food and drink is controlled by an awareness that our bodies are the temples of the Holy Spirit.

Another reason we must closely govern our indulgence of food and drink is that the person who overindulges his body at this point will find it more and more difficult to mortify other sinful deeds of the body. The habit of always giving in to the desire for food or drink will extend to other areas. If we cannot say no to an indulgent appetite, we will be hard pressed to say no to lustful thoughts. There must be an attitude of diligent obedience in every area if we are to succeed in mortifying any one expression of sin. Thomas Boston wrote, "They that would keep themselves pure must have their bodies in subjection, and that may require, in some cases, a holy violence."[3]

Along with such sins of the body as sexual immorality, impurity, lust, and evil desires, Paul also mentions greed, which he says is idolatry (Colossians 3:5). While greed often manifests itself in its basic form—the sheer love of money for money's sake—it more often is seen in what we call materialism. Not many of us want to be extremely rich; we just want all the nice things the world around us considers important.

Materialism wars against our souls in a twofold

manner. First it makes us discontent and envious of others. Second, it leads us to pamper and indulge our bodies so that we become soft and lazy. As we become soft and lazy in our bodies, we tend to become soft and lazy spiritually. When Paul talked about making his body his slave, so that after having preached to others he himself would not be disqualified, he was not thinking about physical disqualification, but spiritual. He knew well that physical softness inevitably leads to spiritual softness. When the body is pampered and indulged, the instincts and passions of the body tend to get the upper hand and dominate our thoughts and actions. We tend to do not what we *should* do, but what we *want* to do, as we follow the craving of our sinful nature.

There is no place for laziness and indulgence of the body in a disciplined pursuit of holiness. We have to learn to say no to the body instead of continually giving in to its momentary desires. We tend to act according to our feelings. The trouble is, we seldom "feel" like doing what we should do. We don't feel like getting out of bed to have our morning time with God, or doing Bible study, or praying, or anything else we should do. That is why we have to take control of our bodies and make them our servants instead of our masters.

The place to start controlling the cravings of our physical appetites is to reduce our exposure to temptation. Our sinful cravings are strengthened by temptation. When a suitable temptation is presented to us, our cravings seem to get new vigor and power. Paul had definite words of instruction for us on this subject. He told us, "Flee the evil desires of youth" (2 Timothy 2:22). Some temptations can best be overcome by fleeing. He also said, "Do not think about how to gratify the desires of your sinful nature" (Romans 13:14). Do not plan ahead or make provision for ways to indulge your bodily appetites.

Several years ago I realized I had developed a craving for ice cream. Now there is nothing wrong with ice cream in itself; it was just that I had indulged myself so much that it had become a craving. When I shared this problem with my wife, she stopped keeping ice cream in the freezer. She helped me stop making provision to fulfill that particular desire which, through overindulgence, had become sin for me. Several years ago I also canceled my subscription to a popular magazine because I noticed many of the articles tended to stimulate impure thoughts in my mind.

We are to flee temptation and take positive steps to avoid it, and we are to avoid thinking how to gratify our sinful desires. "The prudent see danger and take refuge, but the simple keep going and suffer for it" (Proverbs 27:12).

We should also study our sinful desires and how they rise up against us. John Owen said, "To labor to be acquainted with the ways, wiles, methods, advantages, and occasions of the success of sin, is the beginning to this warfare."[4] Consider beforehand. It is amazing how often we walk into known areas of temptation without any plan or resolution as to how we will react. If you have a weakness for sweets as I have, and you must go to the church pie social, plan beforehand what you will do. A number of years ago, a friend who was a new Christian was invited to a roller skating party with a Christian youth group. He decided not to go because, before becoming a

Christian, he had frequently made "pick-ups" at roller rinks. He felt that at that time in his growth, to return to that environment would tend to stimulate his old lustful desires. So he decided to "flee," to "make no provision for the flesh." He was able to do this because he considered beforehand the possible consequences of going to a seemingly innocent roller skating party.

God expects us to assume our responsibilities for keeping the sinful desires of the body under control. It is true we cannot do this in our own strength. Our sinful desires, stimulated by all the temptations around us, are too strong for us. But though we cannot do it by ourselves, we can do it. As we set ourselves to the task in dependence upon the Holy Spirit, we will see Him at work in us. We will fail many times, but as we persevere, we will be able to say with Paul, "I can do everything through him who gives me strength" (Philippians 4:13).

---

NOTES

1. Michel Quoist, *The Christian Response* (Dublin: Gill and Macmillan, 1965), page 4.
2. John Kirk, *The Mother of the Wesleys* (Cincinnati: Poe and Hitchcock, 1865), page 178.
3. This quote from Thomas Boston is taken from an old magazine article in the author's files. Unfortunately, neither the title of the magazine nor the date of publication was listed on the clipping.
4. John Owen, *Temptation and Sin*, page 31.

CHAPTER

# Holiness in Spirit

*Since we have these promises,
dear friends, let us purify
ourselves from everything that
contaminates body and spirit,
perfecting holiness out of
reverence for God.*

2 CORINTHIANS 7:1

Anumber of years ago in campus evangelism, we used an illustration calculated to make our collegiate audiences vividly aware that they were personally sinners. We would say, "If I could flash on a screen before us tonight all of your thoughts of this past week, you would have to leave town." This remark not only made the point, but always drew a laugh. But for the Christian such a charge is no laughing matter. Our thoughts are just as important to God as our actions, and are known to God as clearly as our actions (Psalm 139:1-4, 1 Samuel 16:7).

Jesus taught us in the Sermon on the Mount that God's commands are intended not only to regulate outward conduct, but inner disposition as well. It is not enough that we do not kill; we must also not hate. It is not enough that we do not commit adultery; we must not even entertain lustful looks and thoughts.

Just as we must learn to bring the appetites of our bodies under control, so we must also learn to bring our thought lives under obedience to Jesus Christ. In fact, Paul warns us against misguided and wrongly motivated attempts to control the body that leave our thought lives unrestrained (Colossians 2:23). It is possible to curb the natural appetites of the body outwardly and yet be filled with all manner of inner defilement.

The Bible indicates that our thought lives ultimately determine our character. Solomon said, "For as he thinks within himself, so he is" (Proverbs 23:7, NASB). An old well-known verse puts it this way:

Sow a thought, reap an act;
Sow an act, reap a habit;
Sow a habit, reap a character.

It is because of the importance of our thought lives that Paul said, "Finally, brothers, whatever is true, whatever is noble, whatever is right, whatever is pure, whatever is lovely, whatever is admirable—if anything is excellent or praiseworthy—think about such things" (Philippians 4:8).

As Christians we are no longer to be conformed to the pattern of this world but we are to be renewed in our minds (Romans 12:1-2, Ephesians 4:23, 1 Peter 1:14). Holiness begins in our minds and works out to our actions. This being true, what we allow to enter our minds is critically important.

The television programs we watch, the movies we may attend, the books and magazines we read, the music we listen to, and the conversations we have all affect our minds. We need to evaluate the effects of these avenues honestly, using Philippians 4:8 as a standard. Are the thoughts stimulated by these various avenues true? Are they pure? lovely? admirable, excellent, or praiseworthy?

The world around us constantly seeks to conform our minds to its sinful ways. It is earnest and pressing in its endeavors. It will entice and persuade us (Proverbs 1:10-14). When we resist, it will ridicule and abuse us as "old-fashioned" and "puritanical" (1 Peter 4:4).

Too many Christians, instead of resisting, are more and more giving ground to the world's constant pressure. A few years ago sincere Christians were quite selective about the movies they attended, if they attended them at all. Today the same movies that were avoided are being shown on television in the living rooms of Christians across the nation. A friend of mine told me of a young couple in full-time Christian work who came to him wanting to know if it was wrong to attend X-rated movies! That the question should even be entertained illustrates the degree to which the world has infected our minds.

The music we listen to often carries the message of the world, and the world uses the medium of music to squeeze us into its mold. And a Christian cannot help being gradually influenced if he continually listens to the world's music.

Perhaps it should go without saying that Christians are to abstain from indulging in or listening to suggestive stories and jokes. But Paul could not take this for granted among the early churches, and neither can we in this century. Listen to Paul's clear warning on the subject: "But among you there must not be even a hint of sexual immorality, or of any kind of impurity, or of greed, because these are improper for God's holy people. Nor should there be obscenity, foolish talk or coarse joking, which are out of place, but rather thanksgiving" (Ephesians 5:3-4). "Not even a hint of immorality" places any suggestive speech whatsoever outside the bounds of a holy walk.

Another stimulus to impure thoughts we must be alert for is what our eyes see. Jesus warned against the lustful look (Matthew 5:28). Job made a covenant with his eyes (Job 31:1). David's wanton look was almost fatal to his spiritual life (2 Samuel 11:2). Not only must we guard our own eyes; we must be careful that we are not the source of temptation to others. For this reason, modesty of dress and actions is required among both men and women (1 Timothy 2:9, 5:2).

But Philippians 4:8 speaks to more than just immoral and unclean thoughts. Our thoughts must not only be pure—they must also be true, lovely, and praiseworthy. Just as we can commit adultery in our hearts (Matthew 5:28), so we can also commit murder in our hearts (Matthew 5:21-22).

In one of his letters Paul listed some acts of the sinful nature. These included defilements of the body—sexual immorality, impurity, debauchery, drunkenness, orgies, and the like. Others in the list defile the spirit: hatred, discord, jealousy, fits of rage, selfish ambition, and so on. We must purify ourselves not only from the gross sins of the body, but also from the more "acceptable" sins of the spirit.

Alas, here again we Christians have so often failed miserably. Focusing on our particular group's list of do's and don'ts, we neglect the inner life where envy, pride, bitterness, and a critical, unforgiving spirit may reign unchecked.

The elder brother in the story of the prodigal son (Luke 15) is a classic example of one who led an exemplary outward life but who was consumed by a spirit of envy and self-righteousness. He could claim never to have disobeyed his father's commandments; yet his jealousy and anger over his father's joy in the return of his prodigal brother marks him to this day as an example to be shunned rather than followed.

The spirit of envy was the root of King Saul's unrelenting warfare against David. Initially Saul was highly pleased with David and set him over his men of war. But one day Saul heard the women of Israel singing, "Saul has slain his thousands, and David his tens of thousands" (1 Samuel 18:7). Saul was very angry that they had ascribed ten thousands to David and to him only thousands. And the Scripture says, "Saul looked at David with suspicion from that day on" (1 Samuel 18:9, NASB). God has placed each one of us in the body of

Christ as it has pleased Him (1 Corinthians 12:18), and has assigned to each of us a place in life (1 Corinthians 7:17). To some God has assigned a place of prominence, to others a place of obscurity; to some a place of wealth, to others a place of daily struggle to make ends meet. But regardless of our station in life or place in the Body, there is always the temptation to envy someone else. The elder brother would one day inherit all his father's possessions; yet he became jealous over a banquet to celebrate his brother's return. Saul was king over all Israel but could not stand someone else receiving more praise than he.

The cure for the sin of envy and jealousy is to find our contentment in God. Asaph in Psalm 73 was envious of the wicked as he saw their apparent prosperity (verse 3). He felt his pursuit of a holy life was in vain (verse 13). Only when he was enabled to say to God, "Earth has nothing I desire besides you" (verse 25), was he delivered from the sin of envy.

Another defilement of spirit that has shipwrecked many Christians is *bitterness*. Bitterness arises in our hearts when we do not trust in the sovereign rule of God in our lives. If ever anyone had a reason to be bitter it was Joseph. Sold by his jealous brothers into slavery, falsely accused by his master's immoral wife, and forgotten by one he had helped in prison, Joseph never lost sight of the fact that God was in control of all that happened to him. In the end he was able to say to his brothers, "You intended to harm me, but God intended it for good to accomplish what is now being done, the saving of many lives" (Genesis 50:20).

We can become bitter against God or against other people. Asaph was bitter against God because he felt

God was not giving him a fair shake in life (Psalm 73:21). Job was bitter because he felt God was not recognizing his righteousness, and even came to the place where his attitude was described as, "It profits a man nothing when he tries to please God" (Job 34:9).

Bitterness toward people is the result of an *unforgiving spirit*. Someone has wronged us, either apparently or actually, and we refuse to forgive that person. Instead we harbor thoughts of bitterness toward the person. We refuse to forgive because we will not recognize that God has forgiven us of far, far greater wrongs. We are like the servant who, having just been forgiven a debt of several million dollars, had a fellow servant thrown into prison over a debt of a few dollars (Matthew 18:21-35).

Closely akin to bitterness is the *spirit of retaliation*. When we are wronged, the tendency is to retaliate — often in our minds if not in actions. When David was fleeing the insurrection of his son Absalom in Jerusalem, Shimei of the family of Saul came out to curse David and throw stones at him. One of David's men wanted to retaliate by killing Shimei, but David restrained him with these words: "Leave him alone; let him curse, for the Lord has told him to. It may be that the Lord will see my distress and repay me with good for the cursing I am receiving today" (2 Samuel 16:11-12).

Paul wrote, "Do not take revenge, my friends, but leave room for God's wrath, for it is written: 'It is mine to avenge, I will repay,' says the Lord" (Romans 12:19). Peter said of our Lord, "When they hurled their insults at him, he did not retaliate; when he suffered, he made no threats. Instead, he entrusted himself to him who judges justly" (1 Peter 2:23). This is the way to cleanse ourselves from the defiling spirit of retaliation: to entrust ourselves to Him who judges justly and who said, "It is Mine to avenge, I will repay."

One of the most difficult defilements of spirit to deal with is the *critical spirit*. A critical spirit has its root in pride. Because of the "plank" of pride in our own eye we are not capable of dealing with the "speck" of need in someone else. We are often like the Pharisee who, completely unconscious of his own need, prayed, "God, I thank you that I am not like other men" (Luke 18:11). We are quick to see—and to speak of—the faults of others, but slow to see our own needs. How sweetly we relish the opportunity to speak critically of someone else—even when we are unsure of our facts. We forget that "a man who stirs up dissension among brothers" by criticizing one to another is one of the "six things which the Lord hates" (Proverbs 6:16-19).

All of these attitudes—envy, jealousy, bitterness, an unforgiving and retaliatory spirit, and a critical and gossiping spirit—defile us and keep us from being holy before God. They are just as evil as immorality, drunkenness, and debauchery. Therefore, we must work diligently at rooting out these sinful attitudes from our minds. Often we are not even aware our attitudes are sinful. We cloak these defiling thoughts under the guise of justice and righteous indignation. But we need to pray daily for humility and honesty to see these sinful attitudes for what they really are, and then for grace and discipline to root them out of our minds and replace them with thoughts pleasing to God.

# 13

# Holiness
# and Our Wills

*For it is God
who works in you
to will and to act
according to his
good purpose.*

PHILIPPIANS 2:13

In all that has been said so far about our responsibility for holiness—the necessity of conviction and commitment, perseverance and discipline, and of holiness in body and in spirit—the activity of our wills is always implied. It is the will that ultimately makes each individual choice of whether we will sin or obey. It is the will that chooses to yield to temptation, or to say no. Our wills, then, ultimately determine our moral destiny, whether we will be holy or unholy in our character and conduct.

This being true, it is critically important that we understand how our wills function—what causes them to turn in one direction or the other, why they make the choices they do. Above all else, we must learn how to bring our wills into submission and obedience to the will of God, on a practical, daily, hour-by-hour basis.

To help us understand how our wills function, let us review the definition of the heart presented earlier in chapter 6. In that definition Owen said the heart as used in the Bible generally denotes all the faculties of the soul as they work together in doing good or evil—the mind, the emotions, the conscience, and the will.

These faculties were all implanted in man's soul by God, but were all corrupted through man's fall in the Garden of Eden. Our reason (or understanding) was darkened (Ephesians 4:18), our desires were entangled (Ephesians 2:3), and our wills perverted (John 5:40). With new birth our reason is again enlightened, our affections and desires redirected, and our wills subdued. But though this is true, it is not true all at once. In actual experience it is a growing process. We are told to renew our minds

(Romans 12:2), to set our affections on things above (Colossians 3:1),[1] and to submit our wills to God (James 4:7).

Moreover, when God originally created man, the reason, the emotions, and the will all worked in perfect harmony. Reason led the way in understanding the will of God, the will consented to God's will, and the emotions delighted in doing it. But with the entrance of sin into man's soul, these three faculties began to work at cross-purposes to one another and to God. The will has become stubborn and rebellious and will not consent to that which reason knows to be the will of God. Or, more commonly, the emotions get the upper hand and draw away both reason and will from obedience to God.

The point of all this is to emphasize and enable us to understand the interrelation of the mind, emotions, and will. While the will is the ultimate determiner of all choices, it is influenced in its choices by the strongest forces brought to bear upon it.

These compelling forces come from a variety of sources. It may be the subtle suggestions of Satan and his world system (Ephesians 2:2) or the evil enticements of our own sinful nature (James 1:14). It may be the urgent voice of conscience, the earnest reasoning of a loving friend, or the quiet prompting of the Holy Spirit. But from whatever source these compelling forces come, they reach our wills through either our reason or our emotions.

Therefore we must guard what enters our minds and what influences our emotions. Solomon said, "Watch over your heart with all diligence, for from it flow the springs of life" (Proverbs 4:23, NASB). If we diligently guard our minds and emotions, we will see the Holy Spirit working in us to conform our wills to His own (Philippians 2:12-13). How then do we guard our minds and emotions?

David said, "How can a young man keep his way pure? By living according to your word" (Psalm 119:9). David guarded his way with the Word of God. The Bible speaks to us primarily through our reason, and this is why it is so vitally important for our minds to be constantly brought under its influence. There is absolutely no shortcut to holiness that bypasses or gives little priority to a consistent intake of the Bible.

Solomon told us that wisdom, understanding, and discretion will guard us from the evil way (Proverbs 2:10-12). These are qualities of our minds. How do we acquire these qualities? "For the Lord gives wisdom; from his mouth come knowledge and understanding" (Proverbs 2:6). But to whom does the Lord give these qualities? He gives them to the one who receives His sayings, who inwardly treasures His commandments, who makes his ear alert to wisdom and his heart ready for understanding, who prays for discernment and understanding, and who seeks understanding as if it were hidden treasure (Proverbs 2:1-5).

It is obvious from even a casual reading of Proverbs 2:1-12 that the protective influence of the Word of God comes as a result of diligent, prayerful, and purposeful intake of Scripture. To guard our minds, we must give priority to the Bible in our lives—not just for the spiritual information it gives but also for the daily application of it in our workaday lives.

Not only must we guard our minds, we must

also guard our emotions. To do this, it is helpful first to realize that while God most often appeals to our wills through our reason, sin and Satan usually appeal to us through our desires. It is true Satan will attack our reason to confuse and cloud the issues, but that is only to enable him to conquer us through our desires. This is the strategy he employed with Eve (Genesis 3:1-6). He attacked her reason by questioning God's integrity, but his primary temptation was to her desire. We read that Eve saw that the tree was *good* for food, it was a *delight* to the eyes, and *desirable* for making one wise (Genesis 3:6).

Knowing that Satan attacks primarily through our desires, we should watch over them diligently and bring the Word of God to bear on them constantly. This is not asceticism; it is spiritual prudence. Each of us should seek to be aware of how sin attacks us through our desires, and take preventive actions. This is what Paul urged Timothy to do when he instructed him to "flee the evil desires of youth" (2 Timothy 2:22).

But the guarding of our desires is more than fighting a rear-guard defensive action against temptations from the world, the flesh, and the devil. We must take the offensive. Paul directs us to set our hearts on things above, that is, on spiritual values (Colossians 3:1). The psalmist encourages us to *delight* ourselves in the law of God (Psalm 1:2), and it was said prophetically of Jesus, "I *delight* to do Thy will, O my God" (Psalm 40:8, NASB). So we see that we are to set our desires on spiritual things, and delight ourselves in the law and will of God.

So we have come full circle to discipline—to a structured plan. Normally our reason, wills, and emotions should work in that order, but since we so often reverse the order, giving attention to our desires, we must work at directing those desires toward God's will.

When I first began jogging as an exercise, I was unmotivated, and therefore inconsistent in doing it. I knew I should jog, that my body needed the physical conditioning, and that I would probably be more healthy as a result. But I was out of condition, it required time I didn't think I had, and above all it was painful. So I started, stopped, started, and stopped, never making consistent progress. Then I read Dr. Kenneth Cooper's book *Aerobics*, which documents the importance of strenuous activities, such as jogging, that exercise the heart. Dr. Cooper explained why jogging was important, gave a few simple guidelines for doing it, and sprinkled his facts and instructions with many illustrations of people whose physical lives were changed dramatically as a result of jogging.

I found myself reading through that book perhaps a half dozen times. I didn't need to be convinced of the importance of jogging; I was already convinced. And I didn't need to reread the few simple rules; they were clear the first time through the book. What I needed was motivation. And those "success" stories—what I call "before and after" stories—motivated me to go out and jog. Reading and rereading them finally succeeded in making me consistent. I influenced my will through my emotions (by motivation) when I could not through my reason (by understanding the importance of jogging).

Now in addition to giving us instructions and guidelines for living, the Bible is filled with "success" stories of real people who trusted God and obeyed

Him and whose lives were changed dramatically or who significantly influenced the course of history. The eleventh chapter of Hebrews gives us a brief and partial index of some of these stories. But there are many more not mentioned (as the writer of Hebrews himself acknowledges in Hebrews 11:32). The exploits of men such as Daniel, Nehemiah, and Elijah as well as Abraham, Noah, and David can motivate us to go and do likewise. So we would do well to constantly include the accounts of some of these men in our Bible reading to motivate us in areas of holiness.

In addition to the Scriptures, we can be alert for the few classic books that really motivate us to a holy and godly life. The number will probably not exceed a half dozen that uniquely meet our needs.[2] These books should be reread frequently just as I reread *Aerobics*. The basic idea is to have a plan—a disciplined approach—that will enable us to stay motivated to holiness.

In the final analysis it is God who works in us to will and to act according to His good purpose. But we are expressly told by Paul to work at this ourselves (Philippians 2:12). Our responsibility regarding our wills is to guard our minds and emotions, being aware of what influences our minds and stimulates our desires. As we do our part, we will see the Spirit of God do His part in making us more holy.

---

NOTES

1. In the *New International Version* the phrase from this verse reads, "Set your *heart* on things above." However, Paul evidently used *heart* here in its more limited meaning of affections or emotions, since in verse 2 he told us to set our minds—that is, our intellect— on things above. Thus he exhorted us to set both our affections and our reason on spiritual values.

2. The list of books which uniquely meet each person's needs will of course vary. My own list will not necessarily motivate the reader, but, for whatever it is worth, it includes *Romans: An Exposition of Chapter 6 — The New Man* by D. Martyn Lloyd-Jones, and *Temptation and Sin* by John Owen (both previously cited in this book); and two other short, readable books: *Power Through Prayer* by E. M. Bounds (Zondervan), and *The Life of Robert Murray McCheyne* by Andrew Bonar (Banner of Truth Trust). I must say, however, that day-in and day-out the Scriptures themselves motivate me more to holiness than all the books in my library.

# 14

# Habits
of Holiness

❧

*Just as you used to offer
the parts of your body in slavery
to impurity and to ever-
increasing wickedness, so now
offer them in slavery
to righteousness leading
to holiness.*

❧

ROMANS 6:19

The more we sin, the more we are inclined to sin. John Owen expressed it this way, in his quaint seventeenth-century style: "Repeated acts of the consent of the will unto sin may beget a disposition and inclineableness of the will unto a proneness and readiness to consent unto sin upon easy solicitation."[1]

Every sin we commit reinforces the habit of sinning and makes it easier to sin. In the previous chapter we discussed the importance of guarding our minds and emotions, since these faculties are the channels through which the various compelling forces reach our wills. But it is also important that we understand how our habits influence our wills.

Habit is defined as the "prevailing disposition or character of a person's thoughts and feelings."[2] Habits are the thought and emotional patterns engraved on our minds. These internal habit patterns play just as forceful a role as external influences on our actions — in fact, perhaps more so. Owen said, "Every lust is a depraved habit or disposition continually inclining our hearts to do evil."[3]

As unbelievers, we formerly gave ourselves to developing habits of unholiness — what Paul called "ever-increasing wickedness" (Romans 6:19). Every time we sinned — every time we lusted, coveted, hated, cheated, or lied — we were developing habits of ever-increasing wickedness. These repeated acts of unrighteousness became habits that made us, in fact, slaves to sin.

But now, Paul declared, just as we formerly gave ourselves to these wicked habits, so we are to give ourselves to developing habits of holiness (Romans 6:19). We are to put off our old self — our sinful dis-

position and its habits—and put on the new self—
with its character and habits of holiness. To train
ourselves in godliness (1 Timothy 4:7) is to discipline and structure our lives so that we develop
godly habits. Putting off these sinful habits is what
Paul calls mortifying or putting to death the deeds of
the body (Romans 8:13).

Though we are to deal with these habits of
unholiness, we must not try to do it in our own
strength. Breaking sinful habits must be done in
cooperation with the Holy Spirit and in dependence
upon Him. The determination that "I'll not do that
anymore," based upon sheer human resolve, has
never once broken the shackles of sin. But there are
practical principles which we can follow to train ourselves in godliness.

The first principle is that habits are developed
and reinforced by *frequent repetition*. Another definition of habit is "a behavior pattern acquired by frequent repetition."[4] This is the principle underlying
the fact that the more we sin the more we are inclined
to sin. But the converse is also true. The more we say
no to sin, the more we are inclined to say no.

Therefore, in dependence on the Holy Spirit,
we must systematically work at acquiring the habit
of saying no to the sins that so easily entangle us.
We all know what these sins are; the sins to which
we are particularly vulnerable. We begin by concen-
trating on saying no to these. Then God will lead us
on to work on other sins which we may not even be
aware of at this time. The more we succeed in saying no to our sinful desires, the easier it becomes to
say no.

In the same manner we can develop positive

habits of holiness. We can develop the habit of thinking thoughts that are pure, true, and good. We can develop the habits of prayer and meditating on the Scriptures. But these habits will only be developed through frequent repetition.

The second principle in breaking sinful habits and acquiring new ones is to *never let an exception occur*. When we allow exceptions we are reinforcing old habits, or else failing to reinforce the new one. At this point we must watch the "just this once" type of thinking, which is a subtle, dangerous trap. Because we are unwilling to pay the price of saying no to our desires, we tell ourselves we will indulge only once more, and tomorrow will be different. Deep inside we know that tomorrow it will be even more difficult to say no, but we don't dwell on this fact.

The third principle is that *diligence in all areas is required to ensure success in one area*. Owen said, "Without a sincere and diligent effort in every area of obedience, there will be no successful mortification of any one besetting sin."[5] We may feel that a particular habit "isn't too bad," but continually giving in to that habit weakens our wills against the onslaughts of temptation from other directions. This is the reason, for example, that it is so important for us to develop habits of self-control over our physical appetites. We may think indulging these appetites isn't so bad, but such indulgences weaken our wills in every other respect of our lives.

Last, *don't be discouraged by failure*. There is a vast difference between failing and becoming a failure. We become a failure when we give up—when we stop trying. But as long as we are working on those sinful habits, regardless of how often we fail, we have not become a failure, and we can expect to see progress.

It is vain to guard our minds and emotions against that which comes from without if we do not at the same time deal with habits of sin which are within. The battle for holiness must be fought on two fronts—without and within. Only then will we see progress toward holiness.

---

NOTES
1. John Owen, *Temptation and Sin*, page 253.
2. *Webster's New Collegiate Dictionary*, page 514.
3. Owen, *Temptation and Sin*, page 28.
4. *Webster's New Collegiate Dictionary*, page 514.
5. Owen, *Temptation and Sin*, page 40, author's paraphrase.

# 15

# Holiness
# and Faith

~

*By faith Abraham,
when called to go to a place he
would later receive as his
inheritance, obeyed and went,
even though he did not know
where he was going.*

~

HEBREWS 11:8

In the pursuit of holiness Christians are often called on to perform duties that appear unreasonable and even absurd to an unbelieving world. A Christian farmer in Kansas is a case in point. When wheat is exactly ready to be harvested, it is important that the work be completed quickly lest bad weather arise and damage the crop or reduce its quality. Because of this, harvesting is often done on a seven-day-a-week schedule. But this particular farmer, believing Sunday should be observed as the Lord's Day, would never work his harvest crew on Sunday, even when an impending storm threatened. To his neighboring farmers this action appeared strange and unreasonable. Interestingly enough, however, over the years this Christian farmer was the most prosperous in his area. Like Abraham, he obeyed by faith what he believed to be the will of God, even though such obedience must undoubtedly have been difficult at times.[1]

Though we often think of holiness in a more narrow sense of separation from impurity and moral evil, in its broader sense holiness is obedience to the will of God in whatever God directs. It is saying with Jesus, "Here I am . . . I have come to do your will, O God" (Hebrews 10:7). No one can pursue holiness who is not prepared to obey God in every area of his life. The holiness described in the Bible calls us to do more than separate ourselves from the moral pollution of the world around us. It calls us to obey God even when that obedience is costly, when it requires deliberate sacrifice and even exposure to danger.

During my service in the Navy, I was once in charge of an operation where a mishap occurred in which a valuable boat was lost and a dozen or more lives were endangered. It was a situation that could have seriously jeopardized my future naval service. Though the cause of the mishap was mechanical failure, it was also true that we were not conducting the operation exactly according to the rules. During the ensuing investigation, the temptation to protect myself by covering up this fact was extremely strong, but I knew I had to be completely truthful and trust God for the consequences. God blessed that obedience—the investigation focused totally on the mechanical failure, and my career was not harmed.

Obedience to the revealed will of God is often just as much a step of faith as claiming a promise from God. In fact, one of the more intriguing thoughts from the Book of Hebrews is the way the writer appears to use obedience and faith interchangeably. For example, he speaks of the Old Testament Hebrews who would never enter God's rest because they *disobeyed* (3:18). Yet they were not able to enter because of their *unbelief* (3:19). This interchange of unbelief and disobedience also occurs later in the book (4:2,6).

These heroes of faith were said to be "still living by faith when they died" (Hebrews 11:13). But we will see that the element of obedience—responding to the will of God—was just as prominent in their lives as was claiming the promises of God. The important point, however, is that they obeyed *by faith*. And since obedience is the pathway to holiness—a holy life being essentially an obedient life—we may say that no one will become holy apart from a life of faith.

Faith is not only necessary to salvation, it is also necessary to live a life pleasing to God. Faith enables us to claim the promises of God—but it also enables us to obey the commands of God. Faith enables us to obey when obedience is costly or seems unreasonable to the natural mind.

Several illustrations from Hebrews 11, the great "faith" chapter, bring out this truth. For example, by faith Abel offered to God a better sacrifice than Cain did, and through this received God's approval (verse 4). We can assume that God had revealed to Cain and Abel the duty of offering sacrifices and the acceptable way of performing that duty. It is apparent from the rest of Scripture that God's acceptable way was through the sacrifice of a lamb—through the shedding of blood. Now *by faith* Abel believed what God said. He took Him at His word and obeyed, even though it is likely he did not understand why the sacrifice of the lamb was the only acceptable sacrifice. Cain, on the other hand, did not believe God's revelation regarding an acceptable sacrifice—perhaps because it did not appear reasonable to him—so he did not obey and thus failed to obtain God's blessing.

The world's values surround us on every hand. Fame, fortune, and present happiness are held as the most desirable goals in life. But the Bible flatly contradicts the value of these goals: "Whoever wants to be great among you must be your servant, and whoever wants to be first must be your slave" (Matthew 20:26-27). The rich should not "put their hope in wealth, which is so uncertain," but are told to hope in God, "to be rich in good deeds and to be generous and willing to share" (1 Timothy 6:17-18). It takes faith to pursue such biblical values when the society around us is pursuing goals that are totally opposite. This faith focuses on believing that God ultimately upholds and blesses those who obey Him, and who trust Him for the consequences of obedience.

Noah's life is an example of this kind of faith: "By faith Noah, when warned about things not yet seen, in holy fear built an ark to save his family. By his faith he condemned the world and became heir of the righteousness that comes by faith" (Hebrews 11:7). God's revelation to Noah concerning the forthcoming judgment on the world was first of all a warning. By faith Noah believed that warning. He had conviction about things not yet seen based solely upon the revealed Word of God. Noah also had confidence that the way of salvation from the impending judgment was through God's appointed means—the ark. He responded to that promise, and so saved both himself and his family.

Noah's building of the ark may well be considered one of the greatest examples the world has ever witnessed of perseverance in a difficult duty of obedience. For 140 years he labored because he both heeded the warning of God and believed the promise of God.

Abraham's life also illustrates the obedience element of faith. The call of Abraham consisted of two parts—a command and a promise. The command was to leave his father's house and go to a land God would show him. The promise was that God would make of him a great nation, and through him bless all the families of the earth. Abraham believed that both the command and the promise came from God, so he obeyed the command and expected fulfillment of the promise. It is recorded of him, "By faith Abraham . . . obeyed" (Hebrews 11:8).

The Bible records the story of Abraham's faith and obedience in such a matter-of-fact way that we can easily overlook the difficulty of his obedience and the faith it required. John Brown likens the case of Abraham to "a person, previous to the discovery of America, leaving the shores of Europe, and committing himself and his family to the mercy of the waves, in consequence of a command of God and a promise that they should be conducted to a country where he should become the founder of a great nation, and the source of blessing to many nations."[2]

The path of obedience in the pursuit of holiness is often contrary to human reason. If we do not have *conviction* in the necessity of obeying the revealed will of God as well as *confidence* in the promises of God, we will never persevere in this difficult pursuit. We must have conviction that it is God's will that we seek holiness—regardless of how arduous and painful the seeking may be. And we must be confident that the pursuit of holiness results in God's approval and blessing, even when circumstances make it appear otherwise.

Often in our lives a specific act of obedience will require both conviction and confidence. God's commandments to Israel to keep the sabbatical year was one such instance. He commanded that every seventh year the land should have a sabbath rest to the Lord, during which no sowing or pruning was to be done (Leviticus 25:3-4). Along with this command God promised that He would bless their crops in the sixth year so that they would have enough to eat till crops in the eighth year were harvested (Leviticus 25:20-22). Only as the Israelites had confidence in the promise of God would they dare to obey the command of God. Sadly, the Old Testament record seems to indicate they had neither the confidence in God's promise nor the conviction that His revealed will on this matter was important to their national and spiritual prosperity.

A New Testament application of this spiritual principle is found in the words of Jesus, "But seek first his kingdom and his righteousness, and all these things will be given to you as well" (Matthew 6:33). The command is to seek God's kingdom first. The promise is that as we do, God will provide for our temporal needs. Because we are often fainthearted regarding the promise of God, we find it difficult to obey His command. Consequently we often give the affairs of this life top priority in the basic decisions of our lives.

Jeroboam, the first king of the Northern Kingdom of Israel, also illustrates how lack of faith leads to disobedience. God promised: "If you do whatever I command you and walk in my ways and do what is right in my eyes by keeping my statutes and commands as David my servant did, I will be with you. I will build you a dynasty as enduring as the one I built for David and will give Israel to you" (1 Kings 11:38).

Did Jeroboam believe God and obey Him? We read that he did not: "Jeroboam thought to himself, 'The kingdom will now likely revert to the house of David. If these people go up to offer sacrifices at the temple of the Lord in Jerusalem, they will again give their allegiance to their lord, Rehoboam king of Judah. They will kill me and return to King Rehoboam.' After seeking advice, the king made two golden calves. He said to the people, 'It is too much for you to go up to Jerusalem. Here are your gods, O Israel, who brought you up out of Egypt'" (1 Kings 12:26-28).

We could well think that Jeroboam had not even heard God's command and promise, so flagrantly did he disregard them. He certainly heard, but the message he heard was of no value to him because it was not combined with faith (Hebrews 4:2). But before we condemn Jeroboam, let us consider our own lives. How often do we fail to obey God's clearly revealed will because we do not exercise faith?

Because we do not believe that humility is the path to God's exaltation (1 Peter 5:6), we jockey for a place of position and power in our relations with others. Because we do not believe that God takes note of and will in His time avenge all wrongs done to us (Romans 12:19), we study in our own minds how we can "get back" at someone we feel has wronged us. Because we are not convinced of the deceitfulness of sin (Hebrews 3:13), we play with it, thinking we will thereby find satisfaction. And because we do not have a firm conviction that "without holiness no one will see the Lord" (12:14), we do not seriously pursue holiness as a priority in our lives.

Faith and holiness are inextricably linked. Obeying the commands of God usually involves believing the promises of God. One definition of faith might be "Obeying the revealed will of God and trusting Him for the results."

"Without faith it is impossible to please God" (Hebrews 11:6). If we would pursue holiness we must have faith to obey the will of God revealed in the Scripture and faith to believe that the promises of God will then be ours.

---

NOTES

1. We have already observed in chapter 9 that sincere Christians disagree on what activities are appropriate for Sunday; nevertheless, this man was obeying God's will for him.
2. John Brown, *An Exposition of Hebrews* (1862; reprint edition, Edinburgh: The Banner of Truth Trust, 1961), page 508.

# 16

# Holiness in an Unholy World

*My prayer is not
that you take them out
of the world but that you
protect them from
the evil one.*

All believers must live their Christian lives in the context of an unholy world. Some face extra-ordinary temptation as they live in the midst of a flagrantly sinful atmosphere. The student in the university dormitory, or the man or woman on a military base or aboard ship must often live in an environment polluted with sensuality, wantonness, and lust. The businessman or woman is often under tremendous pressure to compromise ethical and legal standards to satisfy the greed and dishonesty of associates. Unless the Christian is prepared for such evil assaults on his mind and heart, he will have great difficulty maintaining personal holiness.

James said that part of true religion consists in keeping ourselves "from being polluted by the world" (James 1:27), and Paul urged us to "come out from them and be separate" (2 Corinthians 6:17). How should the believer respond when he finds himself surrounded on every hand by the unrelenting pressures of a sinful world?

It is clear from our Lord's prayer that He does not intend for us to withdraw from contact with the world of nonChristians (John 17:15). Instead, He said we are to be "the salt of the earth" and "the light of the world" (Matthew 5:13-14). The writers of the New Testament take it for granted that Christians will live in the midst of an unholy world. (See such passages as 1 Corinthians 5:9-10; Philippians 2:14-15; 1 Peter 2:12, and 3:15-16). And we are never told that it will be easy to live in a godless environment. Instead, we are warned to expect ridicule and abuse (John 15:19, 2 Timothy 3:12, 1 Peter 4:3-4).

Instead of withdrawing from contact with the

world, we must strive to resist its influence. To do this we must first of all resolve to live by the convictions God has given us from His Word. We cannot be like Mr. Talkative in *Pilgrim's Progress* who prided himself on being adaptable to any kind of company and any kind of talk. He was like a chameleon who changes his color every time he changes his environment. Some of us have known people who had two vocabularies—one among Christians and another among their associates of the world.

The convictions we develop about God's will for a holy life must be rock-ribbed enough to withstand the ridicule of the ungodly, and the pressures they put on us to conform to their unholy ways. I still remember the taunts of my fellow officers aboard ship who teased me unmercifully about a large obscene picture they had prominently displayed in the officers' dining room.

One helpful reinforcement to living according to our convictions is to identify ourselves with Christ openly, wherever we find ourselves in the world. This must be done in a gracious yet clear-cut manner. Going aboard a new ship, I sought to identify myself as a Christian by the simple, wordless act of carrying my Bible openly when going ashore on "liberty." A student in a university dormitory can do the same thing by leaving his Bible out to be seen by all who come into his room. This open identification with Christ helps to spare us from the temptation of adapting to our sinful environment as Mr. Talkative did.

But even though we resolve to live in the world by the convictions God has given us from His Word, and we openly identify ourselves with Christ, we still are often subjected to the pollution of unholy surroundings. The lewd pictures everywhere, the obscene jokes told in our presence, and the endless recounting and boasting of immoral activities by those who do them all serve to drag our minds down into the filth of this world. To this list we could add the dishonest shortcuts taken by business associates, the constant gossiping of our neighbors and coworkers, and the lies and half-truths we hear all around us.

The Bible is our best defense against this pollution. David said, "How can a young man keep his way pure? By living according to your word" (Psalm 119:9). The Bible will cleanse our minds of the defilement of the world if we meditate on its teachings. It will also serve as a continual warning to us not to succumb to frequent temptations to indulge our eyes and thoughts in the immorality around us. I know a man who attended a godless, humanistic university. To guard his mind from the corrupting influences of that environment, he determined to spend as much time in the Word of God as he did in his studies. Today that man is a missionary leader who has had a profound impact on hundreds of lives.

Such passages of Scripture as "Hell and destruction are never full; so the eyes of man are never satisfied" (Proverbs 27:20, KJV), and "Nor should there be obscenity, foolish talk, or coarse joking, which are out of place, but rather thanksgiving" (Ephesians 5:4) are verses we can memorize and meditate on as we find ourselves in corrupt surroundings.

Our reaction to the sinful world around us, however, must be more than just defensive. We must be concerned not only for our own purity of mind and heart, but also for the eternal destiny of those who would pollute us. God has left us in the world to be both salt and light (Matthew 5:13-14). The use of salt as a metaphor to describe our relationship to the world teaches us that Christians are to be a preserving power, an antiseptic, an agent to prevent and retard decay. Dr. William Hendriksen says, "Salt combats deterioration. Similarly Christians, by showing themselves to be Christians indeed, are constantly combatting moral and spiritual decay. . . . To be sure, the world is wicked. Yet God alone knows how *far more* corrupt it would be without the restraining example, life, and prayers of the saints."[1]

As the "light of the world" we are the bearers of the Good News of salvation. Jesus Himself is the true light and, just as it was said of John the Baptist, we are to be "a witness to testify concerning that light" (John 1:7-9). A Christian who witnesses in a spirit of genuine concern for another person is not likely to be corrupted by that person's immorality. And through gracious, loving concern, he may perhaps win that person to the Savior.

We do not act as the salt of the earth or shine as the light of the world by necessarily denouncing the sins of our worldly associates. Our own holy life will serve as a sufficient rebuke, and our interest in others at this point is not their conduct but their need of Jesus Christ as their Savior. Henry Clay Trumbull was, among other things, a great personal evangelist. One day he found himself seated on a train next to a young man who was drinking quite heavily. Each time the young man opened his bottle, he offered a drink to Mr. Trumbull, who declined with thanks. Finally the young man said to Mr. Trumbull, "You must think I'm a pretty rough fellow." Mr. Trumbull's gracious reply, "I think you're a very generous-hearted fellow," opened the way for an earnest conversation with the young man about his need to commit himself to Christ.[2]

After Jesus called Matthew the tax collector to Himself and was eating in Matthew's house with a number of his friends, the Pharisees complained, "Why do you eat and drink with tax collectors and sinners?" Jesus answered them, "It is not the healthy who need a doctor, but the sick. I have not come to call the righteous, but sinners to repentance" (Luke 5:30-32). Surely this is what God would have us do as we shine as lights in the world.

Finally, despite all the suggestions in this chapter, there may be a time when the corrupt environment becomes intolerable; where we, like Lot, become tormented by the lawless deeds we see and hear (2 Peter 2:7-8, Genesis 19). Such a situation may occur, for example, in a coed dormitory where unmarried couples are living in open immorality, or in a business situation where there is unceasing pressure to break the law or compromise Christian principles. In these circumstances, we should prayerfully consider the need to leave that ungodly situation. (I realize this may not be humanly possible in a military situation, but we can resort to prayer, since with God all things are possible.)

Maintaining personal holiness in an unholy world is admittedly difficult. The foregoing suggestions are not intended to make the problem seem easy, but to offer some practical help for a tough problem. Above all, we must look to Jesus who, though He ate with tax collectors and sinners, was

Himself "holy, blameless, pure, set apart from sinners, exalted above the heavens" (Hebrews 7:26). And we must claim His promise that "No temptation has seized you except what is common to man. And God is faithful; he will not let you be tempted beyond what you can bear. But when you are tempted, he will also provide a way out so that you can stand up under it" (1 Corinthians 10:13).

---

NOTES
1. From *New Testament Commentary: Exposition of the Gospel According to Matthew* by William Hendriksen (Grand Rapids, Michigan: Baker Book House, 1973), page 282. Used by permission.
2. Charles G. Trumbull, *Taking Men Alive* (1907; reprint edition, Westwood, New Jersey: Fleming H. Revell Co., 1938), page 80.

CHAPTER

# The Joy of Holiness

*For the kingdom of God
is not a matter of eating
and drinking,
but of righteousness,
peace and joy
in the Holy Spirit.*

ROMANS 14:17

God intends the Christian life to be a life of joy—not drudgery. The idea that holiness is associated with a dour disposition is a caricature of the worst sort. In fact, just the opposite is true. Only those who walk in holiness experience true joy.

Jesus said, "If you obey my commands, you will remain in my love, just as I have obeyed my Father's commands and remain in his love. I have told you this so that my joy may be in you and that your joy may be complete" (John 15:10-11). In this statement Jesus links obedience and joy in a cause and effect manner; that is, joy results from obedience. Only those who are obedient—who are pursuing holiness as a way of life—will know the joy that comes from God.

In what way does holiness produce joy? For one thing, there is the joy of *fellowship with God*. David said, "You will fill me with joy in your presence, with eternal pleasures at your right hand" (Psalm 16:11). True joy comes only from God and He shares this joy with those who walk in fellowship with Him. When David committed the awful sins of adultery and murder, he lost his sense of God's joy because he lost fellowship with God. After this, in his penitential prayer he asked God to "restore to me the joy of your salvation" (Psalm 51:12). A life of disobedience cannot be a life of joy.

The daily experience of Christ's love is linked to our obedience to Him. It is not that His love is *conditioned* on our obedience. That would be legalism. But our *experience* of His love is dependent upon our obedience.

Dr. William Hendriksen observes that God's love

both precedes and follows our obedience. God's love, he says, "by *preceding* our love . . . creates in us the eager desire to keep Christ's precepts; then, by *following* our love, it rewards us for keeping them."[1]

Another cause of joy is knowing that I am obeying God—that I am no longer resisting Him in some particular area of my life. This joy is especially apparent when, after a long struggle between the Spirit and our sinful natures, we have by His grace finally and radically dealt with some besetting sin that had previously mastered us. We might call this the joy of victory; I prefer to call it the joy of obedience.

In addition to the joy of fellowship with the Holy God, a holy life also produces the joy of *anticipated reward*. The writer of Hebrews said, "Let us throw off everything that hinders and the sin that so easily entangles, and let us run with perseverance the race marked out for us. Let us fix our eyes on Jesus, the Author and Perfecter of our faith, who *for the joy set before him* endured the cross, scorning its shame, and sat down at the right hand of the throne of God" (Hebrews 12:1-2). Jesus was motivated to endure by anticipating the joy of His reward. No amount of hardship and struggle could deprive Him of that anticipation.

In the parable of the talents, the Lord said to the two servants who used their talents, "Well done, thou good and faithful servant. . . . Enter thou into the joy of thy Lord" (Matthew 25:21,23, KJV). One of the "talents" God has given to every Christian is the possibility of walking in holiness, being free from the dominion of sin. We, too, can look forward to entering into the joy of the Lord as we walk in holiness to the end of our days.

Joy not only *results* from a holy life, but there is also a sense in which joy helps *produce* a holy life. Nehemiah said to the dispirited exiles who returned to Jerusalem, "The joy of the Lord is your strength" (Nehemiah 8:10). The Christian living in disobedience also lives devoid of joy and hope. But when he begins to understand that Christ has delivered him from the reign of sin, when he begins to see that he is united to Him Who has all power and authority, and that it is possible to walk in obedience, he begins to have hope. And as he hopes in Christ, he begins to have joy. In the strength of this joy he begins to overcome the sins that so easily entangle him. He then finds that the joy of a holy walk is infinitely more satisfying than the fleeting pleasures of sin.

But to experience this joy, we must make some choices. We must choose to forsake sin, not only because it is defeating to us, but because it grieves the heart of God. We must choose to count on the fact that we are dead to sin, freed from its reign and dominion, and we can now actually say no to sin. We must choose to accept our responsibility to discipline our lives for obedience.

God has provided all we need for our pursuit of holiness. He has delivered us from the reign of sin and given us His indwelling Holy Spirit. He has revealed His will for holy living in His Word, and He works in us to will and to act according to His good purpose. He has sent pastors and teachers to exhort and encourage us in the path of holiness; and He answers our prayers when we cry to Him for strength against temptation.

Truly the choice is ours. What will we choose? Will we accept our responsibility and discipline ourselves to live in habitual obedience to the will of God? Will we persevere in the face of frequent failure, resolving never to give up? Will we decide that personal holiness is worth the price of saying no to our body's demands to indulge its appetites?

In the Preface we considered the farmer who, in dependence on God, fulfills his responsibility to produce a harvest. He does not sit back and wait for God to act; rather he acts himself, trusting God to do His part. If we are to attain any measure of holiness we must have a similar attitude. God has clearly said, "Be holy, because I am holy."

Surely He has not commanded us to be holy without providing the means to be holy. The privilege of being holy is yours, and the decision and responsibility to be holy is yours. If you make that decision, you will experience the fullness of joy which Christ has promised to those who walk in obedience to Him.

---

NOTE
1. From *New Testament Commentary: Exposition of the Gospel According to John* by William Hendriksen (Grand Rapids, Michigan: Baker Book House, 1953), page 281. Used by permission.

# A Further Word

In Ephesians 4:20-24, Paul urges us to put off our old self and to put on the new self. To put off the old self is to deal with sin patterns in our lives. To put on the new self is to develop Christlike character traits such as love, compassion, generosity, and forgiveness.

*The Pursuit of Holiness* deals largely with putting off the old self—dealing with sin in our lives. A sequel to this book is available that focuses on putting on the new self—the development of Christian character. It is just as important that we put on the new self as it is that we put off the old. Therefore, I encourage you to consider the sequel book, *The Practice of Godliness*.

# The *Pursuit* of *Holiness*
## BIBLE STUDY

# Contents

# Before You Begin

What is holiness? Do I fully understand my responsibility for living a holy life? Why do I experience defeat in the struggle against sin? What has God provided to help me overcome sin?

To help you in a personal discovery of God's principles for holy living, this Bible study course serves as a companion to the book *The Pursuit of Holiness*. Its objective is to guide you into direct study of many Scripture passages on which the book is based.

The course consists of twelve lessons, which encompass all seventeen chapters in *The Pursuit of Holiness*. For each you will read a chapter or chapters from the book, look up Scripture passages and answer questions about the lesson's topic. Then you will plan a way to apply the truths of the lesson to your life. Within each lesson is an optional question for further study of the Scriptures.

Before beginning each lesson, ask God to clarify the Scriptures to you and to reveal Himself in new ways as you study His Word.

Use a pen or pencil to underline or mark key statements as you read the book, and have this Bible study booklet opened to the lesson. During your reading, jot down in the appropriate space any observations about the text you want to remember, as well as other Scripture passages or incidents from your life or the lives of others that illustrate the truths of the chapter, and any questions that come to your mind. This section can be one of the most profitable for you in each lesson, allowing you to expand upon the material presented in the text.

As you study the Scripture passages in the lesson and answer the questions, and as you prepare to write an application at the end, ask yourself these questions:

❖ What do these passages teach about God's will for a holy life?

5

❖ How does my life measure up to Scripture? Where and how do I fall short?

❖ What definite steps of action do I need to take to obey God?

Write down not only the scriptural truth you want to apply, but also a practical, specific statement and plan for making the application.

The most profitable way of doing this study is to do it yourself first, then meet with a group of others who are doing it also. Discuss your discoveries, questions, and applications in the group.

As you learn more about our calling from "the high and exalted One, who lives forever, whose name is Holy" (Isaiah 57:15), may you experience new commitment and joy in holy living.

*LESSON 1*
# Holiness Is for You

1. Read chapters 1 and 2 of *The Pursuit of Holiness*. Record below the major observations, illustrations, or questions that come to your mind as you read the chapters.

_____

_____

_____

_____

_____

_____

_____

_____

_____

2. Look again at the three reasons why we do not experience more personal holiness (pages 16-18). Which of them applies most to your life? Can you think of other reasons?

_____

_____

_____

_____

3. Look up the following verses and meditate on what each one says about God's holiness. Copy from your Bible the verse or verses which are the most meaningful to you, and explain why they are.

Exodus 15:11; Leviticus 19:1-2; Psalm 89:35; Isaiah 57:15; 1 Peter 1:14-16

_____

_____

_____

_____

_____

_____

4. Write a sentence for each of the following verses telling what it teaches about God's holiness.

Habakkuk 1:13 _____

_____

_____

Zechariah 8:17 _____

_____

_____

James 1:13 _____

_____

_____

5. *(For additional study)* Look up the following verses, analyzing what each one teaches about God's holiness or holiness in the Christian. Copy from your Bible the passages which are most helpful to you, and explain why they are.

1 Samuel 13:13-14; Psalm 51:4; Isaiah 6:1-5, 40:25; Jeremiah 51:5; Ezekiel 39:7; Romans 6:14; 1 John 1:5; Revelation 4:8, 22:11

_____

_____

_____

_____

_____

_____

_____

_____

_____

_____

_____

_____

_____

_____

6. In your own words write a definition of holiness.

_____

_____

_____

_____

7. What application of the truths of this lesson do you want
to make in your life?

_____

_____

_____

_____

_____

_____

_____

_____

# Holiness Is Not an Option

1. Read chapter 3 of *The Pursuit of Holiness*. Record below the major observations, illustrations, or questions that come to your mind as you read the chapter.

_____

_____

_____

_____

_____

_____

_____

_____

_____

2. What do the following verses teach about our holy *standing* before God? (Note: The word *sanctified*, used in some Bible versions, means "made holy.")

Romans 5:19 _____

through obedience to God
we are made righteous

_____

Hebrews 10:10 _he paid the preçe with his lyfe_

1 Peter 3:18 _____

_____

_____

3. What do the following verses teach about holy *living*?

Ephesians 4:1,30 _____

_____

_____

1 Thessalonians 4:7 _____

_____

_____

Titus 2:11-12 _____

_____

_____

4. Look up the verses below. From each one write a brief statement on why holiness is not optional for a Christian.

Psalm 66:18 _____

_____

_____

Romans 8:13-14 _____

_____

_____

2 Timothy 2:21 _____

_____

_____

1 John 1:6 _____

_____

_____

5. Consider Hebrews 12:14. What further efforts do you
   need to make toward holiness in your life?

_____

_____

_____

_____

_____

_____

6. *(For additional study)* Look up the following verses, analyzing what each one teaches about our holy standing
   before God and the need for holy living. Copy from your
   Bible the passages which are the most helpful to you, and
   explain why they are.

   Psalms 15:1-5, 32:3-4; Isaiah 64:6-7; Matthew 1:21, 7:21-23;

13

1 Corinthians 1:2; 2 Corinthians 5:17; Ephesians 1:4; James 2:14-26; 1 John 3:2-5

_____

_____

_____

_____

_____

_____

_____

_____

_____

7. What application of the truths of this lesson do you want to make in your life?

_____

_____

_____

_____

_____

_____

_____

# The Holiness of Christ

1. Read chapter 4 of *The Pursuit of Holiness*. Write down the major observations, illustrations, or questions you have from reading the chapter.

_____

_____

_____

_____

_____

_____

_____

_____

_____

2. After studying the following verses, write a statement of what the holiness of Christ means to you in your personal pursuit of holiness.

   Isaiah 6:5-7; Ephesians 5:1-2; 1 Timothy 1:15; 1 Peter 2:21

_____

_____

_____

_____

3. Look up the following verses about the holiness of Jesus Christ. Copy from your Bible those which are the most meaningful to you, and explain why they are.

Isaiah 53:11; John 8:29; 2 Corinthians 5:21; Hebrews 1:9, 4:15; 1 Peter 2:22; 1 John 3:5

_____

_____

_____

_____

_____

_____

_____

_____

4. If Satan questions your salvation with the thought, "A true Christian wouldn't think the evil thoughts you've been thinking today," how should you respond?

_____

_____

_____

_____

5. (For additional study) Look up the following verses about the holiness of Christ. Which are the most significant to you? Why?

John 4:34, 6:38, 8:45-49; Hebrews 10:7; 1 Peter 1:18-19

_____

_____

_____

_____

_____

_____

_____

_____

6. What application of the truths of this lesson do you want
   to make in your life?

_____

_____

_____

_____

_____

_____

_____

_____

# The Battle for Holiness

1. Read chapters 5 and 6 of *The Pursuit of Holiness*. Record the major observations, illustrations, or questions you have from your reading.

_____

_____

_____

_____

_____

_____

_____

_____

2. Study Romans 6:1-12 and Colossians 1:13. In your own words, what does it mean to have died to sin?

_____

_____

_____

_____

3. What does each of the following verses teach about our hearts and sin?

Jeremiah 17:9-10 _____

_____

_____

Mark 7:21-23 _____

_____

_____

Romans 7:18 _____

_____

_____

4. Using the following verses, explain the nature of our desires and why we need to watch them closely.

Ephesians 4:20-22; Titus 3:3; James 1:14-15

_____

_____

_____

_____

_____

5. *(For additional study)* Look up the following verses about our struggle against sin, write down those which are the most helpful to you, and explain why they are.

Genesis 6:5-6; Psalm 139:23-24; Proverbs 4:23; Luke 6:45; Acts 26:18; Romans 6:17-23; 1 Corinthians 10:12; Galatians 5:17, 6:1; Hebrews 4:12; James 1:22; 1 John 3:9

_____

_____

_____

_____

_____

_____

_____

_____

_____

_____

_____

6. Why, if we died to sin, do we still sin?

_____

_____

_____

_____

7. As those who have died to sin, what is our responsibility with regard to sin now?

_____

_____

_____

_____

8. What application of the truths of this lesson do you want to make in your own life?

_____

_____

_____

_____

_____

_____

_____

_____

_____

_____

# God's Provision and Our Responsibility

1. Read chapters 7 and 8 of *The Pursuit of Holiness*. Write down the major observations, illustrations, or questions you have from your reading.

_____

_____

_____

_____

_____

_____

_____

_____

_____

2. Carefully consider Romans 6:11. What does this verse mean to you, and how can you apply it to your life?

_____

_____

_____

3. Review Isaiah 66:2 and 1 Thessalonians 5:23-24. How should we express our dependence on the Holy Spirit for holiness? What do you want to do to improve in this area?

_____

_____

_____

_____

_____

4. From each of the following verses, write a brief statement of how the Holy Spirit helps us in our pursuit of holiness.

Romans 8:9 _____

_____

_____

Romans 8:13 _____

_____

_____

Galatians 5:16 _____

_____

_____

Ephesians 3:16 _____

_____

_____

Philippians 2:12-13 _____

_____

_____

5. Read the following verses, and write a statement describing your personal responsibility for holiness.

Hebrews 12:1; James 4:7; 2 Peter 3:14

_____

_____

_____

_____

6. *(For additional study)* Look up the following verses about the Holy Spirit's work in us, write down those which are the most helpful to you, and explain why they are.

1 Corinthians 6:18-19; Ephesians 3:14-21; Philippians 4:11-13; Colossians 1:9-11; 1 Thessalonians 4:7-8

_____

_____

_____

_____

_____

_____

_____

7. How can we express at the same time both an attitude of dependence on the Holy Spirit and acceptance of our own responsibility for holiness?

_____

_____

_____

_____

_____

8. What application of the truths of this lesson do you want to make in your life?

_____

_____

_____

_____

_____

_____

_____

_____

*LESSON 6*
# Putting Sin to Death

1. Read chapter 9 of *The Pursuit of Holiness*. Write down the major observations, illustrations, or questions you have from your reading.

_____

_____

_____

_____

_____

_____

_____

_____

_____

2. After considering Romans 8:13 and Colossians 3:5, write in your own words what it means to "put to death" the sinful deeds in our lives.

_____

_____

_____

_____

3. How do the following verses help us develop personal convictions about issues that are not specifically mentioned in the Bible?

1 Corinthians 6:12-13 _____

_____

_____

1 Corinthians 8:4-13_____

_____

_____

1 Corinthians 10:23-33 _____

_____

_____

4. Read through Romans 14, and list the principles that can help us in areas in which Christians have different convictions.

_____

_____

_____

_____

_____

_____

_____

5. What do the following verses teach about the importance of commitment to holiness?

Proverbs 27:20 _____

_____

_____

Luke 14:33 _____

_____

_____

1 John 2:1 _____

_____

_____

6. *(For additional study)* Consider what these verses teach about commitment, conviction, and obedience. Write down those which are the most helpful to you, and explain why they are.

Deuteronomy 17:18-20; Psalm 119:9-11; John 14:21; Romans 12:1-2

_____

_____

_____

_____

_____

_____

7. Using at least one Scripture passage to document your answer, explain how we develop conviction about the necessity of living a holy life and about obedience to God in specific areas of our lives.

_____

_____

_____

_____

_____

8. How do you think Scripture memory can help in developing conviction?

_____

_____

_____

9. What application of the truths of this lesson do you want to make in your life?

_____

_____

_____

_____

_____

_____

_____

LESSON 7
# The Place of Personal Discipline

1. Read chapter 10 of *The Pursuit of Holiness*. Write down the major observations, illustrations, or questions you have from your reading.

_____

_____

_____

_____

_____

_____

_____

_____

_____

_____

2. What does each of the following passages teach about Christian discipline?

1 Corinthians 9:24-27 _____

_____

_____

1 Timothy 4:7-8 _____

_____

_____

2 Timothy 3:16 _____

_____

_____

3. Look up the following verses. Why is perseverance needed in Christian discipline? How can these verses help us to persevere?

Proverbs 24:16; 1 Corinthians 15:58; Hebrews 12:3

_____

_____

_____

_____

_____

_____

_____

_____

4. *(For additional study)* Examine how each of these verses relates to discipline in the Christian life. Write down those which are the most helpful to you, and explain why they are.

Joshua 1:8-9; Romans 7:15; Ephesians 4:20-24; Hebrews 12:1-2; James 1:22-25

_____

_____

_____

_____

_____

_____

_____

_____

_____

5. What does it mean to meditate on Scripture? Suggest a plan for meditation that would be suitable for you and your schedule.

_____

_____

_____

_____

_____

_____

_____

6. In your own words, write a definition of discipline.

_____

_____

_____

_____

7. What application of the truths of this lesson do you want
to make in your life?

_____

_____

_____

_____

_____

_____

_____

_____

_____

_____

# Holiness in Body

1. Read chapter 11 of *The Pursuit of Holiness*. Write down the major observations, illustrations, or questions you have from your reading.

_____

_____

_____

_____

_____

_____

_____

_____

_____

2. The following three verses give practical ways to resist temptation. In what areas of your life can these verses help you?

Proverbs 27:12 _____

_____

_____

_____

Romans 13:14_____

_____

_____

2 Timothy 2:22_____

_____

_____

3. *(For additional study)* Examine how each of these verses
   relates to bodily holiness. Write down those which are the
   most helpful to you, and explain why they are.

   Philippians 3:17-19; Colossians 3:5-7; 1 Timothy 6:17;
   Hebrews 13:5; 1 John 2:15-16

   _____

   _____

   _____

   _____

   _____

   _____

   _____

   _____

   _____

   _____

4. After reading the following verses, write a statement about the importance of holiness in body.

Romans 6:12-13, 12:1-2; 1 Corinthians 6:19-20, 9:27

_____

_____

_____

_____

_____

_____

_____

5. Why is it important for the Christian to govern his indulgence of food and drink?

_____

_____

_____

_____

6. In what ways does materialism affect our holiness of body?

_____

_____

_____

_____

7. What application of the truths of this lesson do you want to make in your life?

_____

_____

_____

_____

_____

_____

_____

_____

_____

# Holiness in Spirit

1. Read chapter 12 of *The Pursuit of Holiness*. Write down the major observations, illustrations, or questions you have from your reading.

   _____

   _____

   _____

   _____

   _____

   _____

   _____

   _____

   _____

   _____

2. From each of the following verses, write a statement about the importance of holiness in our thoughts.

   1 Samuel 16:7 _____

   _____

   _____

Psalm 139:1-4 _____

_____

_____

2 Corinthians 7:1_____

_____

_____

3. Compare your own thought life with the standard set for us in Philippians 4:8. What types of thoughts do you need to avoid? What types of thoughts do you want to cultivate?

_____

_____

_____

_____

_____

4. How we think is affected by what we see and hear. From the following verses, explain the Bible's standards in these two areas.

Matthew 5:27-28; Ephesians 5:3-4; 1 Timothy 2:9-10

_____

_____

_____

_____

40

5. Study Galatians 5:19-21. Which of these acts of the sinful nature listed in the passage are most apt to be present in Christians? Which do you think are the most dangerous to you in your life?

_____

_____

_____

_____

6. Describe the unholy thinking referred to in each of the following passages.

1 Samuel 18:6-12 _____

_____

Psalm 73:12-14,21 _____

_____

Matthew 18:21-35 _____

_____

Luke 15:22-32 _____

_____

Luke 18:9-14 _____

_____

7. *(For additional study)* Examine how each of the following verses relates to holiness in spirit, write down those which are the most helpful to you, and explain why they are.

Genesis 37:3-11; Job 31:1; Proverbs 1:10-16; Matthew
5:21-22; Romans 12:19; 1 Peter 2:21-23, 4:3-5

_____

_____

_____

_____

_____

_____

_____

_____

8. What application of the truths of this lesson do you want
to make in your life?

_____

_____

_____

_____

_____

_____

## LESSON 10
# Holiness and Our Wills

1. Read chapters 13 and 14 of *The Pursuit of Holiness*. Write down the major observations, illustrations, or questions you have from your reading.

_____

_____

_____

_____

_____

_____

_____

_____

2. How do the following verses describe our responsibility concerning our reason, emotions, and will?

Romans 6:19 _____

_____

_____

Romans 12:2 _____

_____

_____

Colossians 3:1-2 _____

_____

_____

James 4:7-8 _____

_____

_____

3. Carefully read Proverbs 2:1-12. If we desire to guard our minds from evil, what must we do?

_____

_____

_____

4. List at least two "success" stories from the Bible (see page 128-129 in *The Pursuit of Holiness*) that especially appeal to you and which you can continually refer to for motivation to holiness.

_____

_____

_____

_____

_____

_____

5. *(For additional study)* Examine how each of these verses relates to holiness and our wills, emotions, or reason. Write down those which are the most meaningful to you, and explain why they are.

Genesis 3:1-6; Psalm 1:1-2; John 5:39-40; Ephesians 4:17-19; Philippians 2:12-13; 2 Timothy 2:22

_____

_____

_____

_____

_____

_____

_____

_____

_____

6. Explain in your own words how the reason, emotions, and will are related, and how they work together.

_____

_____

_____

_____

_____

7. Review the four principles for acquiring or breaking a habit listed in chapter 14. Select a habit you want to acquire or break, and write how each of the four principles can help you.

_____

_____

_____

_____

_____

_____

_____

8. What other application of the truths in this lesson do you want to make in your life?

_____

_____

_____

_____

_____

_____

_____

_____

## LESSON 11
# Holiness and Faith

1. Read chapter 15 of *The Pursuit of Holiness*. Write down the major observations, illustrations, or questions you have from your reading.

_____

_____

_____

_____

_____

_____

_____

_____

_____

2. Explain the relationship you see between faith and obedience in Hebrews 3:17-19 and 4:2,6.

_____

_____

_____

_____

47

3. Read through Hebrews 11, noting the instances of obedience by faith. List five things which some of the persons mentioned in this chapter believed. Which is the most meaningful for you, and why?

_____

_____

_____

_____

_____

_____

_____

4. List five ways in which the persons mentioned in Hebrews 11 obeyed God. Which is the most challenging example for you, and why?

_____

_____

_____

_____

_____

_____

_____

5. *(For additional study)* Review the principles given in the
   following verses. Explain how faith is required to follow
   each one, and under what circumstances the principle
   would be the most difficult for you to believe.

   Matthew 20:26-27; Luke 6:30-31; Romans 12:19; 1 Timothy
   6:17-18; Hebrews 3:13

   _____

   _____

   _____

   _____

   _____

   _____

   _____

   _____

   _____

   _____

   _____

   _____

6. In *The Pursuit of Holiness* we have seen holiness defined
   as the state of being "morally blameless" (page 16), "conformity to the moral precepts of the Bible" (page 16),
   "conformity to the character of God" (page 22), and "obedience to the will of God in whatever God directs" (page
   138). From what you have learned in this and the previous

lessons, write a summary definition of holiness which is meaningful to you, then compare it with the definition you wrote in lesson 1, question 6.

_____

_____

_____

_____

_____

_____

7. What application of the truths in this lesson do you want to make in your life?

_____

_____

_____

_____

_____

_____

_____

_____

_____

# Holiness in an Unholy World

1. Read chapters 16 and 17 of *The Pursuit of Holiness*. Write down the major observations, illustrations, or questions you have from your reading.

_____

_____

_____

_____

_____

_____

_____

_____

2. After studying the following verses, summarize what they teach about the Christian's relationship to an unholy world.

Matthew 5:13-14; John 17:14-16; 1 Peter 3:15-16

_____

_____

_____

_____

_____

3. From the following verses, explain what the Christian's response should be when he is ridiculed or abused for his holy life.

   Matthew 5:11-12; John 15:19; 2 Timothy 3:12; 1 Peter 2:12, 4:12-13

   _____

   _____

   _____

   _____

4. How can we follow the example of Jesus in associating with unholy people (read Luke 5:29-32) and at the same time keep ourselves holy as He did (Hebrews 7:26)? List some actual situations you might face in which this would be difficult.

   _____

   _____

   _____

   _____

   _____

5. Read 1 Corinthians 10:13. How can this promise help you in some unholy environment you may be in?

   _____

   _____

   _____

6. *(For additional study)* Examine how each of the following verses relates to holiness in an unholy world, or to the joy of holiness. Write down those which are the most helpful to you, and explain why they are.

Psalm 51:10-12; 1 Corinthians 5:9-10; Ephesians 5:5-12; Philippians 2:14-15; 1 Peter 4:3-4; 2 Peter 2:7-9; Hebrews 12:1-2

_____

_____

_____

_____

_____

_____

_____

_____

_____

_____

7. What does each of the following verses teach about the joy of a holy life?

Nehemiah 8:9-10 _____

_____

_____

Psalm 16:11 _____

_____

_____

John 15:10-11 _____

_____

_____

Romans 14:17 _____

_____

_____

8. What application of the truths in this lesson do you want
to make in your life?

_____

_____

_____

_____

_____

_____

_____

_____

# THE PRACTICE
# GODLINESS
OF

# Contents

*To my wife*
*Eleanor,*
*God's gracious provision*
*of a helper suitable for me*

# Preface

This book is a sequel to an earlier book, *The Pursuit of Holiness*. In Ephesians 4:20-24, Paul urges us to put off our old self and to put on the new self. *The Pursuit of Holiness* dealt largely with putting off the old self—dealing with sin in our lives. *The Practice of Godliness* focuses on putting on the new self—growing in Christian character.

The most well-known list of Christian character traits is the ninefold list in Galatians 5:22-23, which Paul calls the fruit of the Spirit. But there are other lists in passages such as Colossians 3:12-16, Ephesians 4:2-3 and 32, James 3:17, and 2 Peter 1:5-7 that are just as important to our understanding of what constitutes Christian character. I've incorporated most of these in this series of studies.

While in the process of doing a series of Bible studies on Christian character traits, I became interested in the subject of godliness. As my knowledge of that topic grew, I became convinced that any treatment of Christian character would be incomplete without the inclusion of a study on godliness.

Godliness is more than Christian character. It covers the totality of the Christian life and provides the foundation upon which Christian character is built. Thus the first four chapters deal with the general theme of godliness, and the remaining chapters consider important character traits of the godly person.

The order in which the studies of the various character traits appear is deliberate. The first four—humility, contentment, thankfulness, and joy—deal largely with our relationship to God. The next group of three—holiness, self-control, and faithfulness—are qualities that require us to deal sternly with ourselves. The final six—peace, patience, gentleness, kindness, goodness, and love—are qualities that enable us to deal graciously and tenderly with others. These last two divisions reflect the seeming dichotomy of Christian character: sternness with ourselves and tenderness toward others. Only the Holy Spirit can create such a beautiful diversity of sternness and tenderness within a single human personality.

The variety of topics covered in a book of this nature requires that each subject be treated only briefly. My objective is to create an awareness of the importance of each of the aspects of godliness and provide some practical suggestions for growing in them. Hopefully, many readers will be stimulated to do further study on some of the topics of particular interest to them.

As I studied the subjects of both godliness and Christian character, I was somewhat amazed that I could find so little that has been previously written on these subjects. Consequently, I have had to plow new ground in some areas. This has forced me back to the Scriptures more than if I had had the advantage of the writings of previous generations. My one qualification for presenting these studies, then, lies in thirty years of personal Bible study using methods and tools available to any layman.

There is a certain sense of anxiety in committing these studies to print which comes from the warning of James that, "Not many of you should presume to be teachers, my brothers, because you know that we who teach will be judged more strictly" (James 3:1). I am keenly aware of the need for more growth in my own life in many of the areas covered in this book. It is my prayer, however, that both author and readers will grow together as we practice godliness.

This book should be studied more than read. To facilitate that study, I have prepared a companion Bible study to be used in conjunction with this book. Though the book text is complete in itself, the use of the companion Bible study will enable the reader and student to gain a better grasp of the scriptural truths taught.

I am deeply indebted to the staff of NavPress for their encouragement to write this book and for their help in preparing the manuscript for final production.

# 1
# Value for All Things

*For physical training is of some value,*
*but godliness has value for all things,*
*holding promise for both the present life*
*and the life to come.*

1 Timothy 4:8

There is no higher compliment that can be paid to a
Christian than to call him a godly person. He might be a
conscientious parent, a zealous church worker, a dynamic
spokesman for Christ, or a talented Christian leader; but
none of these things matters if, at the same time, he is not a
godly person.

The words *godly* and *godliness* actually appear only a
few times in the New Testament; yet the entire Bible is a
book on godliness. And when those words do appear they
are pregnant with meaning and instruction for us.

When Paul wants to distill the essence of the Christian
life into one brief paragraph, he focuses on godliness. He
tells us that God's grace "teaches us to say 'No' to *ungod-*
*liness* and worldly passions, and to live self-controlled,
upright and *godly* lives," as we await the coming of our
Lord Jesus Christ (Titus 2:11-13). When Paul thinks of his

11

own job description as an apostle of Jesus Christ, he describes it as being called to further the faith of God's elect and their knowledge of the truth that leads to *godliness* (Titus 1:1).

In his first letter to Timothy, Paul emphasizes godliness. We are to pray for those in authority, that we may live peaceful and quiet lives in all *godliness* and holiness. We are to train ourselves to be *godly*. We are to pursue *godliness*—the word *pursue* indicating unrelenting, persevering effort. *Godliness* with contentment is held forth as great gain; and finally, *godliness* has value for all things, holding promise for both the present life and the life to come.

When Peter, in looking forward to the day of the Lord when the earth and everything in it will be destroyed, asks what kind of people we ought to be, he answers that we are to live holy and *godly* lives (2 Peter 3:10-12). Here Peter uses the most momentous event of all history to stir us up to our Christian duty—to live holy and *godly* lives.

Surely, then, godliness is no optional spiritual luxury for a few quaint Christians of a bygone era or for some group of super-saints of today. It is both the privilege and duty of every Christian to pursue godliness, to train himself to be godly, to study diligently the practice of godliness. We don't need any special talent or equipment. God has given to each one of us "everything we need for life and godliness" (2 Peter 1:3). The most ordinary Christian has all that he needs, and the most talented Christian must use those same means in the practice of godliness.

What then is godliness? What are the marks of a godly person? How does a person become godly? I have asked a number of people the question, "What do you think of when you think of godliness?" The answers, though varied, always end up expressing some idea of Christian character, using such expressions as "Godlike," "Christlike," or "the

12

fruit of the Spirit." Godliness certainly includes Christian character, but it is more than that. There is another, even more fundamental aspect of godliness than godly character. It is the foundation, in fact, on which godly character is built.

DEVOTION IN ACTION

The Bible begins to give us some clues about godliness in its earliest pages. Genesis 5:21-24 tells us about Enoch, the father of Methuselah. In a very short three-verse summary of Enoch's life, Moses twice describes him as one who "walked with God." The author of Hebrews gives Enoch a place in his great "Faith's Hall of Fame" in chapter 11, but he sees Enoch from a slightly different perspective. He describes him as "one who pleased God." Here, then, are two important clues: Enoch walked with God, and Enoch pleased God. It is evident from these two statements that Enoch's life was centered in God; God was the focal point, the polestar of his very existence.

Enoch walked with God; he enjoyed a relationship with God; and he pleased God. We could accurately say he was devoted to God. This is the meaning of godliness. The New Testament word for godliness, in its original meaning, conveys the idea of a personal attitude toward God that results in actions that are pleasing to God.[1] This personal attitude toward God is what we call devotion to God. But it is always *devotion in action*. It is not just a warm, emotional feeling about God, the kind of feeling we may get while singing some grand old hymn of praise or some modern-day chorus of worship. Neither is devotion to God merely a time of private Bible reading and prayer, a practice we sometimes call "devotions." Although this practice is vitally important to a godly person, we must not think of it as defining devotion for us.

FOCUSED ON GOD

Devotion is not an activity; it is an attitude toward God. This attitude is composed of three essential elements:

- ❖ the fear of God
- ❖ the love of God
- ❖ the desire for God

We will look at these elements in detail in chapter 2; but for now, note that all three elements focus upon God. *The practice of godliness is an exercise or discipline that focuses upon God.* From this Godward attitude arises the character and conduct that we usually think of as godliness. So often we try to develop Christian character and conduct without taking the time to develop God-centered devotion. We try to please God without taking the time to walk with Him and develop a relationship with Him. This is impossible to do.

Consider the exacting requirements of a godly lifestyle as expounded by the saintly William Law. Law uses the word *devotion* in a broader sense to mean all that is involved in godliness — actions as well as attitude:

> Devotion signifies a life given, or devoted to God. He therefore is the devout [godly] man, who lives no longer to his own will, or the way and spirit of the world, but to the sole will of God, who considers God in everything, who serves God in everything, who makes all the parts of his common life, parts of piety [godliness], by doing everything in the name of God, and under such rules as are conformable to his Glory.[2]

Note the totality of godliness over one's entire life in Law's description of the godly person. Nothing is excluded.

God is at the center of his thoughts. His most ordinary duties are done with an eye to God's glory. In Paul's words to the Corinthians, whether he eats or drinks or whatever he does, he does it all for the glory of God.

Now it is obvious that such a God-centered lifestyle cannot be developed and maintained apart from a solid foundation of devotion to God. Only a strong personal relationship with the living God can keep such a commitment from becoming oppressive and legalistic. John writes that God's commands are not burdensome; a godly life is not wearisome, but this is true only because a godly person is first of all devoted to God.

Devotion to God, then, is the mainspring of godly character. And this devotion is the only motivation for Christian behavior that is pleasing to God.

This motivation is what separates the godly person from the moral person, or the benevolent person, or the zealous person. The godly person is moral, benevolent, and zealous because of his devotion to God. And his life takes on a dimension that reflects the very stamp of God.

It is sad that many Christians do not have this aura of godliness about them. They may be very talented and personable, or very busy in the Lord's work, or even apparently successful in some avenues of Christian service, and still not be godly. Why? Because they are not devoted to God. They may be devoted to a vision, or to a ministry, or to their own reputation as a Christian, but not to God.

Godliness is more than Christian character: It is Christian character that springs from a devotion to God. But it is also true that devotion to God *always* results in godly character. As we study the three essential elements of devotion in the next chapter, we will see that all of them, individually and collectively, must express themselves in a life that is pleasing to God. So the definition of godliness we will use in this book is *devotion to God which results in a life that is pleasing to Him*.

In the first few chapters of this book we will concentrate on this devotion, seeking to understand what it is and why it results in Christian character. In the later chapters we will look at individual traits of godly character. But we must never lose sight of the fact that devotion to God is the mainspring of Christian character and the only foundation upon which it can be successfully built.

---

NOTES
1. Vine's *Expository Dictionary of New Testament Words* defines godliness as, "to be devout, denotes that piety which, characterized by a Godward attitude, does that which is well-pleasing to Him" (Nashville, Tenn.: Royal Publishers, n.d., page 492). J.C. Connell defines godliness as a personal attitude to God and the actions that spring directly from it (*New Bible Dictionary*, London: Inter-Varsity Fellowship, 1962, page 480).
2. William Law, *A Serious Call to a Devout and Holy Life* (Grand Rapids, Mich.: Sovereign Grace Publishers, 1971), page 1.

# 2

# Devotion to God

*Who will not fear you, O Lord,*
*and bring glory to your name?*
*For you alone are holy.*
*All nations will come and worship before you,*
*for your righteous acts have been revealed.*

Revelation 15:4

Enoch walked with God, and Enoch pleased God. His walk with God speaks of his relationship with God, or his devotion to God; his pleasing God speaks of the behavior that arose from that relationship. It is impossible to build a Christian behavior pattern without the foundation of a devotion to God. The practice of godliness is first of all the cultivation of a relationship with God, and from this the cultivation of a life that is pleasing to God. Our concept of God and our relationship with Him determine our conduct.

We have already seen that devotion to God consists of three essential elements: the fear of God, the love of God, and the desire for God. Think of a triangle representing devotion to God, with these three elements as each of its three points.

The fear of God and the love of God form the base of the triangle, while the desire for God is at the apex. As we

17

study these elements individually, we will see that the fear of God and the love of God form the foundation of true devotion to God, while the desire for God is the highest expression of that devotion.

## THE GOD-FEARING CHRISTIAN

The late professor John Murray said, "The fear of God is the soul of godliness."[1] Yet the fear of God is a concept that seems old-fashioned and antiquated to many modern-day Christians. There was a time when an earnest believer might have been known as a "God-fearing man." Today we would probably be embarrassed by such language. Some seem to think the fear of God is strictly an Old Testament concept that passed away with the revelation of God's love in Christ. After all, doesn't perfect love drive out fear, as John declares in 1 John 4:18?

Although it is true that the concept of the fear of God is treated more extensively in the Old Testament, it would be a mistake to assume that it is not important in the New Testament. One of the blessings of the new covenant is the implanting in believers' hearts of the fear of the Lord. In

Jeremiah 32:40 God said, "I will make an everlasting covenant with them: I will never stop doing good to them, and I will inspire them to *fear me*, so that they will never turn away from me."

"Nothing could be more significant," observed John Murray, "than that the fear of the Lord should be coupled with the comfort of the Holy Spirit as the characteristics of the New Testament church: 'So the church . . . walking in the fear of the Lord and in the comfort of the Holy Spirit was multiplied' (Acts 9:31)."[2] Paul and Peter both use the fear of the Lord as a motive to holy and righteous living.[3] The example of the Lord Jesus Himself, of whom Isaiah said, "and he will delight in the fear of the Lord" (11:3), should put the question beyond all doubt. If Jesus in His humanity delighted in the fear of God, surely we need to give serious thought to cultivating this attitude in our lives.

Some of the aversion to the phrase "fear of God" may be due to a misunderstanding of its meaning. The Bible uses the term "fear of God" in two distinct ways: that of anxious dread, and that of veneration, reverence, and awe. Fear as anxious dread is produced by the realization of God's impending judgment upon sin. When Adam sinned he hid from God because he was afraid. Although this aspect of the fear of God should characterize every unsaved person who lives each day as an object of God's wrath, it seldom does. Paul's concluding indictment of ungodly mankind was, "There is no fear of God before their eyes" (Romans 3:18).

The Christian has been delivered from fear of the wrath of God (see 1 John 4:18). But the Christian has not been delivered from the *discipline* of God against his sinful conduct, and in this sense he still fears God. He works out his salvation with fear and trembling (Philippians 2:12); he lives his life as a stranger here in reverent fear (1 Peter 1:17).

For the child of God, however, the primary meaning of

the fear of God is veneration and honor, reverence and awe. Murray says this fear is the soul of godliness. It is the attitude that elicits from our hearts adoration and love, reverence and honor. It focuses not upon the wrath of God but upon the majesty, holiness, and transcendent glory of God. It may be likened to the awe an ordinary but loyal citizen would feel in the close presence of his earthly king, though such awe for an earthly potentate can only distantly approximate the awe we should feel toward God, the blessed and only Ruler, the King of kings and Lord of lords.

The angelic beings of Isaiah's vision in chapter 6 demonstrated this awe when, with two of their wings, they covered their faces in the presence of the exalted Lord. We see this same awe in Isaiah himself and in Peter when they each realized they were in the presence of a holy God. We see it most vividly in the reaction of the beloved disciple John in Revelation 1:17, when he saw his Master in all of His heavenly glory and majesty, and fell at His feet as though dead.

It is impossible to be devoted to God if one's heart is not filled with the fear of God. It is this profound sense of veneration and honor, reverence and awe that draws forth from our hearts the worship and adoration that characterizes true devotion to God. The reverent, godly Christian sees God first in His transcendent glory, majesty, and holiness before he sees Him in His love, mercy, and grace.

There is a healthy tension that exists in the godly person's heart between the reverential awe of God in His glory and the childlike confidence in God as heavenly Father. Without this tension, a Christian's filial confidence can easily degenerate into presumption.

One of the more serious sins of Christians today may well be the almost flippant familiarity with which we often address God in prayer. None of the godly men of the Bible ever adopted the casual manner we often do. They always addressed God with reverence. The same writer who tells us that we have confidence to enter the Most Holy Place, the throne room of God, also tells us that we should worship God acceptably with reverence and awe, "for our God is a consuming fire" (Hebrews 10:19 and 12:28-29). The same Paul who tells us that the Holy Spirit dwelling within us causes us to cry, "*Abba*, Father," also tells us that this same God lives in "unapproachable light" (Romans 8:15 and 1 Timothy 6:16).

In our day we must begin to recover a sense of awe and profound reverence for God. We must begin to view Him once again in the infinite majesty that alone belongs to Him who is the Creator and Supreme Ruler of the entire universe. There is an infinite gap in worth and dignity between God the Creator and man the creature, even though man has been created in the image of God. The fear of God is a heartfelt recognition of this gap—not a putdown of man, but an exaltation of God.

Even the redeemed in heaven fear the Lord. In Revelation 15:3-4, they sing triumphantly the song of Moses the servant of God and the song of the Lamb:

> Great and marvelous are your deeds,
>     Lord God Almighty.
> Just and true are your ways, King of the ages.
> Who will not fear you, O Lord,
>     and bring glory to your name?
> For you alone are holy.
> All nations will come and worship before you,
>     for your righteous acts have been revealed.

Note the focus of their veneration upon God's attributes of power, justice, and holiness. It is these attributes, which particularly set forth the majesty of God, that should elicit from our hearts a reverence for Him. This same reverence was drawn forth from the children of Israel when they saw the great power the Lord displayed against the Egyptians. Exodus 14:31 says, "the people feared the Lord and put their trust in him and in Moses his servant." Along with Moses, they sang a song of worship and gratitude. The heart of that song is found in 15:11: "Who among the gods is like you, O Lord? Who is like you—majestic in holiness, awesome in glory, working wonders?" To fear God is to confess His absolute uniqueness—to acknowledge His majesty, holiness, awesomeness, glory, and power.

Words fail us to describe the infinite glory of God portrayed in the Bible. And even that portrayal is dim and vague, for now we see but a poor reflection of Him. But one day we will see Him face to face, and then we will fear Him in the fullest sense of that word. No wonder, then, that with that day in view, Peter tells us to live holy and godly lives now. God is in the process of preparing us for heaven, to dwell with Him for eternity. So He desires that we grow in both holiness and godliness. He wants us to be like Him and to reverence and adore Him for all eternity. We must be learning to do this now.

In our day we seem to have magnified the love of God almost to the exclusion of the fear of God. Because of this preoccupation we are not honoring God and reverencing Him as we should. We should magnify the love of God; but although we revel in His love and mercy, we must never lose sight of His majesty and His holiness.

Not only will a right concept of the fear of God cause us to worship God aright, it will also regulate our conduct. As John Murray says, "What or whom we worship determines our behavior."[4] The Reverend Albert N. Martin has said that the essential ingredients of the fear of God are (1) correct concepts of the character of God, (2) a pervasive sense of the presence of God, and (3) a constant awareness of our obligation to God.[5] If we have some comprehension of God's infinite holiness and His hatred of sin, coupled with this pervasive sense of God's presence in all of our actions, yes, even our thoughts, then such a fear of God must influence and regulate our conduct. Just as obedience to the Lord is an indication of our love for Him, so is it also a proof of our fear of God. "[You shall] fear the Lord your God as long as you live by keeping all his decrees and commands . . ." (Deuteronomy 6:2).

Leviticus 19 contains a series of laws and regulations for the nation of Israel to observe in the promised land. This is the chapter from which Jesus quoted the well-known second commandment of love, "Love your neighbor as yourself" (verse 18; see also Matthew 22:39). The expression "I am the Lord" or "I am the Lord your God" appears sixteen times in Leviticus 19. Through this frequent repetition of His sacred name, God reminds the people of Israel that their obedience to His laws and regulations is to flow out of a reverence and fear of Him.

The fear of God should provide a primary motivation for, as well as result in, obedience to Him. If we truly reverence God we will obey Him, since every act of disobedience is an affront to His dignity and majesty.

GRIPPED BY GOD'S LOVE

Only the God-fearing Christian can truly appreciate the love of God. He sees the infinite gulf between a holy God and a sinful creature, and the love that bridged that gulf through the death of the Lord Jesus Christ. God's love for us is many-faceted, but He supremely demonstrated it by sending His Son to die for our sins. All other aspects of His love are secondary, and in fact are made possible for us through the death of Christ.

The apostle John says, "God is love" (1 John 4:8). He

explains this statement by saying, "This is how God showed his love among us: He sent his one and only Son into the world that we might live through him. This is love: not that we loved God, but that he loved us and sent his Son as an atoning sacrifice for our sins" (1 John 4:9-10). The *New International Version* of the Bible gives as a marginal rendering for "atoning sacrifice" the phrase, "as the one who would turn aside his wrath, taking away" our sins.

The truly godly person never forgets that he was at one time an object of God's holy and just wrath. He never forgets that Christ Jesus came into the world to save sinners—and he feels along with Paul that he is himself the worst of sinners. But then as he looks to the cross he sees that Jesus was his atoning sacrifice. He sees that Jesus bore his sins in His own body, and that the wrath of God—the wrath which he, a sinner, should have borne—was expended completely and totally upon the Holy Son of God. And in this view of Calvary, he sees the love of God.

The love of God has no meaning apart from Calvary. And Calvary has no meaning apart from the holy and just wrath of God. Jesus did not die just to give us peace and a purpose in life; He died to save us from the wrath of God. He died to reconcile us to a holy God who was alienated from us because of our sin. He died to ransom us from the penalty of sin—the punishment of everlasting destruction, shut out from the presence of the Lord. He died that we, the just objects of God's wrath, should become, by His grace, heirs of God and co-heirs with Him.

How much we appreciate God's love is conditioned by how deeply we fear Him. The more we see God in His infinite majesty, holiness, and transcendent glory, the more we will gaze with wonder and amazement upon His love poured out at Calvary. But it is also true that the deeper our perception of God's love to us in Christ, the more profound our reverence and awe of Him. We must see God in the glory of all His attributes—His goodness as well as His holiness—if we are to ascribe to Him the glory and honor and reverence that is due Him. The psalmist caught this truth when he said to God, "If you, O Lord, kept a record of sins, O Lord, who could stand? But with you there is forgiveness; therefore you are feared" (Psalm 130:3-4). He worshiped God with reverence and awe because of His forgiveness. In our practice of godliness, then, we must seek to grow both in the fear of God and in an ever-increasing comprehension of the love of God. These two elements together form the foundation of our devotion to God.

This awareness of God's love for us in Christ must be *personalized* in order for it to become one of the solid foundational corners of our "triangle of devotion" to God. It is not enough to believe that God loved the world. I must be gripped by the realization that God loves *me*, a specific person. It is this awareness of His individual love that draws out our hearts in devotion to Him.

There was a period in my early Christian life when my concept of God's love was little more than a logical deduction: God loves the world; I am a part of the world; therefore, God loves me. It was as if God's love were a big umbrella to protect us all from His judgment against sin, and I was under the umbrella along with thousands of other people. There was nothing particularly personal about it. Then one day I realized, "God loves *me*! Christ died for *me*."

Our awareness of God's love for us must also be constantly growing. As we mature in our Christian lives we are increasingly aware of God's holiness and our own sinfulness. In Paul's first letter to Timothy he reflects upon God's mercy in appointing him to the gospel ministry. He recalls that he once was a blasphemer and a persecutor and a violent man. This description no longer applies to Paul; it is all past tense.

But as he continues to reflect upon the grace of God, he slips, almost unconsciously it seems, into the present tense of his experience. "Christ Jesus came into the world to save sinners—of whom I am the worst" (1:15). He is no longer thinking about his past as a persecutor of Christ. Now he is thinking about his present daily experience as a believer who falls short of the will of God for him. He doesn't think about other Christians, whom we know were way behind Paul in their devotion to God and their attainment of godly character. Paul never wastes time trying to feel good about himself by comparing himself favorably with less mature Christians. He compares himself with God's standard, and he consequently sees himself as the worst of sinners.

Through this present sense of his sinfulness Paul sees God's love for him. The more he grows in his knowledge of God's perfect will, the more he sees his own sinfulness, and the more he comprehends God's love in sending Christ to die for him. And the more he sees God's love, the more his heart reaches out in adoring devotion to the One who loved him so.

If God's love for us is to be a solid foundation stone of devotion, we must realize that His love is *entirely of grace*, that it rests completely upon the work of Jesus Christ and flows to us through our union with Him. Because of this basis His love can never change, regardless of what we do. In our daily experience, we have all sorts of spiritual ups and downs—sin, failure, discouragement, all of which tend to make us question God's love. That is because we keep thinking that God's love is somehow conditional. We are afraid to believe His love is based entirely upon the finished work of Christ for us.

Deep down in our souls we must get hold of the wonderful truth that our spiritual failures do not affect God's love for us one iota—that His love for us does not fluctuate according to our experience. We must be gripped by the truth that we are accepted by God and loved by God for the sole reason that we are united to His beloved Son. As the *King James Version* translates Ephesians 1:6, "He hath made us accepted in the beloved."

This is why Paul could rejoice so greatly in the love of God. Listen to the triumphant ring of his voice in Romans 8 as he asks these questions:

- ❖ "If God is for us, who can be against us?"
- ❖ "Who will bring any charge against those whom God has chosen?"
- ❖ "Who is he that condemns?"
- ❖ "Who shall separate us from the love of Christ?"

Then hear his exultant conclusion as he says, "For I am convinced that . . . [nothing] . . . will be able to separate us from the love of God that is in Christ Jesus our Lord."

Does this apprehension of God's personal, unconditional love for us in Christ lead to careless living? Not at all. Rather, such an awareness of His love stimulates in us an increased devotion to Him. And this devotion is active; it is not just a warm, affectionate feeling toward God.

Paul testified that Christ's love for us compelled him to live not for himself, but for Him who died for us and rose again (2 Corinthians 5:14-15). The word for "compel" which Paul used is a very strong verb. It means to press in on all sides and to impel or force one to a certain course of action. Probably not many Christians can identify with Paul in this depth of his motivation, but this surely should be our goal. This is the constraining force God's love is intended to have upon us.

John speaks similarly of the constraining force of God's love when he says, "We love because he first loved us"

(1 John 4:19). Whether it is love for God or love for other people that John had in mind, both are prompted by the realization of God's love for us.

So we see that devotion to God begins with the fear of God—with a biblical view of His majesty and holiness that elicits a reverence and awe of Him. And then we see that the fear of God leads naturally to an apprehension of the love of God for us as shown in the atoning death of Jesus Christ. As we contemplate God more and more in His majesty, holiness, and love, we will be progressively led to the apex of the triangle of devotion—the desire for God Himself.

A THIRST FOR GOD

True godliness engages our affections and awakens within us a desire to enjoy God's presence and fellowship. It produces a longing for God Himself. The writer of Psalm 42 vividly expressed this longing when he exclaimed, "As the deer pants for streams of water, so my soul pants for you, O God. My soul thirsts for God, for the living God. When can I go and meet with God?" What could be more intense than a hunted deer's thirst for water? The psalmist does not hesitate to use this picture to illustrate the intensity of his own desire for God's presence and fellowship.

David also expresses this intense desire for God: "One thing I ask of the Lord, this is what I seek: that I may dwell in the house of the Lord all the days of my life, to gaze upon the beauty of the Lord and to seek him in his temple" (Psalm 27:4). David yearned intensely for God Himself that he might enjoy His presence and His beauty. Since God is a spirit, His beauty obviously refers not to a physical appearance but to His attributes. David enjoyed dwelling upon the majesty and greatness, the holiness and goodness of God. But David did more than contemplate the beauty of God's attributes. He sought God Himself, for elsewhere he says, "earnestly I seek you; my soul thirsts for you, my body longs for you . . ." (Psalm 63:1).

The apostle Paul also experienced this longing for God: "I want to know Christ . . ." (Philippians 3:10). The *Amplified Bible* forcefully catches the intensity of Paul's desire in this passage: "[For my determined purpose is] that I may know Him—that I may progressively become more deeply and intimately acquainted with Him, perceiving and recognizing and understanding [the wonders of His person] more strongly and more clearly." This is the heartbeat of the godly person. As he contemplates God in the awesomeness of His infinite majesty, power, and holiness, and then as he dwells upon the riches of His mercy and grace poured out at Calvary, his heart is captivated by this One who could love him so. He is satisfied with God alone, but he is never satisfied with his present experience of God. He always yearns for more.

Perhaps this idea of a desire for God sounds strange to many Christians today. We understand the thought of serving God, of being busy in His work. We may even have a "quiet time" when we read the Bible and pray. But the idea of longing for God Himself, of wanting to deeply enjoy His fellowship and His presence, may seem a bit too mystical, almost bordering on fanaticism. We prefer our Christianity to be more practical.

Yet who could be more practical than Paul? Who was more involved in the struggles of daily living than David? Still, with all their responsibilities, both Paul and David yearned to experience more fellowship with the living God. The Bible indicates that this is God's plan for us, from its earliest pages right through to the end. In the third chapter of Genesis God walks in the garden, calling out for Adam that He might have fellowship with him. In Revelation 21, when John sees the vision of the new Jerusalem coming down from heaven, he hears the voice of God say, "Now the dwelling of God is with men, and he will live with them" (verse 3). For all of eternity God plans to have fellowship with His people.

And during our present day, Jesus still says to us as He did to the church at Laodicea, "Here I am! I stand at the door and knock. If anyone hears my voice and opens the door, I will come in and eat with him, and he with me" (Revelation 3:20). In the culture of John's day, to share a meal meant to have fellowship, so Jesus is inviting us to open our hearts to Him that we may fellowship with Him. He desires that we come to know Him better; therefore, the desire and yearning for God is something that He plants within our hearts.

In the life of the godly person, this desire for God produces an aura of warmth. Godliness is never austere and cold. Such an idea comes from a false sense of legalistic morality that is erroneously called godliness. The person who spends time with God radiates His glory in a manner that is always warm and inviting, never cold and forbidding.

This longing for God also produces a desire to glorify God and to please Him. In the same breath, Paul expresses the desire to know Christ as well as to be like Him. This is God's ultimate objective for us and is the object of the Spirit's work in us. In Isaiah 26:9, the prophet proclaims his desire for the Lord in words very similar to the psalmist's: "My soul yearns for you in the night; in the morning my spirit longs for you." Note that immediately before this expression of desire for the Lord, he expresses a desire for His glory: "Your name and renown are the desire of our hearts" (verse 8). Renown has to do with one's reputation, fame and eminence—or in God's case, with His glory. The prophet could not separate in his heart his desire for God's glory and his desire for God Himself. These two yearnings go hand in hand.

This is devotion to God—the fear of God, which is an

attitude of reverence and awe, veneration and honor toward
Him, coupled with an apprehension deep within our souls
of the love of God for us, demonstrated preeminently in the
atoning death of Christ. These two attitudes complement
and reinforce each other, producing within our souls an
intense desire for this One who is so awesome in His glory
and majesty and yet so condescending in His love and mercy.

NOTES
1. John Murray, *Principles of Conduct* (Grand Rapids, Mich.:
   Eerdmans, 1978), page 229.
2. Murray, page 230.
3. See, for example, 2 Corinthians 7:1, Ephesians 5:21, Colossians
   3:22, and 1 Peter 1:17. The *New International Version* of the
   Bible uses the word *reverence* for "fear" in some of these passages. It is, however, the same Greek word translated as "fear"
   in other places.
4. Murray, page 231.
5. Albert N. Martin, cassette tape series, "The Fear of God" (Essex
   Fells, N.J.: The Trinity Pulpit). This series consists of nine mes-
   sages on the fear of God. I highly recommend it to those who
   wish to pursue this subject in greater detail. I am indebted to
   the Reverend Martin for the definition of the fear of God used
   in this chapter.

# 3
# Train Yourself to Be Godly

*Have nothing to do with godless myths and old wives'
tales; rather, train yourself to be godly.*

1 Timothy 4:7

The apostle Paul did not take for granted the godliness of
his spiritual son Timothy. Though Timothy had been his
companion and co-laborer for a number of years, Paul still
felt it necessary to write to him, "train yourself to be godly."
And if Timothy needed this encouragement, then surely we
also need it today.

In urging Timothy to train himself in godliness, Paul bor-
rowed a term from the realm of athletics. The verb which is
variously translated in different versions of the Bible as "exercise," "discipline," or "train" originally referred to the training
of young athletes for participation in the competitive games of
the day. Then it took on a more general meaning of training or
discipline of either the body or the mind in a particular skill.

PRINCIPLES FOR TRAINING
There are several principles in Paul's exhortation to Timothy
to train himself to be godly that are applicable to us today.

The first is *personal responsibility*. Paul said, "Train yourself." Timothy was personally responsible for his progress in godliness. He was not to trust the Lord for that progress and then relax, though he certainly understood that any progress he made was only through divine enablement. He would have understood that he was to work out this particular aspect of his salvation in confidence that God was at work in him. But he would get Paul's message that he must work at this matter of godliness; he must *pursue* it.

We Christians may be very disciplined and industrious in our business, our studies, our home, or even our ministry, but we tend to be lazy when it comes to exercise in our own spiritual lives. We would much rather pray, "Lord, make me godly," and expect Him to "pour" some godliness into our souls in some mysterious way. God does in fact work in a mysterious way to make us godly, but He does not do this apart from the fulfillment of our own personal responsibility. We are to train ourselves to be godly.

The second principle in Paul's exhortation is that *the object of this training was growth* in Timothy's personal spiritual life. Elsewhere Paul encourages Timothy to progress in his ministry, but the objective here is Timothy's own devotion to God and the conduct arising from that devotion. Even though he was an experienced, well-qualified Christian minister, Timothy still needed to grow in the essential areas of godliness—the fear of God, the comprehension of the love of God, and the desire for the presence and fellowship of God.

I have been in a full-time Christian ministry for well over twenty-five years and have served both overseas and in the United States. During this time I have met many talented and capable Christians, but I think I have met fewer godly Christians. The emphasis of our age is on serving God, accomplishing things for God. Enoch was a preacher of righteousness in a day of gross ungodliness, but God saw fit that the brief account of his life emphasized that he walked with God. What are we training ourselves for? Are we training ourselves only in Christian activity, as good as that may be, or are we training ourselves first of all in godliness?

The third principle in Paul's words of exhortation to Timothy is the importance of *minimum characteristics necessary for training*. Many of us have watched various Olympic competitions on television, and as the commentators have given us the backgrounds of the various athletes, we become aware of certain irreducible minimums in the training of all Olympic competitors. It is very likely that Paul had these minimum characteristics in mind as he compared physical training with training in godliness.

THE COST OF COMMITMENT

The first of these irreducible minimums is *commitment*. No one makes it to the level of Olympic, or even national, competition without a commitment to pay the price of rigorous, daily training. And similarly, no one ever becomes godly without a commitment to pay the price of the daily spiritual training which God has designed for our growth in godliness.

The concept of commitment occurs repeatedly throughout the Bible. It is found in David's cry to God, "earnestly I seek you" (Psalm 63:1). It is found in God's promise to the captives in Babylon, "You will seek me and find me when you seek me with all your heart" (Jeremiah 29:13). It occurs in Paul's pressing on to take hold of that for which Christ Jesus took hold of him (Philippians 3:12). It lies behind such exhortations as "Make every effort . . . to be holy" (Hebrews 12:14), and "make every effort to add to your faith . . . godliness" (2 Peter 1:5-7). None of this seeking, pressing on, or making every effort will occur without commitment on our part.

There is a price to godliness, and godliness is never on

sale. It never comes cheaply or easily. The verb *train*, which Paul deliberately chose, implies persevering, painstaking, diligent effort. He was well aware of the total commitment those young athletes made to win a crown that would not last. And as he thought of the crown that would last—the godliness that has value for all things, both in the present life and the life to come—he urged Timothy, and he urges us today, to make the kind of commitment necessary to train ourselves to be godly.

LEARNING FROM A SKILLED TEACHER

The second irreducible minimum in training is *a competent teacher or coach*. No athlete, regardless of how much natural ability he has, can make it to the Olympics without a skillful coach who holds him to the highest standard of excellence and sees and corrects every minor fault. In the same way we cannot train ourselves to be godly without the teaching and training ministry of the Holy Spirit. He holds us to the highest standard of spiritual excellence as He teaches, rebukes, corrects, and trains us. But He teaches and trains us through His word. Therefore we must consistently expose ourselves to the teaching of the word of God if we are to grow in godliness.

In Titus 1:1 Paul refers to "the knowledge of the truth that leads to godliness." We cannot grow in godliness without the knowledge of this truth. This truth is to be found only in the Bible, but it is not just academic knowledge of Bible facts. It is spiritual knowledge taught by the Holy Spirit as He applies the truth of God to our hearts.

There is a type of religious knowledge that is actually detrimental to training in godliness. It is the knowledge that puffs up with spiritual pride. The Corinthian Christians had this kind of knowledge. They knew that an idol was nothing and that eating food sacrificed to an idol was a matter of spiritual indifference. But they did not know about their responsibility to love their weaker brother. Only the Holy Spirit imparts that type of knowledge—the type that leads to godliness.

It is possible to be very orthodox in one's doctrine and very upright in one's behavior and still not be godly. Many people are orthodox and upright, but they are not devoted to God; they are devoted to their orthodoxy and their standards of moral conduct.

Only the Holy Spirit can pry us loose from such positions of false confidence, so we must sincerely look to Him for His training ministry as we seek to grow in godliness. We must spend much time in exposure to His word, since it is His means of teaching us. But this exposure must be accompanied by a sense of deep humility regarding our ability to learn spiritual truth and a sense of utter dependence upon His ministry in our hearts.

PRACTICE, AND MORE PRACTICE
The third irreducible minimum in the training process is *practice*. It is practice that puts feet to the commitment and applies the teaching of the coach. It is practice, where the skill is developed, that makes the athlete competitive in his sport. And it is the practice of godliness that enables us to become godly Christians. There is no shortcut to Olympic-level skill, there is no shortcut to godliness. It is the day in and day out faithfulness to the means which God has appointed and which the Holy Spirit uses that will enable us to grow in godliness. We must *practice* godliness, just as the athlete practices his particular sport.

We must practice the fear of God, for example, if we are to grow in that aspect of godly devotion. If we agree with the Reverend Martin that the essential elements of the fear of God are correct concepts of His character, a pervasive sense of His presence, and a constant awareness of our responsibility to Him, then we must work at filling our minds with the biblical expressions of these truths and applying them in our lives until we are transformed into God-fearing people.

If we become convinced that humility is a trait of godly character, then we will frequently meditate upon such Scripture passages as Isaiah 57:15 and 66:1-2, where God Himself extols humility. We will pray over them, asking the Holy Spirit to apply them in our lives to make us truly humble. This is the practice of godliness. It is not some ethereal exercise. It is practical, down-to-earth, and even a bit grubby at times as the Holy Spirit works on us. But it is always rewarding as we see the Spirit transforming us more and more into godly people.

USING THE WORD OF GOD

It is evident that the word of God plays a crucial role in our growth in godliness. A prominent part of our practice of godliness, therefore, will be our time in the word of God. How we spend that time varies according to the method of intake. The Navigators use the five fingers of the hand as mental pegs on which to hang the five methods of intake of the word of God—hearing, reading, studying, memorizing, and meditating. These methods are important for godliness and need to be considered one by one.

The most common method of scriptural intake is *hearing* the word of God taught to us by our pastors and teachers. We are living in a day when this method tends to be lightly regarded by many people as being a somewhat ineffective means of learning spiritual truth. This is a serious error. The Lord Jesus Christ Himself has given to His church people who are gifted to teach us the truths of His word, to remind us of the lessons we are prone to forget, and to exhort us to constancy in application. We need to heed those whom He has given to us for this purpose.

None of us ever becomes so spiritually self-sufficient that he does not need to hear the word taught by others. And most of us do not have the ability or the time to search out on our own the "whole will of God" (Acts 20:27). We need to sit under the regular teaching of a man gifted by God and trained to expound the word of God to us.

One reason the hearing of the word of God has fallen into such low esteem is that we do not obey God's teaching in Revelation 1:3—"blessed are those who hear it and take to heart what is written in it." Too often today we listen to be entertained instead of instructed, to be moved emotionally rather than moved to obedience. We do not take to heart what we hear and apply it in our daily lives.

We present-day Christians are hardly different from the Jews of Ezekiel's time, of whom God said, "My people come to you, as they usually do, and sit before you to listen to your words, but they do not put them into practice" (Ezekiel 33:31). God goes on to tell Ezekiel that to his audience, Ezekiel is nothing more than a singer with a beautiful voice who plays an instrument well. To the Jews he was just an entertainer, because they had no intention of putting into practice what they heard.

The type of hearing of the word that God commends is illustrated by the Berean Christians, who "received the message with great eagerness and examined the Scriptures every day to see if what Paul said was true" (Acts 17:11). They did not hear and forget; they did not listen just to be entertained. They realized eternal issues were at stake, so they listened, studied, and applied. Considering that they probably did not have their own personal copies of the Scriptures, their studying of Paul's teaching is remarkable. It is a rebuke to us today, who scarcely remember beyond the church door what we heard in the sermon on Sunday morning.

We have already considered briefly the thought expressed in Titus 1:1—it is the knowledge of the truth that leads to godliness. But that is not all the verse says. In the same passage, Paul says he is an apostle of Jesus Christ for the purpose of furthering the faith of God's elect and their knowledge of the truth that leads to godliness. Paul was called to be a teacher for the express purpose of promoting faith and godliness among God's elect. God called Paul to that task, and He calls pastors and teachers today for the same purpose. But if we are to profit from their ministry so that we grow in the knowledge of the truth that leads to godliness, we must hear their word as the Berean Christians heard Paul—with great eagerness and an intent to obey.

The second method of scriptural intake is *reading* the Bible ourselves. Through Bible reading we have the opportunity to learn directly from the Master Teacher, the Holy Spirit. As helpful and profitable as it is to learn from the teaching of others, there is an unmatched joy in having the Holy Spirit speak to us directly from the pages of His word.

We have already seen that Enoch walked with God, which implies that he enjoyed personal communion with God. Bible reading enables us, too, to enjoy communion with God as He speaks to us from His word, encouraging us, instructing us, and revealing Himself to us. It was said of Moses that "the Lord would speak to [him] face to face, as a man speaks with his friend" (Exodus 33:11). Today we do not have that particular privilege, but we can enjoy the same effect as God speaks to us during our times of personal Bible reading. Our practice of godliness would be very incomplete without a regular Bible reading program of some type.

A second value of Bible reading is the opportunity to gain an overall perspective of the entire Bible. No pastor could—or should—preach through the Bible in the short space of a year or two. But all of us can *read* through the entire Bible in a year. Many Bible reading plans are available to help us do so. As we read through the Bible, the various pieces of spiritual truth begin to fit together. The book of Hebrews doesn't make sense unless one is at least knowledgeable of the Old Testament priesthood and sacrificial system. The New Testament writers' many allusions to the Old Testament would remain a mystery unless we had read the passages in their original setting. The doctrine of original sin through Adam, as taught by Paul in Romans 5, cannot be understood apart from a knowledge of the events recorded in Genesis 3.

Without a reading program of the entire Bible, we would be not only spiritually ignorant, but spiritually impoverished. Who can fail to learn from Abraham's faith, David's love for God, Daniel's righteousness, and Job's trial? How can we become godly without the heartbeat of the Psalms and the practical wisdom of Proverbs? Where better can we learn of both the majesty and the faithfulness of God than from the prophet Isaiah? If we are not periodically reading through the Bible, we will miss these outstanding passages in the Old Testament as well as others in the New Testament.

All Scripture is profitable for us, even passages that seem so difficult to understand. We can choose from among various Bible reading programs to help us maintain consistency in our reading and understand the more difficult passages.[1]

The third method of Bible intake is *studying* the Scriptures. Reading gives us breadth, but study gives us depth. The value of Bible study lies in the opportunity to dig more deeply into a passage or topic than we can do in Bible reading. Greater diligence and mental intensity are required for study, in which we analyze a passage, compare Scripture with Scripture, ask questions, make observations, and finally organize the fruit of our study into some kind of logical presentation. The discipline of writing down our study material helps to clarify our thoughts. All of this strengthens our knowledge of the truth and helps us to grow in godliness.

Every Christian should be a student of the Bible. The Hebrew Christians were rebuked, because although they should have been able to teach others, they still needed to be taught the elementary truths of God's word. They needed milk, not solid food! Unfortunately, many of us are like those Christians.

There are numerous methods of Bible study available for every level of student. There are certain principles that should be applied, however, whatever method is used. These principles are set forth in Proverbs 2:1-5. Note the verbs that have been italicized for emphasis:

> My son, if you *accept* my words and *store up* my
> commands within you, *turning* your ear to wisdom
> and *applying* your heart to understanding, and if you
> *call out* for insight and *cry aloud* for understanding,
> and if you *look* for it as for silver and *search* for it as
> for hidden treasure, then you will understand the fear
> of the Lord and find the knowledge of God.

The verbs that are italicized give us an idea of the principles involved in Bible study, such as,

- ❖ teachability—accept my words
- ❖ intent to obey—store up my commands
- ❖ mental discipline—apply your heart
- ❖ prayerful dependence—call out, cry aloud
- ❖ diligent perseverance—search as for hidden treasure.

The results of applying these principles in Bible study are located in verse 5: "Then you will understand the fear of the Lord and find the knowledge of God"—two of the concepts essential in our devotion to God. If we are to train ourselves to be godly we must give Bible study priority in our lives.

Where can we find the time for quality Bible study? I once heard that question asked of a chief of surgery in a large hospital. Twenty-five years later, his answer continues to challenge me. He looked his questioner squarely in the eye and said, "You always find time for what is important to you." How important is the practice of godliness to you? Is it important enough to take priority over television, books, magazines, recreation, and a score of activities that we all somehow find time to engage in? Once again we are brought face to face with that key element of training we discussed earlier—commitment.

*Memorization* of key passages is a fourth method of scriptural intake. Without doubt the classic verse for Scripture memorization is Psalm 119:11: "I have hidden your word in my heart that I might not sin against you." The word that is translated in verse 11 as "hidden" is elsewhere translated as "stored up," a phrase which is more descriptive of the actual meaning. In Proverbs 7:1, for example, Solomon says, "My son . . . *store up* my commands within you," and in Proverbs 10:14 he says, "Wise men *store up* knowledge." In Psalm 31:19 David speaks of the goodness which God has *stored up* for those who fear Him. From these passages it is clear that the central idea of the psalmist in Psalm 119:11 was that of storing up God's word in his heart against a time of future need—a time when he would encounter temptation and would be kept from that temptation by the word of God.

But the word of God stored in the heart does more than keep us from sin. It enables us to grow in every area of the Christian life. Specifically for our practice of godliness, it enables us to grow in our devotion to God and in the Godlike character that makes our lives pleasing to Him.[2]

The fifth method for taking in God's word is *meditation*. The word *meditate* as used in the Old Testament literally means to murmur or to mutter and, by implication, to talk to oneself.[3] When we meditate on the Scriptures we talk to ourselves about them, turning over in our minds the meanings, the implications, and the applications to our own lives.

Though we use Psalm 119:11 in connection with Scripture memorization, it may be more supportive of the practice of meditation. The psalmist says God's word was stored up in his *heart*—his inmost being. Bare memorization only gets the Scriptures into our minds. Meditation on those same Scriptures opens our understanding, engages our affections, and addresses our wills. This is the process of storing up the word in our hearts. But if the process of storing up Scripture applies primarily to meditation, it is also true that memorization is the first step to meditation. Meditation on the word of God is commanded in Joshua 1:8 and commended in Psalm 1:2. Both verses speak of meditation *day and night*, not just when we are having our quiet time. It is impossible to meditate on Scripture day and night without some form of Scripture memorization.

In chapter 1 we defined godliness as devotion to God which results in a life that is pleasing to God. If we had to select one chapter of the Bible that portrays the heartbeat of the godly person, it would probably be Psalm 119. In all but two of its 176 verses, the writer relates his life to the word of God and to the God behind that word. It is always *Your* laws, *Your* statutes, *Your* desires, *Your* precepts, etc. To the psalmist, the law of God was not the cold commands of some far-off deity, but the living word of the God whom he loved, sought, and yearned to please.

Walking with God involves communion with God. His word is absolutely necessary and central to our communion with Him. Pleasing God requires knowing His will—how He wants us to live, what He wants us to do. His word is the only means by which He communicates that will to us. It is impossible to practice godliness without a constant, consistent, and balanced intake of the word of God in our lives.

The intake of the word is our foundational means of practicing godliness, but it is not our only means. In the next chapter we will consider how to develop a devotion to God. In subsequent chapters we will consider how to grow in some individual traits of godly character, including a look at some practical steps we can take in the practice of godliness.

THE NATURE OF TRAINING

Paul said, "Train yourself to be godly." You and I are responsible to train ourselves. We are dependent upon God for His divine enablement, but we are responsible; we are not passive in this process. Our objective in this process is godliness—not proficiency in ministry, but God-centered devotion and Godlike character. We do want to develop proficiency in ministry, but for training in godliness we want to focus on our relationship with God.

Training in godliness requires commitment, the teaching ministry of the Holy Spirit through His word, and practice on our part. Are we prepared to accept our responsibility and make that commitment? As we ponder that question let us remember, "Godliness has value for all things, holding promise for both the present life and the life to come," and "Godliness with contentment is great gain" (1 Timothy 4:8 and 6:6).

NOTES
1. One of the best aids to daily Bible reading is *The Daily Walk*, available free upon request from The Navigators Daily Walk, P.O. Box 6000, Colorado Springs, Colorado 80934. This publication provides both a program for reading through the Bible as well as short explanatory notes on each day's reading portion.
2. Information on materials for Bible study and Scripture memorization may be obtained from NavPress, P.O. Box 35002, Colorado Springs, Colorado 80935.
3. William Wilson, *Wilson's Old Testament Word Studies* (MacLean, Va.: MacDonald Publ. Co., n.d.), page 271.

# 4
# Seeking
# a Deeper Devotion

*I seek you with all my heart;*
*do not let me stray from your commands.*

Psalm 119:10

Scripture defines unbelievers as totally godless. Paul tells the Romans that they have no fear of God, are hostile to Him, are unwilling to submit to His law, and are unable to please Him. This is just as true of the morally upright unbeliever as it is of the most corrupt profligate. The former worships a god of his own mind, not the God of the Bible. When confronted with the claims of the Sovereign God of the universe, he often reacts with greater hostility than an unbeliever living in open sin.

At the time of our salvation, God through His Holy Spirit deals with this godless spirit within us. He gives us a new heart and moves us to obey Him, He gives us a singleness of heart and inspires us to fear Him, and He pours out His love into our hearts so that we begin to comprehend His love for us. All of this is bound up in the blessings of the new birth, so we may safely say that all Christians possess, at least in embryonic form, a basic devotion to God. It is impossible to be a Christian and not have it. The work of the Holy Spirit at regeneration assures this. God has given us everything we need for life and godliness.

But though all of us as Christians possess a basic God-centeredness as an integral part of our spiritual lives, we must grow in this devotion to God. We are to train ourselves to be godly; we are to make every effort to add godliness to our faith. To grow in godliness is to grow both in our devotion to God and in our likeness to His character.

In chapter 2 we illustrated devotion to God by a triangle whose three points represent the fear of God, the love of God, and the desire for God. To grow in our devotion to God is to grow in each of these three areas. And as the triangle is equal on all three sides, so we should seek to grow equally in all of these areas; otherwise our devotion becomes unbalanced.

To seek to grow in the fear of God, for example, without also growing in our comprehension of His love can cause us to begin to view God as far-off and austere. Or to seek to grow in our awareness of the love of God without also growing in our reverence and awe of Him can cause us to view God as a permissive and indulgent heavenly Father who does not deal with our sin. This latter unbalanced view is prevalent in our society today. That is why many Christians are calling for a renewed emphasis on the biblical teaching of the fear of God.

A crucial characteristic of our growth in godly devotion, then, must be a balanced approach to all three of the essential elements of devotion: fear, love, and desire. Another crucial characteristic must be a *vital dependence upon the Holy Spirit* to bring about this growth. The principle of Christian ministry that Paul states in 1 Corinthians 3:7, "neither he who plants nor he who waters is anything, but only God, who makes things grow," is just as true as a principle of growth in godliness. We must plant and water through whatever means of grace God has given us, but only God can make godly devotion increase within our hearts.

## PRAYING FOR GROWTH

We express this vital dependence on God by praying that He will cause us to grow in our devotion to Him. David prayed, "give me an undivided heart, that I may fear your name" (Psalm 86:11). Paul prayed that the Ephesian Christians might be able to grasp how wide and long and high and deep is the love of Christ (Ephesians 3:16-19). And David prayed that he might dwell in the house of the Lord to behold His beauty and to seek Him in His temple (Psalm 27:4). Each of these prayers is a recognition that growth in devotion to God is of Him.

If we are committed to the practice of godliness, our prayer life will reflect it. We will be regularly asking God to increase our fear of Him, to deepen our understanding of His love for us, and to heighten our desire for His fellowship. We would do well, for example, to put the three verses mentioned above, or similar passages, on our list of prayer requests and pray over them regularly.

## MEDITATING ON GOD

We have already discussed the overall importance of the word of God in developing godliness. The word also helps us specifically in the three areas of devotion—the fear of God, the love of God, and the desire for God.

Although all of the Bible should instruct us in the fear of God, I have found there are certain passages that are especially helpful to me in drawing my attention to the majesty and holiness of God—the attributes particularly suited to stimulate our hearts in the fear of God. Here are some passages I refer to frequently:

- ❖ Isaiah 6 and Revelation 4—God's holiness
- ❖ Isaiah 40—God's greatness
- ❖ Psalm 139—God's omniscience and omnipresence
- ❖ Revelation 1:10-17 and Revelation 5—the majesty of Christ.

These Scripture selections are intended only as suggestions. You may find others that are more meaningful to you. Use them. The important point is that God uses His word to create in our hearts the sense of reverence and awe of Him that causes us to fear Him. It is vain to pray for an increase of the fear of God in our hearts without meditating on passages of Scripture that are particularly suited to stimulate that fear.

There are also specific passages that will help us grow in our awareness of God's love. I find these especially helpful: Psalm 103, Isaiah 53, Romans 5:6-11, Ephesians 2:1-10, 2 Corinthians 5:14-21, 1 Timothy 1:15-16, and 1 John 4:9-11.

In commending certain passages of Scripture to you, I cannot emphasize too strongly, however, that it is not just the bare reading, or even memorizing, of these passages that accomplishes the desired result of growth in godliness. We must meditate on them, but even that is not sufficient. The Holy Spirit must make His word come alive to our hearts to produce the growth, so we must meditate in prayerful dependence upon Him to do His work. Neither meditation nor prayer by themselves are sufficient for growth in devotion. We must practice both.

WORSHIPING GOD

Still another essential part of our practice of devotion to God is *worship*. By worship I mean the specific act of ascribing to

God the glory, majesty, honor, and worthiness which are His. Revelation 4:8-11 and 5:9-14 give us clear illustrations of the worship that goes on in heaven and which should be emulated by us here on earth. I almost always begin my daily quiet time with a period of worship. Before beginning my Bible reading for the day, I take a few minutes to reflect upon one of the attributes of God or to meditate upon one of the passages about Him mentioned above, and then ascribe to Him the glory and honor due to Him because of that particular attribute.

I find it helpful to assume a kneeling position for this time of worship as a physical acknowledgment of my reverence, awe, and adoration of God. Worship is a matter of the heart, not of one's physical position; nevertheless, the Scriptures do frequently portray bowing the knee as a sign of homage and adoration. David said, "in reverence will I bow down toward your holy temple" (Psalm 5:7). The writer of Psalm 95 says, "Come, let us bow down in worship, let us kneel before the Lord our Maker" (verse 6). And we know that one day every knee shall bow before Jesus as a sign of homage to His Lordship (Philippians 2:10).

Obviously, it is not always possible to bow before God in our times of worship. God understands this and surely allows for it. But when we can do so, I strongly recommend bowing before God, not only as a sign of reverence to Him, but also for what it does in helping us prepare our minds to worship God in a manner acceptable to Him.

In emphasizing the value of worship, I have dealt solely with the practice of private worship: that which we should do in our personal quiet time. I do not mean to ignore public, corporate worship; I simply do not feel qualified to speak on that subject. I would plead with ministers of congregations to give us more *instruction* in the nature and practice of corporate worship. I sense that many Christians go through the motions of a worship service without actually worshiping God.

## FELLOWSHIP WITH GOD

All that has been said thus far about the importance of prayer, of meditating on the word of God, and of having a specific time of worship, implies the value of a quiet time. The expression "quiet time" is used to describe a regular period each day set aside to meet with God through His word and through prayer. One of the great privileges of a believer is to have fellowship with almighty God. We do this by listening to Him speak to us from His word and by speaking to Him through prayer.

There are various spiritual exercises we may want to accomplish during our quiet time, such as reading through the Bible in a year and praying over certain requests. But the primary objective of our quiet time should be fellowship with God—developing a personal relationship with Him and growing in our devotion to Him.

After I have begun my quiet time with a period of worship, I next turn to the Bible. As I read a passage of Scripture (usually one or more chapters), I talk to God about what I am reading, as I go along. I like to think of the quiet time as a conversation: God speaking to me through the Bible and I responding to what He says. This approach helps to make the quiet time what it is intended to be—a time of fellowship with God.

Having worshiped God and fellowshiped with Him, I then take time to go over various prayer requests I want to bring before Him that day. Following this order prepares me to pray more effectively. I have thought about who God is; therefore, I do not "rush into His presence" casually and demandingly. At the same time I am reminded of His power and love, and my faith regarding His ability and delight to answer my requests is strengthened. In this way, even my time of asking actually becomes a time of fellowship with Him.

In suggesting certain Scriptures for meditation, or certain modes of worship, or a particular practice for a quiet time, I do not want to give the impression that growing in devotion to God is merely following a suggested routine. Neither do I want to suggest that what is helpful to me ought to be followed by others, or will even be helpful to others. All I want to do is demonstrate that growth in devotion to God, although a result of His ministry in us, comes as a result of very concrete practice on our part. We are to train ourselves to be godly; and as we learned in chapter 3, training involves practice—the day-after-day exercise that enables us to become proficient.

## THE ULTIMATE TEST

Thus far we have looked at specific activities that help us grow in our devotion to God—prayer, meditation on the Scriptures, worship, and the quiet time. There is still another area that is not an activity, but an attitude of life: obedience to the will of God. This is the ultimate test of our fear of God and the only true response to His love for us. God specifically states that we fear Him by keeping all His decrees and commands (Deuteronomy 6:1-2), and Proverbs 8:13 tells us that "To fear the Lord is to hate evil." I can know if I truly fear God by determining if I have a genuine hatred of evil and an earnest desire to obey His commands.

In the days of Nehemiah, the Jewish nobles and officials were disobeying God's law by exacting usury from their countrymen. When Nehemiah confronted them he said, "What you are doing is not right. Shouldn't you walk in the fear of our God to avoid the reproach of our Gentile enemies?" (Nehemiah 5:9). He could just as well have said,

"Shouldn't you *obey* God to avoid the reproach of our enemies?" Nehemiah equated walking in the fear of God with
obedience to God. If we do not fear God, we will not think
it worthwhile to obey His commands; but if we truly fear
Him—if we hold Him in reverence and awe—we will obey
Him. The measure of our obedience is an exact measure of
our reverence for Him.

Similarly, as we have already seen in chapter 2, Paul
affirmed that his awareness of Christ's love for him compelled him to live, not for himself, but for Him who died for
us. As God begins to answer our prayer for a deeper realization of His love, one means He often uses is to enable us to
see more and more of our own sinfulness. Paul was nearing
the end of his life when he wrote these words: "Christ Jesus
came into the world to save sinners—of whom I am the
worst" (1 Timothy 1:15). We realize that our sins as
Christians, though perhaps not as outwardly gross as before,
are more heinous in the sight of God because they are sins
against knowledge and against grace. We know better and
we know His love, and yet we sin willfully. And then we go
back to the cross and realize that Jesus bore even those will-
ful sins in His body on the tree, and the realization of that
infinite love compels us to deal with those very sins and to
put them to death. Both the fear of God and the love of God
motivate us to obedience, and that obedience proves they
are authentic in our lives.

A DEEPER LONGING
As we concentrate on growing in our reverence and awe for
God and in our understanding of His love for us, we will find
that our desire for Him will grow. As we gaze upon His
beauty we will desire to seek Him even more. And as we
become progressively more aware of His redeeming love, we
will want to know Him in a progressively deeper way. But we

can also pray that God will deepen our desire for Him. I recall reading Philippians 3:10 a number of years ago and realizing a little bit of the depth of Paul's desire to know Christ more intimately. As I read I prayed, "O God, I cannot identify with Paul's longing, but I would like to." Over the years God has begun to answer that prayer. By His grace I know experientially to some degree Isaiah's words, "My soul yearns for you in the night; in the morning my spirit longs for you" (Isaiah 26:9). I am grateful for what God has done, but I pray I will continue to grow in this desire for Him.

One of the wonderful things about God is that He is infinite in all of His glorious attributes, so never in our desire for Him will we exhaust the revelation of His person to us. The more we come to know Him, the more we will desire Him. And the more we desire Him, the more we will want to fellowship with Him and experience His presence. And the more we desire Him and His fellowship, the more we will desire to be like Him.

Paul's heartfelt cry in Philippians 3:10 vividly expresses this longing. He desires both to know Christ and to be like Him. He wants to experience both His fellowship—even the fellowship of suffering—as well as the transforming power of His resurrection life. He wants both Christ-centeredness and Christlikeness.

This is godliness: God-centeredness, or devotion to God; and Godlikeness, or Christian character. The practice of godliness is both the practice of devotion to God and the practice of a lifestyle that is pleasing to God and that reflects His character to other people.

In the remainder of our studies in this book we will consider the Godlike character that we should display. But we can build Godlike character only upon the foundation of a wholehearted devotion to God. God must be the very focal point of our lives if we wish to have godly character and conduct.

This point cannot be overemphasized. Too many of us focus on the outward structure of character and conduct without taking the time to build the inward foundation of devotion to God. This often results in a cold morality or legalism, or even worse, self-righteousness and spiritual pride. Of course, the foundation of devotion to God and the structure of a life pleasing to God must be developed simultaneously. We cannot separate these two aspects of godliness.

Because of the importance of properly laying the foundation of inward devotion, I encourage you to review the essential elements of devotion (see chapter 2). Then review this chapter and make specific plans for exercising yourself in the area of devotion to God. No one has ever developed a mental or physical skill without a commitment to practice. And no one will ever develop a devotion to God without a commitment to exercise himself in the essential elements of devotion.

The idea of practice may tend to make us think of drudgery, such as dreary drills on piano scales when we wished to be out playing with our friends. But the practice of developing our relationship with God should not be equated with something like childhood music lessons. We are seeking to grow in our devotion to the most wonderful Person in all of the universe, the infinitely glorious and loving God. Nothing can compare with the privilege of knowing Him in whose presence is fullness of joy and in whose hand there are pleasures forever (Psalm 16:11, NASB).

# 5

# Taking on God's Character

*Therefore, as God's chosen people, holy and dearly loved,*
*clothe yourselves with compassion, kindness, humility,*
*gentleness and patience.*

Colossians 3:12

Godliness consists of two distinct but complementary traits, and the person who wants to train himself to be godly must pursue both with equal vigor. The first trait is God-centeredness, which we call devotion to God; the second is Godlikeness, which we call Christian character. Godly character flows out of devotion to God and practically confirms the reality of that devotion.

We may express a reverence for God; we may lift our hearts in worship to Him; but we demonstrate the genuineness of our devotion to God by our earnest desire and sincere effort to be like Him. Paul not only wanted to know Christ, he wanted to be like Him; and he pressed forward with utmost intensity toward that goal.

Thus far in our study of the practice of godliness we have concentrated on the aspect of devotion, of God-centeredness. Now we turn our attention to Godlikeness—the development of Godlike character. What are the character traits that distinguish the godly person? A good place to start is with the list of gracious qualities, which Paul calls the fruit of the Spirit, in Galatians 5:22-23. It seems obvious, however, that Paul did not intend to limit the traits of the fruit of the Spirit to that particular list. Any other trait commended in Scripture as befitting a believer is also a fruit of the Spirit, since its evidence is a result only of the Spirit's ministry in our hearts. So, to the qualities listed in Galatians 5—love, joy, peace, patience, kindness, goodness, faithfulness, gentleness, and self-control—we can also add such traits as holiness, humility, compassion, forbearance, contentment, thankfulness, considerateness, sincerity, and perseverance.

This is a rather awesome list of character traits to pursue, and our first reaction, if we are realistic at all, is probably to say, "I can't work on all of these." That is indeed true, *if* we were left to our own devices. But these traits are the fruit of the Spirit, the result of *His* work within us. This does not mean we bear no responsibility for the development of Christian character, but rather that we fulfill our responsibility under His direction and by His enablement. It is this divine dimension that makes Christian character possible, and it is *only* this divine dimension that can keep us from becoming frustrated and defeated in our desire to exemplify godly character traits in our lives.

In the following chapters we will study some of these traits of godliness individually. There are some basic principles, however, that apply to all aspects of godly character.

THE RIGHT MOTIVE

The first principle of godly character is, *Devotion to God is the only acceptable motive for actions that are pleasing to God*. This devotion may express itself in one of several different ways. We may have a sincere desire to please God or to glorify

Him; we may do or not do a particular action because we love God, or because we sense that He is worthy of our obedience. However our motivation expresses itself, if it is God-centered, it arises out of our devotion to God and is acceptable to Him.

Unfortunately, too often our motives are self-centered rather than God-centered. We want to maintain our reputation before others, or we want to feel good about ourselves. Or we may even seek to live a decent and moral life or to do good deeds because such an ethic has been instilled in us from childhood. But that motivation is never related to God and thus is not acceptable to Him.

When Joseph was enticed by Potiphar's wife, he did not refuse her on the basis, "If I did that and my master found out, he would have my head." No; he said, "How then could I do such a wicked thing and sin against God?" (Genesis 39:9). His motivation for morality was centered in God, and because of that it was acceptable to God.

I recall once being tempted with the opportunity to engage in a questionable business transaction, one of those gray-area situations in which we tend to rationalize our actions. As I pondered the matter I thought, I better not; I might incur the discipline of God. Now when all proper motives fail, it is certainly better to be checked by the fear of God's discipline than to go ahead with our sin. But that is not the right motive. In this situation the Holy Spirit came to my aid and I thought to myself, *Now that [the fear of God's discipline] is certainly an unworthy motive; the real reason why I should not do that is because God is worthy of my most honorable conduct.* The Holy Spirit helped me to recognize the self-centeredness of my initial motivation and to correctly focus my motivation on God.

When God commanded Abraham to offer up Isaac as a sacrifice, he tested his motive. As He stayed Abraham's knife from the fatal plunge, God said, "Now I know that you fear God, because you have not withheld from me your son, your only son" (Genesis 22:12). It was Abraham's fear of God that motivated him to go forward with that supreme act of obedience. We usually associate Abraham's obedience with his faith. It was by faith that Abraham was *enabled* to offer Isaac as a sacrifice, but it was the fear of God that *motivated* him. And it was this Godward motivation that the Lord saw and accepted and commended.

As we look into the New Testament we see this Godward motivation emphasized again and again. Jesus taught that all the Law and the Prophets hang on the two commandments of love for God and love for our neighbor (Matthew 22:37-40). He was not teaching merely that these two commandments of love sum up all the other more specific commandments, but rather that all the other commandments depend upon the motivation of love for their fulfillment. The fear of consequences may keep us from committing the outward acts of murder or adultery, but only love will keep us from committing murder or adultery in our hearts.

In 1 Corinthians 10:31 Paul tells us that even our eating and drinking is to be done for the glory of God. As someone has observed, there is nothing more ordinary and routine than our eating and drinking; yet even this is to be done with a Godward motivation. Slaves were enjoined to obey their earthly masters out of "reverence for the Lord" (Colossians 3:22). All of us are to submit ourselves to human authority "for the Lord's sake" (1 Peter 2:13). And our interpersonal relationships—our mutual submission to one another—is to be done "out of reverence for Christ" (Ephesians 5:21). All of our actions, to be acceptable to God, must be done out of a sense of devotion to God.

THE SOURCE OF POWER
The second principle of godly character is, *The power or enablement for a godly life comes from the risen Christ.*

Paul said in relation to his ministry, "our competence comes from God" (2 Corinthians 3:5), and "I labor, struggling with all his energy, which so powerfully works in me" (Colossians 1:29). He said of his ability to be content in any situation, "I can do everything through him who gives me strength" (Philippians 4:13).

It is very likely that God, in His sovereign calling and preparation of Paul for his tremendous task, had endowed him with more noble qualities and strength of character than any person since; yet Paul consistently attributes his spiritual strength and accomplishments to the Lord's power. I once heard someone say, "When I do something wrong, I have to take the blame, but when I do something right, God gets the credit." This person was complaining, but he was exactly correct. Certainly God cannot be blamed for our sins, but only He can provide the spiritual power to enable us to live godly lives.

As the *source* of power for godliness is Christ, so the *means* of experiencing that power is through our relationship with Him. This truth is Jesus' essential teaching in His illustration in John 15 of the vine and the branches. It is only by abiding in Him that we can bring forth the fruit of godly character.[1] The most helpful explanation I have found of what it means to abide in Christ comes from the nineteenth-century Swiss theologian Frederic Louis Godet: "'To abide in me' expresses the continual act by which the Christian sets aside everything which he might derive from his own wisdom, strength, merit, to draw all from Christ."[2]

Paul expresses this relationship as "living in Christ." He says in Colossians 2:6-7, "So then, just as you received Christ Jesus as Lord, continue to live in him, rooted and built up in him, strengthened in the faith." The context of this statement is that all the wisdom and power for living the Christian life are to be found in Christ rather than in man-made philosophies and moralisms (see verses 2-4 and 8-10).

This is what Godet is saying. We have to set aside any dependence upon our own wisdom and strength of character and draw all that we need from Christ through faith in Him. This faith, of course, is expressed concretely by prayer to Him. Psalm 119:33-37 is a good example of such a prayer of dependence.

This relationship is also maintained by beholding the glory of Christ in His word. In 2 Corinthians 3:18 Paul tells us that as we behold the Lord's glory, we are transformed more and more into His image. Beholding the Lord's glory in His word is more than observing His humanity in the gospels. It is observing His character, His attributes, and His will in every page of Scripture. And as we observe Him, as we maintain this relationship with Him through His word, we are transformed more and more into His likeness; we are enabled by the Holy Spirit to progressively manifest the graces of godly character.

So it is this relationship with Christ, expressed by beholding Him in His word and depending upon Him in prayer, that enables us to draw from Him the power essential for a godly life. The Christian is not like an automobile with a self-contained power source; rather, he is like an electric motor that must be constantly connected to an outside current for its power. Our source of power is in the risen Christ, and we stay connected to Him by beholding Him in His word and depending on Him in prayer.

RESPONSIBILITY AND DEPENDENCE
The third principle of godly character is, *Though the power for godly character comes from Christ, the responsibility for developing and displaying that character is ours*. This principle seems to be one of the most difficult for us to understand and apply. One day we sense our personal responsibility and seek to live a godly life by the strength of our own

willpower. The next day, realizing the futility of trusting in ourselves, we turn it all over to Christ and abdicate our responsibility which is set forth in the Scriptures. We need to learn that the Bible teaches both total responsibility and total dependence in all aspects of the Christian life.

I once read a statement to the effect that there is nothing a Christian can do to develop the fruit of the Spirit in his life; it is all the work of the Holy Spirit. Sensing that at best, such a statement failed to present a balance of scriptural truth, I took out my concordance and looked up various passages that referred to one or more of the nine character traits listed as fruit of the Spirit in Galatians 5. For every one of those traits I found one or more passages in which we are commanded to exhibit them. We are enjoined to love, to rejoice, to live in peace with each other, and so forth. These commands address our responsibility.

We have already seen that Timothy was responsible to train himself in godliness; he was to *pursue* godliness. When Paul describes his own pursuit of a Godlike life, he uses strong verbs such as "press on" and "straining toward" (Philippians 3:12-14). These words convey the idea of intense effort on his part and communicate forcefully his own sense of personal responsibility.

The solution to the seemingly incompatible statements that we are both totally responsible and totally dependent is found in Philippians 2:12-13: "Therefore, my dear friends, as you have always obeyed—not only in my presence, but now much more in my absence—continue to work out your salvation with fear and trembling, for it is God who works in you to will and to act according to his good purpose."

Commenting on this passage, Professor Jac J. Müller says, "The believer is called to self-activity, to the active pursuit of the will of God, to the promotion of the spiritual life in himself, to the realization of the virtues of the Christian life, and to a personal application of salvation."[3] If we stopped at this point, it would appear that we are left to our own devices, to our own strength of character and our own willpower. But Paul does not stop with our responsibility. He says, "for it is God who works in you." The spiritual power that enables us to apply ourselves to the cultivation of Christian graces is of God, who works in us to will and to act.

Nineteenth-century Dutch Reformed pastor George W. Bethune put it this way:

> While, therefore, we grow in the Christian life by divine grace, it is *our duty* to grow in grace. Besides, the quality of grace is such that, though it is strength from God, we must use it. Grace gives no new faculty, but strengthens the faculties which we have. . . . Hence the fruits of the Spirit are the qualities and actions of the renewed man, not produced without him, but wrought through him. . . . Let us then be ever mindful of our entire dependence upon the Spirit of God . . . [but] let us be ever mindful of our duty "to maintain good works."[4]

PUT OFF AND PUT ON
The fourth principle of godly character is, *The development of godly character entails both putting off and putting on character traits*. Paul says, "You were taught, with regard to your former way of life, to *put off your old self*, which is being corrupted by its deceitful desires; to be made new in the attitude of your minds; and to *put on the new self*, created to be like God in true righteousness and holiness" (Ephesians 4:22-24).

In the succeeding verses (4:28–5:4) Paul makes some very specific applications of this principle. We are to put off falsehood and put on truthfulness. We are to put off stealing and put on generosity. Unwholesome talk must be put off and replaced with speech which is helpful for building others up. Bitterness, rage, anger, and slander are to be replaced with kindness, compassion, and forgiveness. Obscene or suggestive speech is to be replaced with thanksgiving. Even Paul's list of gracious qualities in Galatians 5, called the fruit of the Spirit, is set in contrast to a lengthy catalog of vices of the sinful nature which must be put off by the godly person.

It was said of the Lord Jesus that He has both loved righteousness and hated wickedness (Hebrews 1:9). And we are to follow His example, for Paul instructs us to "hate what is evil; cling to what is good" (Romans 12:9). Surely we must put to death, by the aid of the Holy Spirit, the misdeeds of the body. But we must also, again with His enablement, clothe ourselves with compassion, kindness, humility, gentleness, and patience.

Just as we need to learn Scripture's teaching for the dual principle of personal responsibility and total dependence, here also we need to seek the balance of Scripture in putting off and putting on. Some Christians have a tendency to emphasize only putting off traits of the sinful nature. They are usually very morally upright, but lacking in those gracious qualities of love, joy, and compassion. When a fellow Christian falls into sin, they do not seek to restore him gently, but rather ostracize him from their fellowship. A repentant Christian once wrote me that his church knew how to reach out to lost sinners but did not know how to restore one of its own errant members. This is the attitude we tend to develop when we put our entire emphasis in Christian character growth on putting off sinful habits.

But there is equal danger if we focus all our attention on such qualities as love and compassion while neglecting to deal with the vices of the sinful nature. Today, there is a good deal of emphasis on affirming and encouraging one another. We are to help one another "feel good about ourselves." We undoubtedly need such encouragement in the body of Christ, but we must not neglect the equally scriptural emphasis of putting to death the deeds of the sinful nature.

We are to put off the traits of the old self and put on the traits of the new. If we desire to be godly we must not neglect either of these biblical emphases.

## BALANCED GROWTH

The fifth principle of godly character is, *We are to pursue growth in all of the graces that are considered the fruit of the Spirit*. This would include traits such as compassion, forbearance, and humility that are not included in the nine-trait list of Galatians 5 but are obviously a result of His ministry in our lives. Godly character is balanced. It displays with equal emphasis the entire spectrum of graces that are set forth in the Scriptures as characteristic of the godly person.

We tend to emphasize in our lives those traits that seem most natural to our particular temperaments. But the fruit of the Spirit is not a matter of temperament; it is the result of the individual Christian seeking to grow, under the direction and aid of the Spirit, in every area of Christian character.

Author Tim LaHaye tells us that it was Hippocrates, the Greek physician and philosopher, who gave us the fourfold classification of temperaments so widely used today. He identified the jovial sanguine, the strong-willed choleric, the sensitive melancholic, and the dependable phlegmatic.

The sanguine person easily responds to the admonition to rejoice in the Lord or to be compassionate and tenderhearted. At the same time, he finds it difficult to exercise self-control or to be faithful with responsibilities. He must pray more earnestly and strive more diligently for these latter graces. Above all, he must be convinced of the necessity in his life of those graces that are most difficult to display. He must not excuse himself for his lack of faithfulness on the basis of, "That's just the way I am."

Similarly, the even-tempered, often unemotional phlegmatic person easily responds to the need for faithfulness but may have difficulty with the fruit of joy. I personally identify with this type of person. Faithfulness is very high in my value system; when given a responsibility, I am usually conscientious about fulfilling it. But I have to give special attention to joy. A number of years ago, God brought to my attention that "the kingdom of God is not a matter of eating and drinking, but of righteousness, peace and joy in the Holy Spirit" (Romans 14:17). I realized that joy in the Lord was just as important as any other trait of godly character.

Furthermore, even those traits to which we most naturally respond need to be developed under the ministry of the Spirit. God has a way of putting us in situations that exercise our character in those areas in which we feel we are strong, in order that the fruit might be of the Spirit, not of ourselves. For example, the naturally faithful person might stop short of dependability if it becomes inconvenient. But the godly person keeps his word even when it is costly.

The choleric individual can't understand why anyone else has difficulty with self-control. He is usually so self-disciplined that this trait of godly character seems to come naturally to him. But as a godly person seeking to display all the fruit of the Spirit, he may weep over his lack of patience and gentleness in his relationships with others.

The melancholic person is usually sensitive to the needs of others and is often self-sacrificing in his relationships. At the same time, he has a tendency to be critical and unforgiving, so he needs to especially look to the Holy Spirit for his ministry in those areas of need.

I do not intend this section to be an amateur psychological analysis of various temperament types. Rather, I am seeking to demonstrate the varying needs each of us will have in displaying the fruit of the Spirit in our lives. The principle to learn and apply is, *We are responsible to exhibit all of the traits of godly character in a balanced fashion*. Some traits are more difficult to grow in than others. These will require extra prayer and attention on our part, but that is simply the price we must pay to grow in Godlikeness.

GROWTH IS PROGRESSIVE

The sixth principle of godly character is, *Growth in all areas is progressive and never finished*. Even the apostle Paul recognized this truth in his own life. In the context of his great longing to know Christ and to be like Him, he said, "Not that I have already obtained all this, or have already been made perfect, but I press on . . ." (Philippians 3:12). In prison, near the end of his apostolic career, he was still pressing on, exerting every effort to continue growing in his knowledge and likeness of Christ.

Even in those areas in which we have grown, there is always need for further growth. Paul wrote in his first letter to the Thessalonian Christians that they had been taught by God to love one another and, in fact, they did love all the brothers throughout Macedonia. That is quite a commendation! But Paul was not satisfied. He went on to say, "Yet we urge you, brothers, to do so more and more" (4:9-10). Growth in Christian character is never finished until we go to be with Christ and are transformed completely into His likeness.

Growth in godly character is not only progressive and always unfinished, it is absolutely necessary for spiritual survival. If we are not growing in godly character, we are regressing; in the spiritual life we never stand still. The word *train* in Paul's admonition to Timothy, "Train yourself to be godly," occurs only four times in the New Testament: 1 Timothy 4:7, Hebrews 5:14 and 12:11, and 2 Peter 2:14. In three of those instances, the result of such training is positive and God-honoring.

But consider the fourth passage, 2 Peter 2:14. The context is Peter's sharp denunciation of and warning against false teachers. He refers to them as "experts in greed." The word *expert* is the same word translated in the other three passages as "train." In fact, the *New American Standard Bible* renders it, "having a heart trained in greed."

The implication of Peter's use of the word *train* is very sobering. It is possible to train ourselves in the wrong direction! That is what these false teachers had done. They had *practiced* greed so well that they had become experts in it—they had trained their hearts in greed!

So there is a sense in which we are growing in our character every day. The question is, In which direction are we growing? Are we growing toward godly character or ungodly character? Are we growing in love or selfishness; in harshness or patience; in greed or generosity; in honesty or dishonesty; in purity or impurity? Every day we are training ourselves in one direction or the other by the thoughts we think, the words we say, the actions we take, the deeds we do.

This sense of progression in character, in either one direction or the other, is also taught in Romans 6:19. Paul refers to the Roman Christians' former bondage to sin and to *ever-increasing wickedness*. They were well on their way to becoming experts in wickedness. But now, says Paul, having been freed from the slavery of sin, they are to offer their bodies in slavery to righteousness *leading to holiness*. Righteousness refers here to obedience to God, specific "right actions." Holiness refers to the state or character resulting from those actions; right actions, or obedience, leads to holiness. Of course, both the actions and the character are the result of the working of the Holy Spirit, but He works as we work, and we are able to work because He is at work in us.

The relationship between conduct and character is an intimate one. In the form of repeated actions over time, conduct produces character. That is the teaching of 2 Peter 2:14 and Romans 6:19. But it is also true that character determines actions. What we do, we become. What we are, we do. This truth can be illustrated by a circle formed by two curved arrows feeding into each other.

conduct
what we do
what we are
character

Conduct is always feeding character, but character is also always feeding conduct. Paul's experience while shipwrecked on the Island of Malta furnishes a good example of this relationship. The islanders built the refugees a fire because of the rain and cold. Luke relates in Acts 28 that Paul gathered a pile of brushwood, and, as he put it on the fire, a snake came out of the brushwood and fastened itself on Paul's hand. Under the adverse circumstances of shipwreck, why would Paul have gone about gathering fuel for a fire built and tended by someone else? Why didn't he just stand by the fire and warm himself? He didn't because it was his character to serve (see Acts 20:33-35 and 1 Thessalonians 2:7-9). He had learned well the lesson Jesus taught us when He washed His disciples' feet. Because it was Paul's character to serve, he gathered the brushwood instinctively. He probably did not even think about it. He just did what his servant character dictated at the moment.

Since conduct determines character, and character determines conduct, it is vitally important—extremely necessary—that we practice godliness every day. That is why Peter says, "Make every effort to add to your faith . . . godliness" (2 Peter 1:5-6). There can be no letup in our pursuit of godly character. Every day that we are not practicing godliness we are being conformed to the world of ungodliness around us. Granted, our practice of godliness is imperfect and falls far short of the biblical standard. Let us, nevertheless, press on to know Christ and to be like Him.

FORM REASONABLE EXPECTATIONS
There is a very important truth you should know and keep in mind as you pursue godliness. Otherwise, as you get into the following chapters on godly character, you may feel overwhelmed. As you study the twelve different traits of godly character, each one with several different potential applications, you could easily end up with a list of twenty or so areas of need in which you should grow in Christian character.

Don't fall into such a trap. It will cause you to diffuse your spiritual energies over much too broad an area. Your efforts would be general, scattered, and wasteful, and you would probably not make progress in any area of need. Then the devil would use that to discourage you.

The apostle Paul twice describes Christians as people who are *led* by the Holy Spirit (Romans 8:14 and Galatians 5:18). Both of these passages refer to His leading, not in some decision we must make, but in the conduct and character issues of our lives. If we are led by the Spirit, we will put to death the misdeeds of the body, and we will not gratify the desires of the sinful nature.

The Holy Spirit leads us *objectively* through the general teaching of His word. There is where we learn His will for all Christians. But the Holy Spirit also leads us *subjectively* as He impresses certain Scriptures on our minds, applying them to specific situations in our lives. This is His way of showing us what He wants us to give attention to at a particular time; this is the way He leads us to establish a priority of applications. And this is the important truth we must grasp hold of in our quest for godliness.

As you read the following chapters on godly character, take note of the general principles set forth. Seek to memorize at least one passage of Scripture on each character trait to store up the essence of the biblical teaching on that trait. These Scripture passages will then be available in your mind for the Holy Spirit's use in particular applications.

In addition to the general principles, ask the Holy Spirit to impress upon your mind the two or three traits of godly character He wants you to work on and pray about now. Concentrate on these. Later on, the Spirit will lead you to work on others. Remember, He is in charge of our growth in godly character; He is our teacher and coach. And He will never lead us in a way that will overwhelm or confuse us.

---

NOTES
1. I believe it is the fruit of godly character and conduct that is primarily in view in this passage (John 15:1-6). When Jesus and Paul speak of the fruit of evangelism, they speak of harvesting or gathering, as opposed to producing, fruit (John 4:36, Romans 1:13). Certainly Jesus' use of the term *fruit* in Matthew 7:15-23 relates primarily to character and conduct.
2. Frederic Louis Godet, *Commentary on John's Gospel* (Grand Rapids, Mich.: Kregel Publications, 1978), page 855.
3. Jac J. Müller, "The Epistles of Paul to the Philippians and to Philemon," *The New International Commentary on the New Testament* (Grand Rapids, Mich.: Eerdmans, 1978), page 91.
4. George W. Bethune, *The Fruit of the Spirit* (1839; rpt. Swengel, Penn.: Reiner Publications), pages 32-34.

# 6

# Humility

❦

*For everyone who exalts himself will be humbled,*
*and he who humbles himself will be exalted.*

Luke 18:14

❦

Devotion to God is the first aspect of godliness; Godlike character is the second. There may be some question about whether or not humility is a Godlike quality, since humility is a trait befitting the creature, not the Creator. But there is no question that God commends humility and delights in it in His people.

Two passages from the book of Isaiah show us very clearly the esteem with which God views the humble person. We read in Isaiah 57:15,

> For this is what the high and lofty One says—
>     he who lives forever, whose name is holy:
> "I live in a high and holy place,
>     but also with him who is contrite and lowly in spirit,
> to revive the spirit of the lowly
>     and to revive the heart of the contrite."

And then we read in Isaiah 66:1-2,

> This is what the Lord says:
> "Heaven is my throne
>     and the earth is my footstool.
> Where is the house you will build for me?
>     Where will my resting place be?
> Has not my hand made all these things,
>     and so they came into being?"
>         declares the Lord.
> "This is the one I esteem:
>     he who is humble and contrite in spirit,
>     and trembles at my word."

Not only does God commend humility in His people; our Lord displayed it in His humanity. "And being found in appearance as a man, he humbled himself and became obedient to death—even death on a cross!" (Philippians 2:8). Jesus Christ exemplified humility in its utmost through His death for us. But He also exemplified humility throughout His life. He was born in the very humblest of circumstances; He was obedient to His earthly parents; He called people to Himself as one who was "gentle and humble in heart"; He said, "I am among you as one who serves"; He washed the disciples' feet on the very night of His betrayal; and He taught, "He who humbles himself will be exalted." If we question whether humility is technically a *Godlike* trait (as we view God in His majesty), we certainly cannot question that it is a *Christlike* trait. And we are to be imitators of Him as He lived out His human life on earth.

The promises of God toward the truly humble are almost breathtaking. The infinitely high and lofty One who lives forever promises to dwell with them, to esteem them, to give them grace, to lift them up, and to exalt them (see

Isaiah 57:15 and 66:2, James 4:6, 1 Peter 5:6, and Luke 18:14). Humility opens the way to all other godly character traits. It is the soil in which the other traits of the fruit of the Spirit grow.

Humility manifests itself in our relationships—to God, to ourselves, to others. We are to be humble toward God and His word, humble in regard to trials and blessings that come our way or abilities and achievements with which we are blessed, and humble toward other people. Humility is the proper attitude with which to approach all these relationships and circumstances. Like love, it defies adequate definition; it can only be described and understood as it is applied to everyday living.

## HUMILITY BEFORE GOD

Humility toward God is akin to the fear of God: it begins with a high view of God's person. As we see God in His majesty, awesomeness, and holiness, we are humbled before Him. In every occasion in the Scriptures in which man was privileged to view God in His glory, he was brought low or humbled in the presence of God. Moses bowed to the ground and worshiped; Isaiah cried, "Woe is me!"; Ezekiel fell face down; John fell at His feet as though dead. Even the four living creatures and the twenty-four elders in heaven of Revelation fell down before the throne of the glorified Lamb.

Humility in every area of life, in every relationship with other people, begins with a right concept of God as the One who is infinite and eternal in His majesty and holiness. We are to humble ourselves under God's mighty hand, approaching every relationship and every circumstance in reference to Him. When relationships with people are good and circumstances are favorable, we are to humbly receive these blessings from His gracious hand. When people are mistreating us and circumstances are difficult, we are to humbly accept them as from an infinitely wise and loving heavenly Father.

This humility before God is basic to all our relationships in life. We cannot begin to experience humility in any other relationship until we experience a deep and profound humility in our attitude toward God. When we are conscious of our (sinful) creature relationship to an infinitely majestic and holy God, we will not wish to selfishly compare ourselves with others. And to the extent that our awareness of our lowly place before God is an abiding one, we will avoid the temptations of pride and competition.

## TREMBLING AT HIS WORD

The person who is truly humble before God is also humble before God's word. God says He esteems the person who is humble and contrite in spirit, and who trembles at His word. When King Josiah heard the words of the Book of the Law, he tore his robes, saying, "Great is the Lord's anger that burns against us because our fathers have not obeyed the words of this book . . ." (2 Kings 22:13). Josiah realized that the word of God was the expression of the will of God, that it was to be obeyed, and that failure to obey would incur the judgment of God. Because Josiah trembled at the word of God, his heart was responsive, he humbled himself, he acknowledged the sin of his people, and God heard him. He did not dispute the word of God; he simply obeyed it.

We also must develop this kind of humility toward the Bible. As we search the Scriptures, we must allow them to search us, to sit in judgment upon our character and conduct. We must not treat the Scriptures only as a source of knowledge about God, but also as the expression of His will for our daily lives. As someone has said, "The Bible was given not just to increase our knowledge, but to guide our conduct." Far too often it seems we approach the Bible just to increase our knowledge of the facts of the Bible. We do need to increase our spiritual knowledge, but it should be for the purpose of obeying God's will. Paul prayed that God would fill the Colossian Christians with the knowledge of His will in order that they might live a life worthy of the Lord and please Him in every way. He wanted them to know God's will so that they would obey God's will and thus please God.

Not only must we develop a spirit of humility toward the Bible in regard to our *conduct*, we must also develop such a spirit in regard to our *doctrines*. We evangelicals are not noted for our humility about our doctrines—our beliefs about what the Bible teaches in various areas of theology. Whatever position we take in a specific area of theology, we tend to feel our position is airtight, and that anyone holding a different view is altogether wrong. We tend to be quite impatient with anyone who differs from us. Ironically, the more our views come from the teachings of someone else instead of from the Bible itself, the more rigidly we tend to hold those views.

It is one thing to be persuaded that what we believe is correct as we understand the Scriptures; it is quite another to believe that our views are *always* correct. Twice in my life I have had to make significant changes in my doctrines as a result of additional understanding of the Scriptures. This is not to suggest that we are to be wishy-washy in our beliefs so that we are "blown here and there by every wind of teaching," but that we are to hold our beliefs in a spirit of true humility. We must remind ourselves that God has not seen fit to make our minds, or even a particular church, the depository of the sum total of His teaching.

At one time in His ministry Jesus prayed, "I praise you, Father, Lord of heaven and earth, because you have hidden these things from the wise and learned, and revealed them to little children. Yes, Father, for this was your good pleasure" (Luke 10:21). Commenting on this passage, Norvel Geldenhuys has aptly remarked,

> The contrast pointed by the Savior is not that between "educated" and "non-educated" but between those who imagine themselves to be wise and sensible—and those who live under the profound impression that by their own insight and their own reasonings they are utterly powerless to understand the truths of God and to accept them.[1]

May God help us to be humble enough toward the Scriptures to be found in that group that Jesus called, "little children."

### HERE BY THE GRACE OF GOD

When a believer is truly humble before God and His word, he will also be humble about his own gifts, abilities, and attainments. He will realize and gratefully acknowledge that all that he is and all that he has comes from the hand of God.

This aspect of humility actually begins with our understanding of personal salvation. All evangelicals agree that we are saved solely by the grace of God, apart from any works of our own. But do we believe, even in some undefined way, that we did contribute something to our salvation, something that implies that we were a little bit wiser, or a little smarter, or a little more responsive to God than others?

Some time ago I read a statement in which the writer said he realized that the only difference between himself and another group of people was that perhaps he had a little more reliance upon the grace of God. I am sure the writer meant this as an expression of humility, but it left me uncomfortable. Somehow I cannot imagine the apostle Paul finding any distinguishing difference in himself, even a little more reliance upon the grace of God. Instead I find him saying, "Christ Jesus came into the world to save sinners — of whom I am the worst" (1 Timothy 1:15). Paul never compared himself favorably with the unbelievers around him. He was too overwhelmed with the fact that the grace of God was sufficient to reach even him.

Our attitude of humility in regard to our salvation should carry over to a recognition that any of our abilities and achievements are equally a result of God's grace. In his first epistle to the Corinthian Christians, Paul minces no words on this subject: "For who makes you different from anyone else? What do you have that you did not receive? And if you did receive it, why do you boast as though you did not?" (4:7). Every ability and every advantage we have comes from God and has been given to us as a stewardship to be used in serving Him. For some time after I went into "full-time" Christian work and was living on a mere subsistence income, I often struggled with thoughts of how much money I could have been making if I had followed the profession I was trained for in college. Finally I began to realize that it was God who had given me the advantage of a good education, and that I was not doing Him a favor by being in His service full-time. All that I had came from Him and was to be used for His glory.

Paul refused to take the credit for his abilities or even his diligent labors. Again in his first letter to the Corinthians he declares, "But by the grace of God I am what I am, and his grace to me was not without effect. No, I worked harder than all of them — yet not I, but the grace of God that was with me" (15:10). This passage used to puzzle me. It seemed as if Paul was trying to be both humble and proud. How could anyone dare to state publicly that he had worked harder than all the other apostles? But then I realized that Paul was ascribing even his hard work to the grace of God. Sometimes we hear some tired Christian describing how hard he has worked in the service of God, teaching Sunday school for ten years straight, or sponsoring a difficult junior high youth group, or being one of the faithful few at Wednesday night prayer meeting. Perhaps we ourselves have been one of those tired Christians. If so, let's remember to credit our hard work and faithful labors strictly to the grace of God.

We should ascribe any attainments, whether secular or spiritual, to the grace of God. When Moses was giving final instructions to the children of Israel prior to entering the promised land, he specifically warned them against the pride that comes with taking credit for successes: "You may say to yourself, 'My power and the strength of my hands have produced this wealth for me.' But remember the Lord your God, for it is he who gives you the ability to produce wealth, and so confirms his covenant, which he swore to your forefathers, as it is today" (Deuteronomy 8:17-18). Paul was just as emphatic about spiritual success when he wrote, "So neither he who plants nor he who waters is anything, but only God, who makes things grow" (1 Corinthians 3:7). The prophet Isaiah succinctly expressed the attitude we are to have toward accomplishments when he said, "Lord . . . all that we have accomplished you have done for us" (26:12).

While writing this chapter I had occasion to express appreciation to a fellow church member for a job well done. I liked his simple, humble response: "It was the Lord who did it." Humility with regard to ourselves, then, consists in ascribing all that we are, all that we have, and all that we have accomplished to the God who gives us grace.

## SUBMISSION, SERVICE, AND HONOR

A believer who is humble before God will also be humble toward other people. One way this humility expresses itself is in mutual submission to one another. Paul instructs us, "Submit to one another out of reverence for Christ" (Ephesians 5:21). Peter likewise says, "Clothe yourselves with humility toward one another" (1 Peter 5:5), and James tells us that submissiveness is characteristic of the wisdom that comes from heaven (James 3:17). What does it mean to submit to one another? Does it mean always giving in to others' demands or opinions? Not at all. It means to submit to *instruction* as well as *correction* from other believers; to be teachable or to be humble enough to admit we have erred when another believer corrects us.

Apollos and Peter are beautiful examples of men who submitted themselves to other believers. Apollos submitted himself to others' instruction. Luke tells us that Apollos was a learned man, with a thorough knowledge of the Scriptures, who had been instructed in the way of the Lord, and who spoke with great fervor and taught about Jesus accurately. Apollos was obviously a gifted and capable man, and apparently a "full-time Christian worker," but he had one defect. His knowledge about Christ was accurate but incomplete; he knew only the baptism of John. When Priscilla and Aquila, a godly "lay" couple in the church at Ephesus, heard Apollos, they invited him to their home and explained the way of God more adequately (Acts 18:24-26). It is evident that Apollos received their instruction because shortly thereafter, when Apollos wanted to go on to minister to the churches in Achaia, the church at Ephesus not only encouraged him but also wrote a letter to the Achaian Christians telling them to welcome him.

What a commentary on the humility of Apollos! What a sermon by example on what it means to submit to one another! Apollos was a capable, gifted minister; yet he was not above receiving instruction from Priscilla and Aquila. (It is not too hard to imagine in passing with what gentleness and consideration Priscilla and Aquila must have instructed Apollos. That is the other side of submission to one another—but more about that when we get to the trait of gentleness in chapter 15.)

Peter provides us with an example of submitting to the correction of another believer. Paul records that when Peter came to Antioch, he found it necessary to rebuke Peter because of his hypocrisy in regard to the Gentile Christians. Not only was Paul's rebuke severe; it was done openly before the other believers. The Scriptures do not tell us what Peter's reaction was, but apparently Peter did not harbor any resentment toward Paul. In one of his own letters he later refers to Paul as "our dear brother" and speaks of Paul's letters as Scripture—that is, as part of the divinely inspired writings of the word of God (2 Peter 3:15-16). Peter had evidently accepted Paul's rebuke. He had humbly submitted himself to the correction of another believer, even though that believer was "younger in the Lord" than he.

There is no question that submission to the unsolicited teaching or correction of others is difficult for our naturally proud hearts. But the context of Paul's instruction on mutual submission in Ephesians 5 indicates it is one of the evidences of being filled with the Spirit. Humility is a fruit of the Spirit, the result of His ministry in our hearts. But this ministry does not occur without deliberate, conscious effort on our part. The Spirit does not make us humble; He enables us to humble ourselves in these difficult situations.

Although submission is probably the most difficult application of humility toward others, it is by no means the only one. A very common occasion for showing humility is through *serving one another*. In this area Jesus is our greatest teacher and pacesetter. The foremost example is His washing the disciples' feet on the night of His betrayal, but

Jesus' whole life was one of serving others. He said He did not come to be served but to serve; He went around doing good for others. Jesus even seems to indicate that He will still be serving us in eternity (Luke 12:37), as incredible as that may seem.[2]

In addition to the example He set for us, Jesus also taught us by precept the importance of serving one another. He indicated that true greatness in the kingdom of God does not consist in position but in serving one another, and He promised blessing to those who followed His example in serving others.

This demonstration of humility in serving others also requires the grace of God. Peter tells us that those who serve "should do it with the strength God provides, so that in all things God may be praised through Jesus Christ" (1 Peter 4:11). We all know people, even unbelievers, who seem to be natural servants. They are always serving others one way or another. But God does not get the glory; they do. It is *their* reputation that is enhanced. But when we, natural servants or not, serve in dependence upon the grace of God with the strength He supplies, God is glorified.

Dependence upon the grace of God not only results in God being glorified; it also makes it possible for those of us who are not natural servants to practice this aspect of humility. His grace is sufficient for all of our needs, whatever they may be. We can, by His enablement, *learn* to serve one another.

A third way we demonstrate humility is by *honoring* one another. Paul says in Romans 12:10, "Honor one another above yourselves," and in Philippians 2:3, "consider others better than yourselves." We are to place the other person above ourselves in matters of position, concerns, or needs.

Jesus rebuked the Pharisees for seeking the places of

honor at a feast, telling them to instead seek out the lowest place. We may condemn the childish self-seeking of the Pharisees, but how about our own attitude? Do we maneuver for first place in line, or for the best seats at public meetings? Do we frequently assert ourselves at the expense of others, or do we consider their interests as well as our own?

If we are to experience the blessings promised to the humble we must work out this humility in our daily relationships with others. We must learn to submit to one another, to serve one another, and to honor or prefer one another above ourselves. Remember: the Spirit does not make us humble, but He enables us to humble ourselves. We must *learn* humility, just as Paul learned contentment, but in our efforts we are assured of the same enabling power he experienced (see Philippians 4:11-13).

PRACTICING HUMILITY

Here are some practical suggestions for learning humility. Begin by renewing your mind. The best way to do this is to memorize one or more passages of Scripture, choosing those you believe address most directly your areas of greatest need.

As we memorize and then meditate on Scriptures in this way, the Holy Spirit transforms us inwardly, changing our values; for example, we may begin to place greater importance on putting others ahead of ourselves. The Holy Spirit will also use these Scriptures we have memorized to convict us in specific situations when we fail to live up to our new values.

Confess any prideful ways, as the Holy Spirit convicts you, and pray for sensitivity to see yourself as God does. Also pray for the Holy Spirit to change you inwardly.

Finally, take whatever specific steps are necessary in order to obey God's direction to humble yourself. We are to humble ourselves before God. The word *humble*, when used in this way, is an action verb. We are to *do* something. It may be a specific act of putting another first, such as in a supermarket check-out line or in an opportunity for a choice job position. It might even be as drastic as telling our friends we have taken the credit for success that rightfully belongs to God. Whatever the area of humility we need to work on, it is important that we do so in dependence upon Him who is at work in us.

NOTES
1. Norvel Geldenhuys, "Commentary on the Gospel of Luke," *The New International Commentary on the New Testament* (Grand Rapids, Mich.: Eerdmans, 1977), pages 306-307.
2. William Hendriksen comments on this passage, "What is promised here, therefore, is that our Lord, at his second coming will, in a manner consonant with his glory and majesty, 'wait on' his faithful servants!" in his "The Gospel of Luke," *New Testament Commentary* (Grand Rapids, Mich.: Baker Book House, 1978), page 677.

# 7
# Contentment

*But godliness with contentment is great gain.*
1 Timothy 6:6

Contentment is one of the most distinguishing traits of the godly person, because a godly person has his heart focused on God rather than on possessions or position or power. As William Hendriksen has observed so well, "The truly godly person is not interested in becoming rich. He possesses inner resources which furnish riches far beyond that which earth can offer."[1]

The words that are rendered as "content" or "contentment" in our English Bibles actually mean "sufficiency."[2] The same word translated "contentment" in 1 Timothy 6:6 is rendered "all that you need" or "all sufficiency" in 2 Corinthians 9:8. When God said to Paul, "My grace is sufficient for you" (2 Corinthians 12:9), He used the same word translated elsewhere as "be content" (see Luke 3:14, 1 Timothy 6:8, Hebrews 13:5).

The contented person experiences the sufficiency of

God's *provision* for his needs and the sufficiency of God's *grace* for his circumstances. He believes God will indeed meet all his material needs and that He will work in all his circumstances for his good. That is why Paul could say, "Godliness with contentment is great gain." The godly person has found what the greedy or envious or discontented person always searches for but never finds. He has found satisfaction and rest in his soul.

The idea of contentment in the Bible is most often associated with possessions or money, but there are other areas of life in which we need to be content. After possessions, probably the most common need is to learn contentment with our place in society or in the body of Christ. Still a third area that demands our practice of contentment is the providence of God in such varied circumstances as physical limitations and afflictions, privations, unpleasant neighbors or living situations, trials, and even persecutions. These circumstances often cause the natural man to murmur and complain and to question the goodness of God in his life.

The very first temptation in the history of mankind was the temptation to be discontent. God had provided for Adam and Eve far beyond all they needed. Genesis states, "God made all kinds of trees grow out of the ground—trees that were pleasing to the eye and good for food." God withheld only one tree from Adam and Eve as a test of their obedience to Him. And Satan used that one tree to tempt Eve by sowing seeds of discontent in her heart. He questioned the goodness of God to Eve, and that is exactly what discontent is—*a questioning of the goodness of God*.

Satan tried the same strategy with Jesus in the wilderness. He sought to make Jesus discontent over His lack of food and covetous for position and power over the kingdoms of the world. If Isaiah 14:13-15 is a veiled reference to Satan, as many scholars believe, then we can conclude that

Satan's own downfall was occasioned by his discontent — his unwillingness to accept his God-ordained position in the hierarchy of angelic beings.

We should note these incidents carefully. Discontent is one of the most satanic of all sins, and to indulge in it is to rebel against God just as Satan did.

## CONTENTMENT WITH POSSESSIONS

To be content with one's possessions is one of the most strongly worded exhortations in Scripture. God deemed it important enough to include a prohibition against covetousness together with prohibitions against the more abhorrent sins of murder, stealing, and adultery (Exodus 20:13-17). In His Sermon on the Mount, Jesus dwelt more extensively on the principle, "You cannot serve God and money," than on any other subject. While later addressing a dispute over an inheritance He said, "Watch out! Be on your guard against all kinds of greed; a man's life does not consist in the abundance of his possessions" (Luke 12:15). His double warning to us — "Watch out! Be on your guard" — alerts us to the extreme danger of being discontent with our possessions.

Paul has a similarly strong warning for us in his first letter to Timothy as he urges us to be content with food and clothing, because the love of money is the root of all kinds of evil. He warns Timothy to "flee from" this love of money and discontentment with possessions (6:11). The writer of Hebrews frames his admonition in the form of encouragement as he urges us to keep our lives free from the love of money and be content with what we have, because God Himself has promised never to leave or forsake us (13:5). So Scripture both warns us of the dangers of discontent and encourages us to pursue contentment on the basis of God's promise to provide for us.

In his letter to the Romans, Paul tells us that everything written in the past was written to teach us (15:4). The historical events recorded in the Old Testament, then, are not merely interesting anecdotes. They were written that we might learn from them. With this truth in mind, we need to give careful heed to the result of covetousness in the lives of Achan and Gehazi, as recorded in Joshua 7 and in 2 Kings 5. Achan's covetousness at the battle of Jericho resulted in the defeat of the army of Israel at Ai and his own untimely death by stoning. The covetousness of Elisha's servant Gehazi resulted in the affliction of the dread disease of leprosy on Gehazi and his descendants forever. In the New Testament, covetousness was the root of sin that brought down God's judgment upon Ananias and Sapphira (Acts 5:1-11).

It may be true that God's judgment upon covetousness and discontentment is not as severe or obvious in our day as it was in the days of Achan, Gehazi, and Ananias and Sapphira. Yet God's *attitude* toward discontentment has not changed, and the spiritual danger of loving the things of this world is far more serious than the judgment of a dreaded disease or an untimely death. John says very plainly that if anyone loves the world, the love of the Father is not in him. In other words, he is not a Christian! John makes it clear that a craving for possessions is being in love with the world.

In view of such strong biblical warnings against covetousness and the earnest exhortations of the New Testament writers to be content with what we have, we must take seriously the need to earnestly pursue contentment as a dominant character trait in our lives. It is not a spiritual luxury. Contentment with what we have is absolutely vital to our spiritual health.

How then can we pursue an attitude of being content with what we have? What are some practical steps we can take? As with every other character trait, begin renewing your mind by memorizing and meditating on one or two passages of Scripture you find especially helpful in this area. You may want to use Luke 12:15, 1 Timothy 6:6-8, or Hebrews 13:5, or perhaps some other passages from your own personal study. As you meditate on these verses, ask God to bring to your mind any specific areas in your life in which you are discontent with what you have. Decide on what definite steps you can and should take to deal with that area, and begin to take those steps.

Keep in mind, however, that only the Holy Spirit can work a lasting and fundamental attitude change deep in your heart, so make contentment a matter of regular, earnest prayer. I often pray as David did in Psalm 119:36-37, "Turn my heart toward your statutes and *not toward selfish gain. Turn my eyes away from worthless things*; renew my life according to your word."

Prayer and meditation on Scripture passages are essential to developing contentment about possessions. I've also found the following scriptural principles especially helpful in this area.

*Our focus should be on the true values of life.* In Mark 8, Jesus teaches that eternal life is more valuable than all the world. David declares in Psalm 19 that the word of God is more precious than gold. Solomon tells us that wisdom (an understanding and application of the moral principles of God) is more profitable than silver or gold or precious jewels (Proverbs 3:13-15). These statements all reflect God's value judgments about what is truly important in life. We have to decide whether we will accept them and make them our own values. To the extent we do, we are well on our way to experiencing contentment about possessions.

*Service to God through service to mankind is the only motivation acceptable to God for diligence and hard work in our vocational calling.* We must avoid selfish ambition (the desire for more money or prestige), and instead make it our

ambition to please God in all of our work. We should, therefore, look at our job or our business not in terms of larger
salaries, greater commissions, or increased sales, but in terms
of how we may best please God. Vocational success should not
be measured in terms of one's bank account or material possessions but in terms of service to others that is acceptable to
God. Such an attitude, rather than fostering indifference to
work, should promote greater diligence. Paul told the
Colossians that slaves were more accountable to God for their
work than they were to their earthly masters. This principle
obviously applies to employment relationships of today.

*All that we have comes from God as a result of His
grace.* As David so wisely acknowledged, "Wealth and honor
come from you . . . in your hands are strength and power to
exalt and give strength to all" (1 Chronicles 29:12). As in
developing humility, we can learn contentment by remembering that it is God who gives anyone the ability to produce
wealth (Deuteronomy 8:18). Humility toward God and contentment toward possessions, in fact, are handmaidens of
each other. If I accept all I have now as a gift of God's grace
and am thankful for it, I will not be secretly feeling that I
deserve more and longing for greater possessions.

*God in His sovereign good pleasure has seen fit to give
some people more wealth and possessions than others;*
consequently we are not to envy them. In an effort to teach
that all reward is of grace, Jesus told the parable of the
workers in the vineyard. He described the situation of
workers who labored for only the last hour of the day
receiving the same pay as those who labored all day. Those
who had worked all day became envious of the generous
treatment accorded the workers who came later, and they
began to grumble. But the master of the vineyard silenced
them with the statement, "Don't I have a right to do what I
want with my own money? Or are you envious because I

am generous?" With this parable Jesus teaches us that God, who owns everything, has a right to dispense the material possessions of this world as He desires, and we are not to question Him or envy the recipients of His favors.

*For those whom God has blessed with wealth or an abundance of possessions, with privilege comes responsibility.* "From everyone who has been given much, much will be demanded; and from the one who has been entrusted with much, much more will be asked" (Luke 12:48). Paul told Timothy to "Command those who are rich . . . to do good, to be rich in good deeds, and to be generous and willing to share" (1 Timothy 6:17-18).

This principle applies to most people who will read this book, because we are in fact wealthy in terms of the vast majority of the people of the world.

We'll find that contentment comes when we share what we have with others. It is in this context of sharing with those in need that Paul declared in 2 Corinthians 9 that God is able to make all grace abound to us, so that we will feel sufficient—or content—in every respect.

Some may feel that we should encourage one another toward a "simplified lifestyle," or one as unencumbered by material possessions as possible. This subject can easily degenerate into legalism, however, in which we begin judging one another by perhaps arbitrary standards of what is and is not acceptable in the way of material goods and possessions. Instead, we should concentrate on being content in all our circumstances, and on living lives that are pleasing to God. The result of this kind of focus will be that our lifestyles will be the kind that God wants us to live.

## CONTENTMENT WITH POSITION
Having to some degree won the battle of contentment regarding possessions, many Christians all too often fail in

the battle of contentment regarding position in the body of Christ. Like Diotrephes of old we love to be first (3 John 9). And if we are not first, or at least prominent, either we envy those in positions of prominence, or else we adopt the attitude, "I'm just a nobody. God can't use me." It was to guard against this type of thinking that led Paul to write to the Roman Christians, "Do not think of yourself more highly than you ought, but rather think of yourself with sober judgment, in accordance with the measure of faith that God has given you" (12:3).

Paul recognized, and wanted the Christians at Rome to recognize, that God has placed each of us in the body of Christ as it pleased Him. Our duty is not to decide what we want to be or to do, but to discover on the basis of our capabilities and gifts what God wants us to do and to be. Contentment lies not in being first, but in being faithful to fulfill the function God has called us to in the body of Christ.

The greatest single help to me in learning to be content about position is to come to terms with the fact that all positions in the church are given by the sovereign grace of God. Paul said, "We have different gifts, according to the grace given to us" (Romans 12:6). We have not only different gifts, but also different capacities for the use of those gifts. In the parable of the talents, one servant was given five talents, another two, and a third only one. The accountability was proportionate to the number of talents. The servant entrusted with only two talents who used them to get two more received the same commendation and reward as the servant entrusted with five talents who used them to get five more. Presumably, the servant entrusted with only one talent would have been similarly rewarded if he had been faithful to use it to get even one more, instead of burying it in the ground.

Whether we have several gifts or only one, whether our gifts put us in a position of prominence or keep us always behind the scenes, the important truth is that those gifts have been given to us by grace. We did not deserve them; we did not earn them; they were sovereignly bestowed upon us. I don't deserve to be where I am in the body of Christ, and the prominent person doesn't deserve to be where he is. We are each in our place by God's grace.

And God *is* sovereign in the bestowal of His grace. Paul again makes this very clear in the ninth chapter of Romans when he asks, "Does not the potter have the right to make out of the same lump of clay some pottery for noble purposes and some for common use?" Although Paul wasn't asking this question within the context of the bestowment of gifts, the principle still applies. God has the right to put each of us where He pleases. He not only has the right, He exercises it, as 1 Corinthians 12 shows us. "All these [gifts] are the work of one and the same Spirit, and he gives them to each one, just as he determines."

How does my acknowledgment of God's sovereign grace in placing each of us in the body of Christ help me to be content? First, I realize that I am where I am not by chance, nor by the favor or disfavor of other people, but by the decision of an all-wise and all-loving heavenly Father. And He has plans for me, plans to prosper and not to harm me, plans to give me hope and a future (Jeremiah 29:11).

Second, I realize I do not deserve to be where I am. However obscure a position it might be, I identify with Paul when he said, "Although I am less than the least of all God's people, this grace was given to me: to preach to the Gentiles the unsearchable riches of Christ" (Ephesians 3:8). I may not be a missionary as Paul was, but whatever my position in the body, it was given to me by God's grace.

Third, I realize that each part of the body is indispensable. Paul says the body grows "as each part does its work" (Ephesians 4:16). I am important to God and I am important to the body. This is true of every single Christian in the world!

As I realize and accept these truths I find not only contentment, but excitement. Paul tells us in Ephesians 2:10 that God has prepared in advance good works for each of us to do. As we accept our place in the body of Christ and seek to do these good works, we do find the fulfillment and contentment of a life lived in accordance with the purpose of God.

Along with accepting our position in the body of Christ, we also need to learn to be content with our position in society—our vocational calling. Vocational calling usually determines status as well as wealth. And because of the world's preoccupation with status, we often face the temptation to be discontent with our position in society. Just as we are tempted to covet possessions, so we are tempted to covet position.

Here again we must go back to the sovereignty of God in all of life. God ultimately rules in the natural realm, just as He does in the spiritual, even though this aspect of His sovereignty may not always be apparent to us.

It is God who has created some to be farmers, some physicians, some building tradesmen, some salesmen, some bus drivers, and some airline pilots. If God did not rule in this manner, even in the lives of unbelievers, the world would be a chaotic place in which to live. We would have an oversupply of workers in some vocations and a critical shortage in others. The vocational imbalances that God does allow to occur arise out of man's greed in constantly pursuing higher paying jobs and professions.

The principles of contentment with our position in the body of Christ will apply with equal force to our vocational position if we realize that our vocational calling is just as much a trust from God as is our spiritual responsibility.

In an excellent article on the Puritan work ethic, Leland Ryken said,

> The Puritans declared the sanctity of all honorable work. In so doing, they rejected a centuries-old division of callings into 'sacred' and 'secular'. . . . This Puritan rejection of the dichotomy between sacred and secular work has far-reaching implications. It judges every honorable job to be of intrinsic value, and integrates every vocation with a Christian's spiritual life. It makes every job consequential by regarding it as the arena for glorifying and obeying God and for expressing love (through service) to a neighbor.[3]

Not only are some jobs more prestigious than others; some are more challenging and exciting than others. What are we to do if God places us in a vocational responsibility that seems dull and unchallenging? We go right back to the principles of contentment in the body of Christ: I am where I am by God's sovereign but loving appointment; I do not deserve to be even here; and my job, however dull, is necessary to the ongoing of society. If I will look to Him, God will give me the grace (in the sense of divine enablement) to be faithful and content in a dull and unchallenging situation.

Does this mean that contentment is incompatible with ambition, that we should never aspire to more responsible or challenging jobs? Not at all. Paul's counsel to the Christian slaves at Corinth provides a principle for us today: "Were you a slave when you were called? Don't let it trouble you—although if you can gain your freedom, do so" (1 Corinthians 7:21). Whatever your situation is, be content—don't let it trouble you. But if you have an opportunity to improve your position, do so (unless, of course, doing so would violate the will of God in some other respect).

Every Christian should pursue excellence of workmanship and service in whatever vocational calling he finds himself. But he should do so to please Christ and to glorify Him, not for the sake of personal ambition. In many instances such faithful service *will* result in promotion, for even the unbelieving world respects and rewards excellence. But faithful service is not a guarantee to a better position. God is sovereign over our position in society, and He places us and keeps us where He wants us to be. As the Scripture says so eloquently, "No one from the east or the west or from the desert can exalt a man. But it is God who judges: He brings one down, he exalts another" (Psalm 75:6-7).

## PAUL'S SECRET OF CONTENTMENT

A Christian may be winning the battle for contentment with regard to possessions and position and still lose the struggle for contentment with the providence of God in his life. We live in a sin-cursed world, where even creation itself is subjected to frustration (Romans 8:20). Christians are not immune from the frustrating, irritating, often overwhelming circumstances of life.

But as Christians we believe that all circumstances come to us, not by chance, but through the often unfathomable will of an all-wise, all-powerful, and all-loving heavenly Father. Because of this we refer to our circumstances as being under the providence of God, the word *providence* basically meaning God's care of and control over all the universe.[4] That the Bible teaches such care and control is affirmed over and over again in the Scriptures. For example, Psalm 33:10-11 says, "The Lord foils the plans of the nations; he thwarts the purposes of the peoples. But the plans of the Lord stand firm forever, the purposes of his heart through all generations."[5]

But God's providence does not always appear favorable toward His children. We are at a loss to understand many events and circumstances that appear to cast doubt on His wisdom and love. As God Himself said through Isaiah, "For my thoughts are not your thoughts, neither are your ways my ways. . . . As the heavens are higher than the earth, so are my ways higher than your ways and my thoughts than your thoughts" (Isaiah 55:8-9).

Other circumstances, though perhaps not severe or tragic, can be perplexing and frustrating: we experience varying physical limitations, chronic illnesses, and nagging injuries. We are placed with an inconsiderate roommate or find ourselves next door to annoying neighbors. We live in a city that is too large and crowded, or in a remote community that is too dull and boring. The climate is too dry or too humid. There are a thousand and one such circumstances that can make us fretful and discontented.

To make matters worse, our unbelieving neighbors often appear to have no problems. With Asaph of old we look at them and say, "This is what the wicked are like— always carefree, they increase in wealth. Surely in vain have I kept my heart pure; in vain have I washed my hands in innocence" (Psalm 73:12-13).

With such situations as these surrounding us, how can we learn, as Paul did, "to be content whatever the circumstances" (Philippians 4:11)? "I have learned the secret of being content," Paul said, "in any and every situation." What "secret" had Paul learned?

The Bible never tells us, but perhaps 2 Corinthians 12 gives us the answer. That chapter records Paul's experience of being caught up into heaven and hearing inexpressible things that man is not permitted to tell. To keep Paul from becoming conceited over these surpassingly great revelations, there was given to him "a thorn in the flesh," a mes-

senger of Satan, to torment him. Three times Paul pleaded
with the Lord to take away the thorn, but God said to him,
"My grace is sufficient for you, for my power is made perfect
in weakness." As we noted earlier, the Greek word translated
"is sufficient" is the same word rendered elsewhere as "be
content."

This must be the secret Paul had learned: *God's grace is
sufficient*, whatever the circumstance. And because God's
grace is sufficient, we can be content. But to experience contentment we must, as Paul did, *accept* that God's grace is in
fact sufficient. By acceptance I mean not just theological
assent to a truth, but an authentic faith in His grace in the
face of trying circumstances.

Since early childhood I have suffered a vision impair-
ment that is often frustrating, and a total hearing loss in one
ear that is often embarrassing (as when people speak to me
and I don't hear them, and thus appear to be ignoring
them). But those are not my only physical problems. One
day I stood before the bedroom mirror and named seven
distinct things that were "wrong" with my body; things I had
often fretted about and murmured over. That day I said,
"Lord, I accept the fact that You made me the way I am, and
that Your grace is sufficient for all these limitations." I cannot
say I have not fretted over these problems since then, but I
can now say I know how to be content with them: by accepting that God's grace is sufficient. Although I do not always
apply this wonderful fact, it is true and it is always available.
The choice to accept it and experience contentment is mine.
And the choice is yours in your particular circumstances.

In all of the areas in which we are called upon to be content—whether possessions, position, or the providence of
God—the grace of God is the ultimate solution for our discontent. Grace, as used in the New Testament, expresses two
complementary thoughts: God's unmerited favor to us

through Christ, and God's divine assistance to us through the Holy Spirit. An understanding and appreciation of both of these meanings is necessary for us to be content. First, we must learn to live by the realization that whatever our situation might be, it is far better than we deserve. Actually, we deserve God's eternal judgment. It's been said, "Anything this side of hell is pure grace." This statement is true, and we must accept it and adjust our attitude accordingly.

Second, we must learn that however difficult and frustrating our circumstances might be, God's divine assistance through the Holy Spirit is available to help us to respond in a godly manner and to be content. When Paul said, "I can do everything through him who gives me strength," he was referring to God's divine enablement. He could have said, "I can do everything by His grace," and he would have been saying the same thing.

This is the secret of being content: to learn and accept that we live daily by God's unmerited favor given through Christ, and that we can respond to any and every situation by His divine enablement through the Holy Spirit.

---

NOTES

1. William Hendriksen, *Commentary on I & II Timothy and Titus* (London: The Banner of Truth Trust, 1959), page 198.
2. W.E. Vine, *An Expository Dictionary of New Testament Words*, pages 226 and 1105.
3. Leland Ryken, "Puritan Work Ethic: The Dignity of Life's Labors," *Christianity Today*, 19 October 1979, page 15.
4. Providence is defined theologically as "the unceasing activity of the Creator whereby, in overflowing bounty and goodwill, he upholds his creatures in ordered existence, guides and governs all events, circumstances, and free acts of angels and men, and directs everything to its appointed goal, for his own glory." *The New Bible Dictionary* (London: Inter-Varsity Fellowship, 1962; rpt. Grand Rapids, Mich.: Eerdmans, 1973), pages 1050-1051.
5. Other passages that affirm the truth of God's providence include Genesis 12:17, 20:6, and 50:20; Exodus 3:21, 8:22, and 9:29; Ezra 1:1; Proverbs 21:1; Daniel 4:34-55; Acts 16:6-7; and Romans 8:28.

# 8
# Thankfulness

*Enter his gates with thanksgiving
and his courts with praise;
give thanks to him and praise his name.
For the Lord is good and his love endures forever;
his faithfulness continues through all generations.*

Psalm 100:4-5

Some virtues of Christian character, such as holiness, love, and faithfulness, are godly traits because they *reflect* the character of God. They are Godlike qualities. Other virtues are godly traits because they *acknowledge and exalt* the character of God. They are God-centered qualities that enhance our devotion to God. Such are the virtues of humility, contentment, and thankfulness. In humility we acknowledge God's majesty, in contentment His grace, and in thankfulness His goodness.

Thankfulness to God is a recognition that God in His goodness and faithfulness has provided for us and cared for us, both physically and spiritually. It is a recognition that we are totally dependent upon Him; that all that we are and have comes from God.

HONORING GOD

To fail to be thankful to God is a most grievous sin. When

100

Paul recounts the tragic moral downfall of mankind in Romans 1, he begins with the statement, "Although they knew God, they neither glorified him as God nor gave thanks to him, but their thinking became futile and their foolish hearts were darkened." To glorify God is to acknowledge the majesty and dignity of His person. To thank God is to acknowledge the bountifulness of His hand in providing and caring for us. And when mankind in their pride failed to give God the glory and thanks due Him, God gave them up to ever-increasing immorality and wickedness. God's judgment came because man failed to honor Him and to thank Him. If failure to give thanks is such a grievous sin, then, it behooves us to cultivate a spirit of thankfulness that permeates our entire lives.

One of the most instructive passages on the subject of thankfulness is Luke 17:11-19, the account of the healing of the ten lepers. Here were ten men in the most pitiful of all human misery. Not only were they afflicted with a terrible and loathsome disease; they were outcasts from society because of their disease. They had no one to relieve either their physical or emotional suffering. And then Jesus healed them.

As these men went to show themselves to the priest and thus be restored to their families and friends, only one of them, realizing what had happened, turned back to give thanks to Jesus. Ten men were healed, but only one gave thanks. How prone we are to be like the other nine. We are anxious to receive but too careless to give thanks. We pray for God's intervention in our lives, then congratulate ourselves rather than God for the results. When one of the American lunar missions was in serious trouble some years ago, the American people were asked to pray for the safe return of the astronauts. When they were safely back on earth, credit was given to the technological achievements and skill of the American space industry. No thanks or credit was publicly given to God. This is not unusual. It is the natural tendency of mankind.

In addition to instructing us about human nature, the account of the ten lepers also instructs us about God. Thanking Him for blessings we receive is very important to Him. Jesus asked, "Were not all ten cleansed? Where are the other nine?" Jesus was very much aware that only one returned to give Him thanks. And God is very much aware today when we fail to thank Him for the ordinary as well as the unusual blessings that come to us daily from His hand.

Even the angelic beings around God's throne give Him thanks. Revelation 4:9 speaks of their giving glory, honor, and thanks to Him who sits on the throne and who lives forever. God has created both angels and men to glorify Him and give Him thanks. When we fail to do this we fail to fulfill one of His purposes for us.

Thanksgiving is taught in the Bible by both precept and example. In 1 Chronicles, the Levites who took part in the temple worship were to stand every morning to thank and praise the Lord. The Psalms contain some thirty-five references to giving thanks to God. In eighteen instances in his letters, Paul expresses thanksgiving to God, and there are ten other instances in which he instructs us to give thanks. In all, there are approximately 140 references in the Bible to giving thanks to God. Thankfulness is no minor principle in God's sight. It is absolutely necessary to the practice of godliness.

One incident from the life of Daniel shows us the importance that this man of God put on giving thanks. We all know the story of Daniel in the lions' den, but do we remember how he got there? King Darius was persuaded by certain officials who were jealous of Daniel's position to issue a decree that for thirty days, anyone who prayed to any god or man other than King Darius would be thrown into the lions' den.

When Daniel knew that the decree had been published, he went to his room and three times a day he got down on his knees and prayed, giving thanks to his God, just as he had done before.

Now if you and I prayed at *all* under those circumstances, we'd be pleading with God for His deliverance. No doubt Daniel did pray for deliverance; but he also gave thanks. Our situation is never so desperate that it is not fitting to give thanks to God. Paul teaches us this principle in Philippians 4:6 when he says, "Do not be anxious about anything, but in everything, by prayer and petition, *with thanksgiving*, present your requests to God."

When Paul wrote his letter to the Colossian Christians, he was seeking to deal with an infiltration of man-made philosophy and wisdom into their church. After declaring that all the treasures of wisdom and knowledge are hidden in Christ, he urges the Colossians, "So then, just as you received Christ Jesus as Lord, continue to live in him, rooted and built up in him, strengthened in the faith as you were taught, and overflowing with thankfulness" (2:6-7). Paul is dealing with the fundamental issues of the Christian life, and he includes the concept of thanksgiving as one of those fundamental issues. He says we are to *overflow* with thanksgiving. Thanksgiving is a normal result of a vital union with Christ, and a direct measure of the extent to which we are experiencing the reality of that union in our daily lives.

## PURPOSES OF THANKSGIVING

The primary purpose of giving thanks to God is to acknowledge His goodness and honor Him. God says in Psalm 50:23, "He who sacrifices thank offerings honors me." Psalm 106:1-2 says, "Praise the Lord. Give thanks to the Lord, for he is good; his love endures forever. Who can proclaim the mighty acts of the Lord or fully declare his praise?" When we give thanks to the Lord we proclaim His mighty acts; we acknowledge His goodness.

God is infinite in goodness to all His creatures. "He causes his sun to rise on the evil and the good, and sends rain on the righteous and the unrighteous"; and "He has compassion on all he has made" (Matthew 5:45, Psalm 145:9).

He is most worthy of our praise and thanksgiving, especially if we are among His redeemed people, for He has blessed us not only in the temporal realm, but also with every spiritual blessing in the heavenly realms (Ephesians 1:3).

Thanksgiving promotes not only the glory of God, but also humility in us. It is the tendency of the sinful human heart—even the regenerated heart—to usurp the credit that rightfully belongs only to God. On several occasions God warned the children of Israel against this tendency (see Deuteronomy 8:11-14, 8:17-18, and 9:4-7). In David's prayer of thanksgiving for the gifts for the temple, he gratefully acknowledged that all of the abundance which the people brought came from and belonged to God. Paul constantly gave thanks to God for the spiritual progress of the churches under his care. He never took the credit for himself.

Thanksgiving also stimulates our faith. In Psalm 50:14-15, God connects thank offerings with calling upon Him in the day of trouble. Remembering God's previous mercies encourages us to trust Him for mercies we need today. Perhaps this idea is included in Paul's cure for anxiety in Philippians 4:6-7.

Finally, thanksgiving promotes contentment. Few things will stir up discontent within us as will our inner spiritual struggle between the sinful nature and the Holy Spirit. Its intensity caused Paul to cry out, "What a wretched man I am!" But then he finds relief and contentment in thanksgiving to God for the deliverance promised to us through Jesus Christ (Romans 7:24-25). Thanksgiving will also promote contentment about possessions, position, and providence by focusing our thoughts on the blessings God has already given, forcing us to stop spending our time yearning for things we do not have. Contentment and thanksgiving strengthen each other.

## CULTIVATING A THANKFUL HEART

The foundation of an attitude of thankfulness is a life lived in fellowship with Christ. As Colossians 2:6-7 suggests, thankfulness is the overflow of being rooted and built up in Christ. As we abide in Him, as we see His power at work in us and through us, as we call upon Him for our needs and experience His provision, our response will be thanksgiving. Like any other trait of godly character, thankfulness is a result of the Holy Spirit's ministry in our hearts. He gives us a thankful spirit, but He does this through our fellowship with Christ.

But though an attitude of thankfulness is the work of the Holy Spirit, it also comes as a result of personal effort on our part. We must cultivate the habit of always giving thanks for everything (Ephesians 5:20). One way we can do this is to expand our mealtime expression of thanks to include other blessings beyond the food before us. Another way is to begin and end the day with a time of thanksgiving. Psalm 92:1-2 says, "It is good to praise the Lord and make music to your name, O Most High, to proclaim your love in the morning and your faithfulness at night." As we arise in the morning we can thank God for His love, which is assured to us throughout the day. As we retire we can thank Him for specific demonstrations of His faithfulness during the day.

Another practical help is to write down the prayer requests you make to God; then keep those answered requests on your list until you feel you have adequately thanked God for His answer. Along with my written prayer requests, I also keep a list of significant blessings for which I am always thankful. I try to go over this list two or three times a week to express my thanks to God for His goodness to me. My thanksgiving list includes the following items:

- ❖ my personal salvation
- ❖ opportunities I have for spiritual growth
- ❖ the availability of the Bible
- ❖ the instruction and fellowship of our church
- ❖ the abundance of helpful Christian books
- ❖ opportunities for ministry and service
- ❖ godly parents
- ❖ a godly wife
- ❖ children who know Christ and are growing in Him
- ❖ health of our family
- ❖ political freedom
- ❖ material provision for family needs

Your personal thanksgiving list may not include all the items on my list, but it will likely include others. The important thing is to make such a list, and then use it. Set aside a period of time when you do nothing but thank God for the blessings on that list, as well as blessings more passing in nature.

Thanksgiving should also be included as a regular part of our intercessory prayer time. Paul seemed to always do this. He makes frequent statements in his letters such as, "We always thank God, the Father of our Lord Jesus Christ, when we pray for you" (Colossians 1:3). Later in that letter he instructs the Colossians, "Devote yourselves to prayer, being watchful and thankful" (4:2). When we pray without giving thanks we impoverish our own souls and render our prayers ineffective.

Along with the practical steps for cultivating an attitude of thankfulness and a habit of giving thanks, we need to remember the place of the word of God and prayer in developing traits of godly character. An ungrateful heart (which all of ours are by nature) must be transformed by the renewal of the mind. This transformation is the work of the Holy Spirit as we fill our minds with the word of God. Again I encourage you to memorize key verses on thanksgiving, using some of the passages cited in this chapter or others of your choosing. As you meditate on these verses, ask God to give you a genuine attitude of thanksgiving so that you, too, may be found in the company of the one leper who returned to give God thanks.

# 9
# Joy

❧

*For the kingdom of God
is not a matter of eating and drinking,
but of righteousness, peace and joy
in the Holy Spirit.*

Romans 14:17

❧

For a number of years the virtue of joy was not very evident in my life nor very high in my value system. As far as Romans 14:17 was concerned, I considered myself a man of peace, and I felt I was seeking after the ethical righteousness that is referred to in that passage. But I really hadn't given much thought to the importance God places on the fruit of joy in our lives.

Then one day as I was reading through Romans 14, I realized that God was not satisfied with only righteousness and peace in our lives. Paul tells us very plainly that the kingdom of God is a matter of not only righteousness and peace, but also *joy*. Furthermore, I learned from verse 18 that without joy, my life was really not very pleasing to God.

The fact is, only Christians have a reason to be joyful, but it is also a fact that every Christian *should* be joyful.

True Christian joy is both a privilege and a duty. Jesus

said, "I have come that they [His sheep] may have life, and have it to the full" (John 10:10). He has come that our lives might be full of joy. Twice in His talk to the disciples on the evening of His betrayal, Jesus referred to the joy that He desired for them to have. He has done all to make it possible for us to live joyful lives.

But we are not to sit around waiting for our circumstances to make us joyful. We are *commanded* to be joyful always (1 Thessalonians 5:16). We are to rejoice always (Philippians 4:4). Paul is quite emphatic about this: "I will say it again: Rejoice!" Like the other character traits we have examined, joy is not an option available only to those whose temperament is conducive to it. God intends that every one of His children exhibit the fruit of joy.

Just being joyful is not enough, however; we should continually be growing in joy. It is a contradiction for a Christian who professes to be a child of the one and only God—who created the universe and who governs it for His glory and the good of His people—to wear a gloomy countenance. As John W. Sanderson says, "It is practical atheism, for it ignores God and his attributes." [1]

Yet if we are honest, most of us must admit that life is so often anything *but* joyful. It often seems that at best life is dull, and at worst it is filled with anxiety, conflict, and tension. What is it that blocks joy in our lives?

STUMBLING BLOCKS
One of the most common hindrances to joy is *sin in our lives*, or sinful attitudes in our hearts. Christian joy is essentially the enjoyment of God, the fruit of communion with Him. Sin obviously breaks that communion and the enjoyment of His presence. When David was confessing his sin of adultery with Bathsheba, he prayed, "Restore to me the *joy* of your salvation" (Psalm 51:12).

Psalm 32:3-4 vividly describes David's lack of joy as he agonized over his sin. When we are not experiencing joy, we should examine our hearts and our lives. Are we doing or have we done something that is displeasing to God that we need to confess and forsake? Or, as is often the case, are we holding on to some sinful attitude such as envy or resentment, or a critical and unforgiving spirit? The fruit of joy cannot exist when such attitudes have control of our hearts. All sin, be it in attitude or action, must be dealt with if we are to display the virtue of joy in our lives.

Another stumbling block to joy is *misplaced confidence*. Paul told the Philippian Christians to "rejoice in the Lord" (3:1). He then made it clear that the opposite of rejoicing in the Lord is to put confidence in the flesh—in our good works or religious attainment. For the believers of Paul's day it was Jewish legalism. For us today it might be our personal disciplines such as a regular quiet time, a consistent Scripture memory program, or faithfulness in witnessing to nonChristians. Whatever it is, if the source of our confidence is anything other than Jesus Christ and His grace, it is a false and oft-interrupted joy. As Sanderson says, "even success in the Lord's work is a broken reed if we lean on it for security."[2]

If we are to have consistent joy, our attitude must be that expressed in the words of the old hymn:

> My hope is built on nothing less
> than Jesus' blood and righteousness;
> I dare not trust the sweetest frame,
> but wholly lean on Jesus' name.

In Luke's account of Jesus' sending out the seventy-two to preach, he says that they returned with joy and said, "Lord, even the demons submit to us in your name." Jesus responded, "However, do not rejoice that the spirits submit to you, but rejoice that your names are written in heaven" (10:17-20). It appears that Jesus was not discouraging joy in the ministry, but cautioning against the grounds of one's joy being in the *success* of a ministry. Success in ministry comes and goes, but our names are written in heaven forever. The circumstances of this life rise and fall, but the assurance of being with Christ one day never changes. It is in this fact that our joy must be grounded.

I have referred earlier to the book *The Pursuit of Holiness*, which I was privileged to write several years ago. God has blessed the ministry of that book far beyond my expectations, and He has done it purely by His grace. I sometimes think I feel as the little boy must have who gave Jesus his five small barley loaves and two small fish, then watched in utter amazement as Jesus used them to feed five thousand people. Although I rejoice at what God has done through *The Pursuit of Holiness*, the fundamental ground for my joy should be not in a book and its ministry, but in the fact that my name is written in heaven.

Perhaps you don't feel you have too much to show for your life. You haven't written a book, or seen scores come to Christ through your witness, or done anything else that seems significant. But is your name written in heaven? If it is, you have as much reason to rejoice as the most well-known and successful Christian. Nothing you or I will ever do can possibly compare with having our names written in heaven. The most humble Christian as well as the most famous Christian stand together on that common ground.

A third area that can choke off joy in our lives is the *chastening* or *discipline* that God often administers to His children. Scripture says, "No discipline seems pleasant at the time, but painful" (Hebrews 12:11). Discipline is never a joyful experience; it is not meant to be, else it would not accomplish its intended results.

If we lose sight of its intended results, or feel we don't deserve it, discipline can lead to self-pity. John Sanderson again provides a helpful insight into the relationship between discipline and joy when he says,

> If we only knew how bad we are, we would welcome chastening because this is God's way of getting rid of sin and its habits. But chastening is resented because we cannot believe that we have done anything worthy of it.[3]

The secret of maintaining some semblance of joy in the midst of discipline is to remember that "the Lord disciplines those he loves," and that "later on, however, it [the discipline] produces a harvest of righteousness and peace for those who have been trained by it" (Hebrews 12:6,11).

*Experiencing trials of faith* is a fourth hindrance to joy. Trials differ from discipline in that their purpose is to exercise our faith, not deal with sin in our lives. In His infinite wisdom, God allows trials in order to develop perseverance in us and to cause us to fix our hopes on the glory that is yet to be revealed.

Trials can come in many forms—nagging health problems, financial reverses, criticism and rejection, outright persecution. Whatever form the trial takes and however severe it may be, it is intended to strengthen our character. I once read of a sign on the entrance to a gymnasium that said, "No pain, no gain." To the weight lifters entering that door, the message was plain. They knew they had to endure the agony of lifting more than their muscles could comfortably handle if they wanted to increase their strength. So it is with faith. Our faith and perseverance can grow only under the pain of trial.

Frequently, our reaction to trials is like Job's. At the beginning of his testing, he reacted positively with the statement, "The Lord gave and the Lord has taken away; may the name of the Lord be praised" (1:21). But as time wore on and the trials, aggravated by the false accusations of his friends, continued, Job's faith and patience gave out. He was finally reduced to saying, "It profits a man nothing when he tries to please God" (34:9). But though Job's faith wore out, God's faithfulness did not. He stayed with Job until Job had learned the lesson of God's sovereignty, and then He gave Job twice as much as he had before.

God's faithfulness should also be of comfort to us in times of trial. "Though he brings grief, he will show compassion, so great is his unfailing love" (Lamentations 3:32).

STEPPING-STONES

Before considering any of the practical steps we can take to cultivate a joyful spirit, we must remind ourselves that joy is a fruit of the Spirit, the effect of His ministry in our hearts. Paul said in his letter to the Romans, "May the God of hope fill you with all joy and peace as you trust in him, so that you may overflow with hope by the power of the Holy Spirit" (15:13). It is by the power of the Holy Spirit that we experience the joy of salvation and are enabled to rejoice even in the midst of trials.

The Holy Spirit uses His word to create joy in our hearts. Romans 15 contains an interesting connection between God and the Scriptures. Verse 4 of that chapter speaks of the endurance and encouragement that come from the Scriptures; verse 5 says God gives endurance and encouragement. That God gives endurance and encouragement through the Scriptures should not surprise us. God is the source; the Scriptures are the means. The same truth applies to joy. Verse 13 speaks of the God of hope filling us with joy and peace as we trust in Him. How would we expect God to fill us with joy and hope? The reasonable answer is by means of the comfort of the Scriptures.

When I have experienced the Lord's discipline, the passage in Hebrews 12:6, "The Lord disciplines those he loves," has been a source of comfort and a means of restoring joy. When I was once experiencing what for me was a rather severe trial, Psalm 50:15 became a source of comfort: "Call upon me in the day of trouble; I will deliver you, and you will honor me." On another occasion when I thought my future looked bleak I was enabled to rejoice in the Lord through the assurance of Jeremiah 29:11, "'For I know the plans I have for you,' declares the Lord, 'plans to prosper you and not to harm you, plans to give you hope and a future.'"

These are the words the Holy Spirit will use to promote joy in our hearts. In order for Him to use the Scriptures, however, they must be in our hearts through regular exposure to and meditation upon them. This is our responsibility and is one of the practical means we must pursue to exhibit the fruit of joy.

But does the word always minister to us in times of need? Are there not times when the Scriptures seem barren and lifeless and utterly powerless to arouse the spirit of joy in the face of difficult trials? Yes, there are those times, but we must remember that it is the Holy Spirit who comforts us and enables us to rejoice. His word is simply His instrument. He works when and how He pleases, so we must look to Him with faith and patience to bring life to His word and apply it to our hearts.

I well remember a time when our family was struggling through a series of financial reverses. There was one thing after another: injuries, emergency hospital care, things breaking down at home, and frequent car repairs. The final straw was when the car broke down on a trip and we had to leave it for repairs at an unknown garage for four days. Assuming the worst, I lost all sense of joy in the Lord because I was focusing on circumstances rather than on Him. But sometime during those four days, the Holy Spirit enabled me to rest on the promise of Romans 8:28: that God was in control and was at work in those circumstances for my good. Romans 8:28 is a passage I had known for years, but it did not help until the Holy Spirit applied it to my heart and enabled me to believe it.

So again we see the principle set forth in chapter 5—we are both responsible and dependent. I was responsible to exhibit the fruit of joy during that time of financial reversal, but I was absolutely dependent upon the Holy Spirit for the power to do it. As we look to Him, though, let us remember that the purpose of rejoicing is not so we can feel better emotionally (though that will happen). The purpose of joy is to glorify God by demonstrating to an unbelieving world that our loving and faithful heavenly Father cares for us and provides for us all that we need.

Now for some specific practical aids to joy in our lives: an obvious one is, *Confess and forsake sin*. I have already referred to the lack of joy, or the strong spirit of oppression, that David experienced when he failed to deal with his sin (Psalm 32:3-4). But as David confessed his sin there was an interesting progression in his thoughts, starting from freedom from guilt, to faith in God's deliverance, to testimony to God's unfailing love, to rejoicing and singing (see verses 5-11).

God's forgiveness is always a source of amazement to me. It seems incredible that in spite of repeated sins, if we confess them, He is faithful and just to forgive them. And the continued faithfulness of God to forgive and to restore me to His fellowship is a source of joy to me. I am ready to sing just as David did.

A second specific aid to joy is, *Trust in God*. Romans 15:13 speaks of God filling us with joy and peace as we trust in Him. It is God who stands behind His word. The promises of the Bible are nothing more than God's covenant to be faithful to His people. It is His character that makes these promises valid.

I remember a friend of mine who, in the midst of a very deep trial, could find no comfort in the Scriptures. He asked God for some words of comfort but none came. He finally concluded that though the promises of the Scriptures seemed dead to him, he could trust in the character of God. God fills us with joy as we trust in Him.

Consider that absolutely amazing statement of Romans 8:28: in all things God works for the good of those who love Him. That statement is true whether you believe it or not. Your faith or lack of it does not determine God's working. He is at work in all the circumstances of your life to bring out the good for you, even if you had never heard of Romans 8:28. His work is not dependent upon your faith. But the comfort and joy that statement is intended to give you is dependent upon your believing it, upon your trusting in Him who is at work, even though you cannot see the outcome of that work. God never explained to Job the reason for his trials. He simply brought Job to the place where Job trusted Him without an explanation.

Another aid to joy is, *Take the long-range view of life*. The Scriptures repeatedly affirm that the focal point of our joy should be our hope of the eternal inheritance that awaits us in Jesus Christ and the final revelation of His glory. Consider, for example, the following passages:

In this [hope] you greatly rejoice, though now for a little while you may have had to suffer grief in all kinds of trials. (1 Peter 1:6)

And we rejoice in the hope of the glory of God. (Romans 5:2)

So we fix our eyes not on what is seen, but on what is unseen. For what is seen is temporary, but what is unseen is eternal. (2 Corinthians 4:18)

You . . . joyfully accepted the confiscation of your property, because you knew that you yourselves had better and lasting possessions. (Hebrews 10:34)

To take the long-range view is to rejoice because our names are written in heaven; it is to rejoice in the Lord in whom alone we have the hope of an eternal inheritance that far outweighs whatever troubles we are now experiencing. To take the long-range view is to follow the example of Jesus Himself, who "for the joy set before him endured the cross, scorning its shame, and sat down at the right hand of the throne of God" (Hebrews 12:2).

A fourth aid to joy is, *Give thanks in all circumstances* (1 Thessalonians 5:18). This refers, of course, to both pleasant and unpleasant circumstances. We are to be thankful all the time. This does not mean we are to be thankful *for* a difficult circumstance, considered in itself. Rather, we are to give thanks *in the midst of* every circumstance, good or bad. We are to be thankful that God is working in this circumstance for our good. We are to be thankful for past deliverances from trials. We are to be thankful that in this present trial God will not allow a greater burden than we can bear, and that His grace is sufficient to enable us to bear it. And as we give thanks to God we will begin to experience once again the joy that is our heritage in Christ.

THE FRUITS OF JOY

One of the results of experiencing this joy is that God is pleased (Romans 14:17-18). If Christ came that we might have joy (life to the full), if the Holy Spirit is at work in us to produce joy, then it is a contradiction of God's purpose for us when we are not joyful. Certainly, some people are more joyful by nature than others, but every Christian is to exhibit a balanced display of all the virtues of Christian character, regardless of his temperament. We must look to God and apply all the means He has given us until we can rejoice in the Lord always.

A second result of joy is that we are strengthened physically, emotionally, and spiritually. Nehemiah said to the returned exiles, "Do not grieve, for the joy of the Lord is your strength" (8:10). Sanderson asks, "How much of our physical weakness, apathy and illness is probably due to a heavy spirit?"[4] I have experienced the direct relationship of physical strength to joy in my personal exercise program. When I am rejoicing in the Lord the strength is there, and the jogging and other exercise go much easier. If I am discouraged I seem to have no energy at all.

What is true in the physical or emotional realm is also true in the spiritual. I recall one morning going into our living room to begin my quiet time. Just prior to that I had been sinning by entertaining resentful thoughts toward a Christian brother. As I started to kneel to pray, the thought came to me, "You cannot enter the presence of God with the thoughts you have been thinking." Thinking of Hebrews 10:19-22, I said, "Lord, I acknowledge my sin, and it is true, I cannot come into Your presence in my own merit. I come in the only way I can come. I come through the blood of Jesus." As I uttered (and believed) those words I thought, "What a wonderful thing that I, a sinner, having just indulged in the sin of resentment, can through the blood of Jesus come into the very presence of a Holy God." Then I thought, "That's not all! Not only can I come into His presence, but I can call him Father."

That little episode changed my whole day. It changed me from a discouraged, resentful person to a joyous and forgiven person. And the joy of God's gracious forgiveness enabled me to deal with the root of that resentment. Joy does give spiritual strength. The joy of discovering the sufficiency of God's grace enabled Paul to delight in weaknesses, in insults, in difficulties (2 Corinthians 12:9-10).

So the choice is ours. We can be joyless Christians, or we can be joyful Christians. We can go through life bored, glum and complaining, or we can rejoice in the Lord, in our names being written in heaven, in the hope of an eternal inheritance. It is both our privilege and our duty to be joyful. To be joyless is to dishonor God and to deny His love and His control over our lives. It is practical atheism. To be joyful is to experience the power of the Holy Spirit within us, and to say to a watching world, "Our God reigns."

Joy is a fruit of the Spirit. It is a result of His work, but it is also something we must do. We must, by His power, rejoice. This is a part of the practice of godliness.

---

NOTES
1. John W. Sanderson, *The Fruit of The Spirit* (Grand Rapids, Mich.: Zondervan, 1972), page 72.
2. Sanderson, pages 65-66.
3. Sanderson, page 71.
4. Sanderson, page 73.

# 10
# Holiness

*This is the message we have heard from him
and declare to you: God is light;
in him there is no darkness at all.*

1 John 1:5

The outward evidence of godliness is Godlike character. Although it is this character that is usually thought of as godliness, as we have seen in earlier chapters, Godlikeness in character is built upon the foundation of God-centeredness—devotion to God.

If we want to develop godly character, we must learn what the Bible says about the character of God Himself. The apostle John gives us two statements about God that together sum up the biblical revelation of God's character: "God is light" (1 John 1:5), and "God is love" (1 John 4:8). The Christian who wants to train himself to be godly must understand the meaning of these statements about the character of God and must appropriate their teachings in his life.

What was John telling us about the character of God when he made the statement, "God is light"? Professor Howard Marshall explains, "Two notions became associated

with God as light. One was that of revelation and salvation
. . . the other is that of holiness; light symbolizes the flawless
perfection of God."[1] In 1 John 1:5, it is the idea of God's holiness that is in view. God is absolutely holy; in Him there is not
the slightest hint of any moral flaw. A well-known soap has
been advertised as being "99.44 percent pure." While that may
be quite an achievement for soap, it would be blasphemous as
a statement about God. God is infinitely perfect in His holiness. Not the slightest degree of sin taints His character.

To be Godlike in our character, then, is first of all to be
holy. The practice of godliness involves the pursuit of holiness because God has said, "Be holy, because I am holy"
(1 Peter 1:16). Paul tells us that we have been called to a holy
life; we have been redeemed for that purpose. Any Christian
who is not earnestly pursuing holiness in every aspect of his
life is flying in the face of God's purpose in saving him.

What is holiness? The best practical definition that I have
heard is simply "without sin." That is the statement that was
made of the Lord Jesus' life on earth (Hebrews 4:15), and
that should be the goal of every person who desires to be
godly. Granted, we will never reach that goal in this life; nevertheless it is to be our supreme objective and the object of
our most earnest efforts and prayers.

John said he wrote his first letter so that his readers
would not sin (1 John 2:1). Most Christians seem content not
to sin very much, but John's goal was that we not sin at all.
Every sin, no matter how small it may seem to us, is an affront
to God's authority, a disregard for His law, a spurning of His
love. Because of this, sin cannot be tolerated in any form, to
any degree. That "inconsequential" lie, that "just a little bit" of
dishonesty, that fleeting lustful look, offends our holy God
and wages war against our own souls (1 Peter 2:11).

When Paul was instructing Timothy about his relationship with younger women, he said to treat them "as sisters,

with absolute purity" (1 Timothy 5:2). His every thought, look, and act toward them was to be conditioned by a perfect standard of holiness—absolute purity. When Paul was instructing the Ephesian Christians about the importance of holiness he said, "So I tell you this, and insist on it in the Lord, that you must no longer live as the Gentiles do" (4:17). He *insisted* on holiness, and he did so with the Lord's authority. Holiness is not an option but a must for every Christian.

Even for the most godly Christian, there will be failure in the pursuit of holiness. The apostle John says, "If we claim to be without sin, we deceive ourselves" (1 John 1:8). We still have a sinful nature within us, and we still live in a wicked world ruled by a wicked devil. Temptation is on every hand, and our old nature responds to it. But what is the desire of our hearts? What is the object of our most earnest prayers? What is the major bent of our lives? If we want to train ourselves to be godly, it must be holiness in every area of our lives.

But let's get specific. When Paul exhorted the Ephesian Christians to a life of holiness, to stop living as the Gentiles did, he dealt with three general areas of morality: honesty (a refusal to lie, steal, or deceive in any way); peaceableness (freedom from bitterness, anger, or strife of any kind); and purity (not even a hint of sexual immorality in word, look, thought, or act).

We all acknowledge the need for Christians to walk circumspectly in each of these areas. At the same time, we recognize how increasingly difficult it is to do so. Honesty and purity are no longer essential elements of our culture. Lying, cheating, and stealing have become commonplace in business, education, and sports. Sexual immorality is no longer an issue; it is an accepted practice in almost every area of society. And our soaring divorce rate and litigious (a tendency toward lawsuits) society are symptoms of our desperate need for peaceableness.

The Christians of Paul's day lived in the same kind of society; quite possibly it was even worse. Paul said of the nonChristians of Ephesus, "Having lost all sensitivity, they have given themselves over to sensuality so as to indulge in every kind of impurity, with a continual lust for more" (4:19). Things couldn't have gotten much worse in the culture those first-century Christians lived in. Yet in the midst of such gross ungodliness, the Christians were expected to put off the traits of their sinful natures and to put on the traits of righteousness and holiness.

God expects no less of us today. Our responsibility to pursue holiness, even in the midst of a wicked society, is just as great as was the first century Christians'. Yes, it gets more difficult each year; the temptations seem more numerous, the ridicule of the ungodly toward those who seek to live a godly life grows more abusive. But we are still called to be holy as He is holy. We cannot and must not evade God's standard for us.

How do we pursue holiness? Some time ago I heard a seminary professor tell of a friend who would frequently write the letters "YBH" in the margins of books he was reading. When asked what they stood for, he replied, "I agree with the author's challenge to a more consistent Christian life, but my heart says, 'Yes, but how?'" I suspect some of you are asking the same question about holiness—"Yes, but how?"

I have previously mentioned that several years ago God gave me the privilege of writing a book on the subject of holiness. Since its publication, I have had many opportunities to speak on the subject of holiness, often in only a single forty-five-minute message. Because of the necessity of covering such a vast subject in a limited time, I have given much thought to what I think are the most essential elements of holiness. They can be summed up in five words: conviction, commitment, discipline, dependence, and desire.[2]

## CONVICTIONS: KNOWLEDGE OF THE TRUTH

In the passage in Ephesians 4 that we have been considering, Paul says, "be made new in the attitude of your minds." To the Christians at Rome he wrote, "Do not conform any longer to the pattern of this world, but be transformed by the renewing of your mind" (12:2). This process of renewing our minds involves establishing convictions. As we prayerfully expose ourselves to the Scriptures, we begin to understand what God's will is regarding our conduct and character. And then as the Holy Spirit applies His word to specific areas of our lives, and as we are obedient to His promptings, we begin to develop Bible-based convictions. Our values begin to change so that God's standard becomes our delight and our desire.

One has only to prayerfully meditate over Ephesians 4:25–5:7, for example, to realize that God has set down very clear standards regarding honesty, peaceableness, and purity. As we progress in our Christian life, however, we begin to realize more and more the extent of these standards. At first we may be convicted of gross lying; later on we realize that speaking truthfully to our neighbor covers any intent to deceive directly or indirectly; then the Holy Spirit convicts us about "white" lies or social lies that are told to save face or avoid embarrassing someone else.

Each year that we practice godliness the Holy Spirit continues to renew our minds, giving increased understanding of His word and enabling us to develop convictions in greater conformity to His will. Without such Bible-based, Spirit-developed convictions, we easily fall prey to manmade convictions which tend toward one of two extremes. At one extreme is a strict code of legalistic "don'ts" that often miss the more weighty issues of Christian character; at the other is a loose permissiveness that too often conforms to the world's values and customs.

The only safe path is to allow the Holy Spirit to establish convictions through His word. Even on this path, however, we need to be careful not to build convictions upon a misunderstanding of some isolated text of Scripture. Here is where the insight of other Christians can help us. One of the values of Bible study discussion groups is the opportunity to test our understanding and application of the Scriptures against the thinking of other believers. Godly pastors and teachers who have a gifted insight into the Scriptures can also help us to correctly understand them. Paul himself stated that a part of his calling was to help God's people grow in the knowledge of the truth that leads to godliness.

This is where holiness begins: with the knowledge of the truth that renews our minds and enables us to understand how God wants us to live.

## A COMMITMENT TO OBEDIENCE

Someone has said, "A belief is what you hold; a conviction is what holds you." A conviction is not truly a conviction unless it includes a commitment to live by what we claim to believe. A commitment is not a vow but a resolution—a determined purpose to live by God's word as He applies it to our lives. First, we need a commitment to holiness as a total way of life. We must decide that holiness is so important to God that it deserves priority attention in our lives. We must commit ourselves to obeying God in all of His commands. We cannot pick and choose according to our own values. A little bit of fudging on one's income tax return is sin just as much as outright theft; an unforgiving spirit toward someone else is sin just as much as murder. I am not suggesting that all sin is equally offensive to God; I am saying that *all* sin is offensive to God. The measure of sin is not just in its effect upon our neighbor, but in its affront to the majesty and holiness of a sovereign God.

Sin is serious business to God, and it becomes serious

business to us when we reflect upon the fact that every sin, regardless of how seemingly insignificant it appears to us, is an expression of contempt toward the sovereign authority of God. There is nothing that so motivates me toward a genuine heartfelt confession of sin and a serious resolve to turn from it, as a reflection upon the fact that sin of any degree is an affront to His dignity and a contempt for His law.

The psalmist recognized the seriousness of any and all sin when he said, "You have laid down precepts that are to be fully obeyed" (Psalm 119:4). He recognized that partial obedience—for example, refraining from outright theft of our neighbor's property while allowing our heart to covet it—is actually disobedience. God's precepts are to be *fully* obeyed. And Jesus clearly taught us in the Sermon on the Mount that obedience in our thought life is as necessary as obedience in our actions.

The psalmist's response to his recognition of the seriousness of all sin was a commitment to obedience. He longs that his ways will be steadfast in obeying God's decrees (verse 5). He even takes an oath that he will follow God's righteous laws (verse 106). Clearly, he solidified his convictions about God's will with a determined commitment to obey it.

We need not only a commitment to holiness as a total way of life, but frequently a commitment regarding specific areas of temptation. Job made a personal covenant not to look lustfully at young women (31:1). Daniel resolved not to defile himself with forbidden food, even though from the king's table (1:8). These two Old Testament saints are commended by God Himself as among the most righteous who ever lived (Ezekiel 14:14); yet both found it necessary to make a commitment regarding some specific area of temptation. Job found his temptation in his own breast; Daniel found his in his particular circumstances. Both responded with a commitment to obey God. They lived up to their convictions.

## THE DISCIPLINE OF CHOICES

The third of the five essential elements of holiness is the discipline of daily choices. We have already looked in chapter 5 at the serious consequences of our daily choices; over time we become what we do. To experience the holiness God calls us to, we must learn to make the right choice in the face of each specific temptation. Paul said the grace of God "teaches us to say 'No' to ungodliness and worldly passions" (Titus 2:11-12). Although he was probably referring to an overall attitude toward sin, and thus to renounce it as a way of life, I find it helpful to take the same attitude toward specific occurrences of temptation. I even go so far as to verbalize (softly or to myself) a firm *no*, at the same time breathing a prayer for the aid of the Holy Spirit to carry through with that choice.

In Romans 8:13, Paul tells us to put to death the misdeeds of the body. We do this by the choices we make—not only to say no to temptations, but also to say yes to the positive steps we must take to pursue holiness. We must exercise ourselves in the disciplines of choosing to feed upon the Scriptures so that our convictions will conform more and more to God's will for us, of choosing to pray constantly for His enabling grace to say no to temptation, of choosing to take all practical steps to avoid known areas of temptation and flee from those that surprise us. These are some of the practical steps we must take to discipline ourselves in holiness. We can easily see that this discipline involves nothing less than an *all-out* effort to turn from every sin and to do the will of God in every area of our lives.

## DEPENDENCE ON THE SPIRIT

Any time we stress the personal responsibility of practical actions, however, we are in danger of thinking that the pursuit of holiness does depend upon our own willpower, our own strength of character. Nothing is further from the truth. We are both *personally responsible and totally dependent* in our practice of godliness. We cannot change our hearts; that is the exclusive work of the Holy Spirit. But we can and must avail ourselves of the means He uses.

In Romans 12:2, we are told to be *transformed* by the renewing of our minds. The word *transformed* means "to be changed within." John Murray says, "The term used here implies that we are to be constantly in the process of being metamorphosed by renewal of that which is the seat of thought and understanding."[3] It is nothing less than a total renovation of our values and desires. This renewal is the exclusive work of the Holy Spirit. Through His ministry we are transformed more and more into the likeness of our Lord. Conceivably, even an unsaved person can change certain actions, but only the Holy Spirit can transform us within; only He can give us new values and desires.

Again the godly writer of Psalm 119 recognizes this dependence upon the Spirit to change his inward thoughts and desires. He prays, "Turn my heart toward your statutes and not toward selfish gain. Turn my eyes away from worthless things; renew my life according to your word" (verses 36-37). This same man who elsewhere in this psalm expresses so strongly his sense of personal responsibility here acknowledges his total dependence upon God for the work of inner transformation. Paul said he had *learned* to be content in every situation. There was no doubt he felt responsible for this changed attitude toward varying circumstances. But he was just as clear that he was totally dependent upon the Holy Spirit working within him to accomplish such a change (Philippians 4:11-13).

This principle of simultaneous personal responsibility and total dependence upon God for fulfillment is one of the most important principles in the practice of godliness. We will not make progress in godliness without consistent application of this principle in our lives.

## A GOD-CENTERED DESIRE

The fifth essential element in the pursuit of holiness is the development of a *God-centered desire* for holiness. We have already considered in chapter 5 the necessity of a Godward motivation in the development of all the graces of Christian character. The need for such a Godward motivation, however, is especially critical in the pursuit of holiness—the putting off of the sinful traits of the old self. We want victory in our lives, whether it is in a Ping-Pong game or in our struggle with sin. We want to feel good about ourselves, and we know we will not as long as we are allowing some sin to gain mastery over us.

To paraphrase a writer from a previous century, so often when we sin we are more vexed at the lowering of our self-esteem than we are grieved at God's dishonor. We are irritated at our lack of self-control in subjecting ourselves to some unworthy habit. We are unable to stand the disappointment of seeing ourselves fail.

God does not honor these self-centered desires. This is one reason we do not experience more of His enabling power in our day-to-day struggles with so-called besetting sins. God does not give us His power so that we might feel good about ourselves; He gives us His power so that we can obey Him for His sake, for His glory. It is not wrong to feel good about ourselves, but this should be a byproduct of obedience which is motivated by a desire to please God.

We have learned in earlier chapters that godliness is first of all God-centeredness. This concept is extremely important in the area of holiness. Our desire for holiness, our motivation to pursue it, must be a God-centered desire and motivation. Developing this God-centered motivation requires practice or training; it does not come naturally or easily. We are by nature self-centered. If we are diligent to examine ourselves, we will often find that our motivation is self-centered. We must confess and renounce this, just as we must any disobedient action, and then seek a God-centered motivation.

NOTES
1. Howard Marshall, "The Epistles of John," *The New International Commentary on the New Testament* (Grand Rapids, Mich.: Eerdmans, 1978), page 109.
2. These five essentials, as well as other aspects of holiness, are more fully developed in *The Pursuit of Holiness* (NavPress, 1978). This book may be obtained from most local Christian bookstores or by contacting NavPress at P.O. Box 35002, Colorado Springs, CO 80935.
3. John Murray, "The Epistles of Romans," *The New International Commentary on the New Testament*, Vol. II (Grand Rapids, Mich.: Eerdmans, 1965), page 114.

# 11

# Self-Control

~

*Like a city whose walls are broken down*
*is a man who lacks self-control.*

Proverbs 25:28

~

I n ancient times the walls of a city were its main defense;
without them the city was easy prey to its enemies. To
godly Nehemiah, a Jewish captive in the faraway city of Susa,
the news that the wall of Jerusalem was broken down signi-
fied the ultimate destruction of his beloved city. When he
heard the news he sat down and wept.

Self-control is the believer's wall of defense against the
sinful desires that wage war against his soul. Charles Bridges
has observed that the person without self-control is easy
prey to the invader: "He yields himself to the first assault of
his ungoverned passions, offering no resistance. . . . Having
no discipline over himself, temptation becomes the occasion
of sin, and hurries him on to fearful lengths that he had not
contemplated. . . . Anger tends to murder. Unwatchfulness
over lust plunges into adultery."[1]

Self-control is control *of* one's self. It is probably best defined as *the governing of one's desires*. D. G. Kehl describes it as "the ability to avoid excesses, to stay within reasonable bounds."[2] Bethune calls it "the healthful regulation of our desires and appetites, preventing their excess."[3] Both of these descriptions imply what we all know to be true; we have a tendency to overindulge our various appetites and consequently need to restrain them.

But self-control involves a much wider range of watchfulness than merely control of our bodily appetites and desires. We also must exercise self-control of thoughts, emotions, and speech. There is a form of self-control that says *yes* to what we should do as well as that which says *no* to what we shouldn't do. For example, I seldom *want* to study the Bible when I first begin a study. There are too many other things that are mentally much easier to do, such as reading the newspaper, a magazine, or a good Christian book. A necessary expression of self-control, then, is to set myself down at the dining room table with Bible and notebook in hand and say to myself, "Get with it!" This may not sound very spiritual, but neither does Paul's exclamation, "I beat my body and make it my slave" (1 Corinthians 9:27).

Self-control is necessary because we are at war with our own sinful desires. James describes those desires as dragging us away and enticing us into sin (1:14). Peter says they war against our souls (1 Peter 2:11). Paul speaks of them as deceitful (Ephesians 4:22). What makes these sinful desires so dangerous is that they dwell within our own heart. External temptations would not be nearly so dangerous were it not for the fact that they find this ally of desire right within our own breast.

Self-control is an essential character trait of the godly person that enables him to obey the words of the Lord Jesus, "If anyone would come after me, he must deny himself and take up his cross daily and follow me" (Luke 9:23). It is impossible to be a follower of Jesus without giving diligent attention in our lives to the grace of self-control.

The translators of the *New International Version* of the Bible have used the expression *self-control* to translate two different words from the original language. The first word, which is used by Paul in his list called the fruit of the Spirit, refers primarily to moderation or temperance in the gratification of our desires and appetites. A friend of mine who is a former teacher of Greek says it has the literal meaning of "inner strength," and refers to that strength of character that enables one to control his passions and desires.

The second word rendered *self-control* by the *New International Version* translators is a word that denotes soundness of mind or sound judgment. It is rendered *sober* or *sensible* by other translations. This word conveys the idea of allowing sound judgment to control our desires and appetites, our thoughts, emotions, and actions.

We can readily see that these two ideas complement one another in the biblical meaning of self-control. Sound judgment enables us to determine what we should do and how we should respond; inner strength provides the will to do it. Both sound judgment and inner strength are thus necessary for Spirit-directed self-control.

Sound judgment is critical to the exercise of self-control. It enables the godly person not only to distinguish good from evil, but also to sort out the good and the best. Sound judgment enables us to determine the boundaries of moderation in our appetites, desires, and habits. Sound judgment helps us regulate our thoughts and keep our emotions under control.

But sound judgment alone is not enough to enable us to practice self-control. Inner strength is also essential. All too often we know very well *what* to do, but we do not do it. We allow feelings or desires to overrule our judgment.

Ultimately, *Self-control is the exercise of inner strength under the direction of sound judgment that enables us to do, think, and say the things that are pleasing to God*.

Since the grace of self-control affects so many aspects of our lives, it is helpful to focus our study of it in three major areas: *body, thoughts*, and *emotions*.

## HONOR GOD WITH YOUR BODY

"And the Lord God made all kinds of trees grow out of the ground—trees that were pleasing to the eye and good for food" (Genesis 2:9). God created man to enjoy sensuous pleasures; that is, things that are pleasant to our senses and bodily appetites. The trees of His creation were not only good for food, but also pleasant to the eyes. There is no doubt that God intends that we enjoy the physical things of this life which He has so graciously provided. As Paul says in 1 Timothy 6:17, "God . . . richly provides us with everything for our enjoyment."

But man in his sin has corrupted all of the natural blessings which God has given. Because our desires have been corrupted, those things which God intended for our use and enjoyment have a tendency to become our masters. Paul had to warn the Corinthian believers against this tendency when he said, "'Everything is permissible for me'—but I will not be mastered by anything" (1 Corinthians 6:12). The moderation resulting from self-control keeps permissible things from becoming masters of our bodies.

In the rather short letter in which Paul instructs Titus in his pastoral duties among the Cretan Christians, Paul frequently refers to the grace of self-control. It is a requirement for elders, it is important for older men, younger men, older women and younger women; it is in fact to be a characteristic of all believers. Why did Paul so stress this trait of self-control? Because the Cretans were "always liars, evil brutes, lazy

134

gluttons" (1:12). They were demonstrably in need of the grace of self-control. Someone characterized as a lazy glutton certainly needs to learn self-control of the body.

Self-control of the body should be aimed primarily at three areas of physical temptation: gluttony (in both food and drink), laziness, and sexual immorality or impurity. Although drunkenness is a widespread sin in the nonChristian culture of today, I do not detect that it is a major problem among Christians. But gluttony surely is. Most of us have a tendency to overindulge in the food which God has so graciously provided for us. We allow the sensual part of our God-given appetite to range out of control and lead us into sin. We need to remember that even our eating and drinking is to be done to the glory of God (1 Corinthians 10:31).

What about laziness? Most of us would no doubt assent to the widespread need for self-control with respect to food and drink among Christians today. But laziness? I suspect we don't particularly think of ourselves collectively as a lazy people like those Cretan Christians. We work hard at our jobs, keep our houses painted and our lawns trimmed. Can we have a problem with laziness?

To answer that question, let's look at an incident in the life of Jesus. Mark records that "Very early in the morning, while it was still dark, Jesus got up, left the house and went off to a solitary place, where he prayed" (1:35). That Jesus got up to pray while it was still dark is challenging enough. But note what had happened the night before. Mark tells us that on the previous evening after sunset the people brought to Jesus all the sick and demon-possessed to be healed; the whole town, in fact, gathered at the door (verses 32-34). Jesus was probably quite weary at the end of that evening.

Now you and I, under those circumstances, would have tended to sleep in the following morning, feeling that after such a full evening of ministry we deserved a rest and a little pampering. But not Jesus. He knew the importance of getting that time of fellowship with His Father, and He disciplined His physical body in order to do it.

I suspect that the number of Christians who have a consistent, productive time of fellowship with God each day is a very small minority. For some, such a time is nonexistent; for others, it is sporadic at best. This is because we tend to be lazy in body and undisciplined in the use of our time.

There are other Christians who have learned the self-control of getting up in the morning to have fellowship with God, but who haven't learned the self-control of caring for their bodies. Some are abusing their bodies through a constant lack of needed rest and recreation; others are allowing their bodies to become soft and flabby through no exercise at all. Both groups need to learn godly self-control of their bodies.

Sexual self-control belongs to both the body and the mind. There was a time, a generation or so ago, when we would hardly have felt it necessary to exhort Christians to exercise self-control in the area of sexual immorality. Control of impure thoughts, yes; but even the more moral segment of nonChristian society condemned the actual physical acts of immorality. This situation no longer exists. Authorities in our social and psychological areas today are telling us that premarital or extramarital sexual activity is okay as long as it is not emotionally harmful.

Many Christians, unfortunately, are falling prey to such thinking. Immorality among both single and married people is becoming a major concern in the Christian community. The need for sexual self-control among Christians has probably never been greater since the rise of the first-century Gentile church out of gross paganism.

God's standard for sexual self-control is *absolute abstinence* outside of the marriage relationship. If, as Kehl suggests, self-control is the ability to stay within reasonable bounds, then we must realize that God's boundary for sexual activity is limited strictly to marriage. As Hebrews 13:4 says, "Marriage should be honored by all, and the marriage bed kept pure, for God will judge the adulterer and all the sexually immoral." Paul's words to the Thessalonian believers also leave no room for compromise on this point: "It is God's will that you should be holy; that you should avoid sexual immorality; that each of you should learn to control his own body in a way that is holy and honorable, not in passionate lust like the heathen, who do not know God" (1 Thessalonians 4:3-5).

The Christian must exercise self-control not only in the area of sexual activity, but in the area of impure thoughts, lustful looks, and suggestive speech as well. Jesus said, "I tell you that anyone who looks at a woman lustfully has already committed adultery with her in his heart" (Matthew 5:28). A lustful look quickly becomes an impure thought. If *acts* of immorality are becoming a problem among Christians, the *thoughts* of immorality are a much greater problem. Sexual lust lies latent in the heart of every Christian. Even righteous Job found it necessary to deal decisively with this temptation; he made a covenant with his eyes not to look lustfully at a girl (31:1). If Job found it necessary to make this kind of commitment in the day in which he lived, how much more do we need it in today's society—where sexual lust is exploited even to advertise spark plugs!

The subject of control of our bodies, then, especially in the area of sexual purity, leads naturally to a second area of self-control: our thoughts.

TAKE CAPTIVE EVERY THOUGHT

Paul said, "We take captive every thought to make it obedient to Christ" (2 Corinthians 10:5). Although the immediate context indicates that he was referring to the thoughts of his opponents at Corinth, it still remains a worthy objective for the control of our own thoughts. Self-control of our thoughts means entertaining in our minds only those thoughts that are acceptable to God.

The best guideline for evaluating the control of our thoughts is that given by Paul in Philippians 4:8: "Finally, brothers, whatever is true, whatever is noble, whatever is right, whatever is pure, whatever is lovely, whatever is admirable—if anything is excellent or praiseworthy—think about such things." Self-control of our thoughts, then, is more than just refusing to admit sinful thoughts—such as lust, greed, envy, or selfish ambition—into our minds. Controlling our thoughts also includes focusing our minds on that which is good and pleasing to God.

Solomon warned us, "Above all else, guard your heart, for it is the wellspring of life" (Proverbs 4:23). The meaning of the Hebrew word for "heart" generally refers to our entire conscious person—understanding, emotions, conscience, and will; the warning is particularly applicable, however, to our thought life. It is in our thought life that our emotions and actions begin, and that sinful desires plant their roots and entice us into sin.

Our minds are mental greenhouses where unlawful thoughts, once planted, are nurtured and watered before being transplanted into the real world of unlawful actions. People seldom fall suddenly into gluttony or immorality. These actions are savored in the mind long before they are enjoyed in reality. The thought life, then, is our first line of defense in the battle of self-control.

The gates to our thought lives are primarily our eyes and our ears. What we see or read or hear largely determines what we think. Memory, of course, also plays a big part in what we think, but our memories only store and feed back what originally comes into our minds through our eyes and ears. Guarding our hearts begins with guarding our eyes and ears. We must not allow that which panders to sexual lust, greed (called materialism in our present society), envy, and selfish ambition to enter our minds. We should avoid television programs, magazine or newspaper articles, advertisements, and conversations that arouse such thoughts. We should not only avoid them, but, to use Paul's words to Timothy, "flee from all this." It is well worth noting that in both of his letters to Timothy, Paul felt it prudent to warn Timothy to *flee* temptation. Although Timothy was a godly leader, he was not exempt from the necessity of exercising self-control.

Solomon said to *guard*; Paul said to *flee*. Both verbs convey a much stronger reaction to temptation than most Christians practice. Instead of guarding the gates of our minds, we actually open them to the flood of ungodly material coming to us through television, newspapers and magazines, and the world's conversations that often surround us. Instead of fleeing from temptations, we too often indulge them in our thoughts.

We allow in our minds what we would not allow in our actions, because other people cannot see our thoughts. But God sees them. David said, "You perceive my thoughts from afar," and "Before a word is on my tongue you know it completely, O Lord" (Psalm 139:2,4). The Christian who fears God, controls his thoughts—not because of what other people think, but because of what God thinks. He prays, "May the words of my mouth and the meditation of my heart be pleasing in *your* sight, O Lord, my Rock and my Redeemer" (Psalm 19:14).

The television and printed media are not the only culprits in leading our thoughts astray. Paul's checklist for controlled thoughts in Philippians 4:8 includes such requirements as "true" and "noble" as well as "pure." A Christian may not be particularly bothered with impure thoughts, but may be tempted to entertain those that are not true or noble. Listening to such things as gossip, slander, or criticism about others needs to be rejected just as strongly as the tendency to pass them over our tongues.

It is impossible to listen in a condoning manner to gossip or criticism about someone else and then think only thoughts that are true and noble about that person. And if we guard our thoughts we will more easily guard our tongues, for Jesus said, "For out of the overflow of the heart the mouth speaks" (Matthew 12:34).

## CURBING OUR EMOTIONS

The emotions that need to be controlled include anger and rage (the so-called "hot temper"), resentment, self-pity, and bitterness. The feelings may be explosive, as in the case of an uncontrolled temper, or they may be only simmering, as in the case of self-pity. But in either case these emotions are displeasing to God and need to be included in our efforts to exercise self-control.

An uncontrolled temper is a contradiction in the life of a person who is seeking to practice godliness. Outbursts of temper are harmful not only because they release our own ungoverned, sinful passions, but more importantly because they wound those who are the recipients of such outbursts. In this respect temper is a unique challenge in the area of self-control. Ungoverned thoughts and other emotions are sins within our own minds; they harm only ourselves, unless of course they lead to sinful words or actions. But an uncontrolled temper damages the self-respect of others, creates bitterness, and destroys relationships.

We are of course talking here about an *uncontrolled* temper. Many believers by temperament have a tendency to lash out at those who incur their displeasure in some way. But the godly person has learned to control this tendency.

Solomon said, "Better a patient man than a warrior, a man who controls his temper than one who takes a city" (Proverbs 16:32). To have a temper that requires control is not a mark of ungodliness; to fail to control it is. To succeed, by God's grace, in controlling an unruly temper is to demonstrate godly self-control.

Someone has said of Proverbs 16:32, "Note what price the Holy Spirit puts on a curbed temper; it is more to be sought than a decisive victory in war." Charles Bridges has commented, "The taking of a city is child's play, compared with this wrestling. . . .That is only the battle of a day. This, the weary, unceasing conflict of a life."[4] The person who painfully struggles, often with failure, to control his temper should take to heart God's evaluation of this struggle and be willing to pay the price necessary to succeed in it.

Although not as harmful to others, other uncontrolled emotions such as resentment, bitterness, and self-pity may be more destructive to ourselves and to our relationship to God. Uncontrolled temper is soon dissipated on others. Resentment, bitterness, and self-pity build up inside our hearts and eat away at our spiritual lives like a slowly spreading cancer.

All of these sinful inner emotions have in common a focus on self. They put our disappointments, our wounded pride, or our shattered dreams on the thrones of our hearts, where they become idols to us. We nurture resentment and bitterness, and we wallow in self-pity. Intellectually we know that in all things God works for our good, that nothing can separate us from His love. But in defiance of those God-given promises, we *choose* to think about that which is dishonoring to God and destructive of our own spiritual health.

Just as the apostle Paul beat his body (figuratively speaking, of course), so we must subdue our sinful emotions. We must deal decisively with them at their first appearance in

141

our thoughts. Keeping a tight rein on our emotions is just as necessary to godliness as keeping the appetites and desires of our bodies under control.

BREAKING THE CHAINS OF SELF-INDULGENCE

The emphasis in the struggle for self-control should be on the word *growing*. We will never fully attain self-control in all areas in this life. Furthermore, we must realize that the battle of self-control is different for each of us. One person may have no problem at all with bodily self-control, but he may struggle with thoughts of spiritual pride. Another may never be bothered with impure thoughts but may indulge his emotions in resentment or in self-pity. As we are tempted to judge others for their lack of self-control in areas where we have no problems, let us remember our own areas of struggle and be charitable in our opinions.

Sound judgment is the beginning of self-control, and the Bible is absolutely essential to its exercise. Sound judgment must be based on a thorough knowledge of God's standard, as revealed in the Scriptures, for our bodies, thoughts, and emotions. Years ago when I first began to grow as a Christian I read the quotation, "God's word will keep you from sin, or sin will keep you from God's word." This is not simply a cliché, nor is the Bible some magical wand to wave at temptation. It is sound judgment, growing out of reflection on the word of God, that warns us when the enemy of sinful desire is assailing the citadel of our hearts.

Sound judgment also enables us to form an accurate estimate of our particular needs in the area of self-control. Paul's admonition, "Think of yourself with sober judgment" (Romans 12:3), is good advice, not only for assessing our spiritual gifts, but also for assessing our spiritual needs. Proverbs 27:12 says, "The prudent see danger and take refuge." Spiritual prudence requires that we know ourselves—our particular weaknesses and vulnerabilities. Only as we study both the Scriptures and ourselves will we be able to exercise sound judgment.

Next, we must face the issue of whether we are truly willing to give up enjoying the fleeting pleasures of sin in return for knowing that our lives are pleasing to God. Kehl points out, "The beginning of self-mastery is to be mastered by Christ, to yield to his lordship. 'Wouldst thou have thy flesh obey thy spirit?' Augustine asked. 'Then let thy spirit obey thy God. Thou must be governed, that thou may'st govern.'"[5] Are you willing to acknowledge Jesus Christ as Lord of your appetites and desires, of your thoughts and emotions? If self-control begins with sound judgment, it must be carried forward by surrender to the authority of Christ in every area of our lives.

Then we must realize that the battle for self-control is fought primarily within our own minds; it is a battle with our own passions, thoughts, and desires. In those areas where we have failed to curb our appetites and emotions, we seem to have invisible antennae sensitively attuned to the corresponding temptations. The proverbial "chip on his shoulder" describes the person whose antenna is constantly searching for the minor incident that he can magnify into an occasion for losing his temper. The person who habitually yields to some bodily appetite or lust is constantly alert for opportunities to indulge that carnal desire. We must learn to say no to those passions when they first enter our minds.

Above all, we must pray for the inner strength of will necessary to curb our passions and desires. It is God who works in us to will and to act. Our own particular areas of vulnerability must be made the subject of earnest, beseeching prayer for God's grace to work in our wills. At the same time we must realize that the will is strengthened by obedience. The more we say no to sinful desires, the more we will *be able* to say no. But to experience this, we must persevere through many failures. A large part of learning self-control is breaking bad habits and replacing them with good ones. And this process always involves a certain amount of failure.

Finally, as Kehl points out, "True spiritual self-discipline holds believers in bounds but never in bonds; its effect is to enlarge, expand and liberate."[6] James describes the word of God as "the perfect law that gives freedom" (1:25). As we grow in the grace of self-control, we will experience the liberation of those who, under the guidance and grace of the Holy Spirit, are freed from the shackles of self-indulgence and are brought into the freedom of true spiritual discipline.

---

NOTES
1. Charles Bridges, *An Exposition of Proverbs* (1846; rpt.
   Evansville, Ind.: Sovereign Grace Book Club, 1959), page 483.
2. D. G. Kehl, *Control Yourself!* (Grand Rapids, Mich.: Zondervan
   Publishing House, 1982), page 25. This is an excellent book for
   those who want to pursue the subject of self-control further.
3. Bethune, *The Fruit of the Spirit*, page 179.
4. Charles Bridges, page 250.
5. Kehl, page 79.
6. Kehl, page 26.

# 12
# Faithfulness

*Many a man claims to have unfailing love,*
*but a faithful man who can find?*
Proverbs 20:6

Opening my concordance to the word *faithfulness*, I quickly ran my finger down the column and counted more than sixty references in the Bible to the faithfulness of God. It is not surprising that some forty of these instances occur in the book of Psalms, which recounts, more than any other book in the Bible, the struggles of the godly and their total dependence upon God's faithfulness.

Consider for a moment the absolute necessity of the faithfulness of God. We are dependent upon His faithfulness for our final salvation (1 Corinthians 1:8-9), for deliverance from temptation (1 Corinthians 10:13), for ultimate sanctification (1 Thessalonians 5:23), for the forgiveness of our sins (1 John 1:9), for deliverance through times of suffering (1 Peter 4:19), and for the fulfillment of our ultimate hope of eternal life (Hebrews 10:23). We can easily see that every aspect of the Christian life rests upon the faithfulness of

God, and we have the assurance, "The Lord is faithful to all his promises" (Psalm 145:13).

No wonder, then, that the psalmist says, in reflecting upon the faithfulness of God, "with my mouth I will make your faithfulness known through all generations. I will declare . . . that you established your faithfulness in heaven itself" (Psalm 89:1-2).

Even the prophet Jeremiah, in the midst of his lamentations over the judgment of God upon Judah, could still proclaim of God, "Great is your faithfulness" (Lamentations 3:23).

Actually, even a study of the sixty references to the faithfulness of God couldn't do justice to the subject: The entire Bible is a treatise on that theme. God's faithfulness appears in precept or illustration on almost every page. It is impossible to describe the acts of God without in some way touching upon His faithfulness to His own.

In our effort to become like God in our character, we must ensure that the grace of faithfulness is very high in our value system. This is not a natural virtue, as indicated by Solomon's lament, "Many a man claims to have unfailing love, but a faithful man who can find?" (Proverbs 20:6). Many people will profess faithfulness, but very few will demonstrate it. The virtue of faithfulness is often costly, and few people are willing to pay the price. But for the godly person, faithfulness is an absolutely essential quality of his character, regardless of what it might cost.

What is faithfulness? How do we practice it, and when do we exhibit it in our lives? The biblical word denotes that which is firm and can be counted upon. The dictionary defines *faithful* as "firm in adherence to promises or in observance of duty."[1] Some common synonyms are "dependable," "reliable," "trustworthy," and "loyal." The word also has the connotation of absolute honesty or integrity.

The faithful person is one who is dependable, trustworthy, and loyal, who can be depended upon in all of his relationships, and who is absolutely honest and ethical in all of his affairs. It was said of Daniel that his rivals "tried to find grounds for charges against Daniel in his conduct of government affairs, but they were unable to do so. They could find no corruption in him, because he was trustworthy [faithful] and neither corrupt nor negligent" (Daniel 6:4).

The words *corrupt* and *negligent* help us define, by contrast, what it means to be faithful in our daily affairs. The word *corrupt* is the opposite of "honest" or "ethical," and the word *negligent* is an antonym of such words as "careful," "thoughtful," and "considerate."

## ABSOLUTE HONESTY

Daniel was not corrupt; he was honest, ethical, and principled. Absolute honesty in speech and in personal affairs has to be the hallmark of a faithful person. The Scriptures tell us, "The Lord detests lying lips, but he delights in men who are truthful," and "The Lord abhors dishonest scales, but accurate weights are his delight" (Proverbs 12:22 and 11:1). The Lord detests lying and abhors dishonest business transactions. Not only are we commanded not to lie; we are also commanded not to deceive in any manner (Leviticus 19:11).

Lying has been defined as "any deceit: in word, act, attitude—or silence; in deliberate exaggerations, in distortions of the truth, or in creating false impressions."[2] We lie or deceive when we pretend to be something we are not; when as students we cheat on an examination, or as taxpayers we fail to report all of our income. My friend Jerry White writes of struggling over how much to tell a prospective buyer about a used car.[3] The issue of honesty pervades every area of our lives.

On Christmas Eve our doorbell rang, and when I answered it, I found a little four-year-old neighbor girl holding out a plate of cookies. "My mommy sent you some cookies," she said with a big smile. I thanked her and put the cookies down someplace—and promptly forgot about them, for we were just leaving for a Christmas Eve church service. A few days later as I was walking out to my car, the little girl came down the sidewalk on her tricycle. "Mr. Bridges, how'd you like the cookies?" she asked in great anticipation. "Oh, they were fine," I said, though I had not even tasted them.

As I drove away I began to think about what I had said. I had lied; there was no question about it. Why had I done it? Because it was expedient; it saved me embarrassment and the little girl disappointment (though mostly I was concerned about myself, not her). Sure, it was only a social lie, of little or no consequence. But it was a lie, and God says without qualification that He detests lying.

As I thought of that incident I began to realize it wasn't an isolated instance. The Holy Spirit reminded me of other occasions of seemingly innocent "social lying," of instances of exaggeration, or manipulating the facts of a story just a bit. I had to face the fact that I was not quite as honest as I had considered myself to be. God taught me a valuable, though humbling, lesson through that plate of cookies.

As I have told the story of the cookies to some audiences, I have gotten a troubled reaction from a few people. Some people, sincere Christians, think I may be nit-picking, going a bit too far in this matter of absolute honesty. But consider Daniel. The record states that his enemies could find no corruption in him. It seems clear that these government officials, from their bitter jealousy and utter hostility toward Daniel, would have seized upon any inconsistency, regardless of how small or insignificant, to bring Daniel into disrepute before King Darius. But they could find none. Daniel, like Elijah, was a man with a nature just like ours (James 5:17), but he had evidently mastered this matter of absolute integrity. We should have the same goal.

Think of the Lord Jesus. One day He asked His enemies, "Can any of you prove me guilty of sin?" (John 8:46). If Jesus had ever distorted the truth even a little bit, He could not have asked that question with such total confidence. We are called to be like Jesus—to be as absolutely honest as He was. How would Jesus have handled the little neighbor girl's question about the cookies? I don't know what He would have said. But one thing I know; He would not have lied. And neither should you or I.

Why do I go into such detail about absolute honesty in the social minutiae of life? Because this is where honesty begins. If we are careful to be honest in the little things, we will certainly be careful to be honest in the more important things of life. If we are honest about the cookies in our lives, we will certainly be honest in our business transactions, our college examinations, and even our sports competitions. As Jesus said, "He who is faithful in a very little thing is faithful also in much; and he who is unrighteous in a very little thing is unrighteous also in much" (Luke 16:10, NASB).

Our age desperately needs to reemphasize honesty in both its business transactions and its social intercourse. I recall reading an article in one of our leading business journals that quoted a number of executives as saying it was impossible to succeed in business today without compromising the truth. Probably the same attitude prevails in politics, sports, and every other aspect of our society. But we Christians are called to be salt in a putrefying society, and we cannot be such if we are not models of absolute honesty.

## UTTER DEPENDABILITY

Daniel was neither corrupt nor negligent: He was reliable and dependable. People could count on him. He undoubtedly was on time for his appointments, kept his commitments, honored his word, and considered how his actions might affect others.

Few things are more vexing than relying on someone who is not dependable. Solomon observed, "As vinegar to the teeth and smoke to the eyes, so is a sluggard to those who send him" (Proverbs 10:26). Though the term *sluggard* refers to a habitually lazy person, it is his unfaithfulness that makes him exasperating. We may be indifferent about a lazy person's habits if we do not have to rely on him. But if we are dependent upon his actions in any way, we see his slothful habits as unfaithfulness.

If our society needs to reemphasize the virtue of honesty, it certainly needs to place great importance on dependability. Dependability has taken a decided back seat to personal desire or convenience. "I'll keep that commitment if it's convenient," seems to be the attitude of our age. John Sanderson has perceptively observed,

> If we probe a bit deeper, we see that "unfaithfulness" is very close to "disobedience," for the man who disobeys God has cast himself loose from the only solid support a man can have, and his direction in life will be controlled by the shifting winds of circumstances and of his whimsical desire. . . . The man who is not controlled by God has no settled reason to keep his word or discharge his obligations.[4]

For the person who is practicing godliness, then, dependability is a duty owed not only to his fellow man, but more importantly to God. Reliability is not just a social obligation; it is a spiritual obligation. God is even more concerned about our faithfulness than the person who is relying on us in some particular situation.

In Psalm 15, David asks the question, "Lord, who may dwell in your sanctuary? Who may live on your holy hill?" There follows a list of ethical standards that a person must keep to enjoy God's fellowship. And in the middle of that list there is this standard: He "who keeps his oath even when it hurts." God wants us to be dependable even when it costs us. This is what distinguishes godly faithfulness from the ordinary dependability of secular society.

Consider the teenager who agrees to baby-sit for a neighbor on a given evening. Then a young man calls and invites her to the football game on that same night. What is she to do? Does she just simply cancel her baby-sitting arrangement and leave the neighbor to find someone else? The godly teenager will keep her commitment even when it hurts. Or, she might seek to find a substitute agreeable to the neighbor. In either case she feels a responsibility before God to honor her commitment and to fulfill her responsibility.

Lest I appear to be singling out teenagers as especially vulnerable to the temptation to treat commitments lightly, consider the businessman who enters into an agreement only to discover that it is quite to his disadvantage. What is he to do? The nonChristian is most apt to contact his lawyer to see if there is some legal loophole through which he can get out of the contract. Unfortunately, many Christians will seek the same relief. Not so the godly businessman. He may indeed see if there is some resolution to his dilemma that is acceptable to the other party. But he will not renege on his word just because it is legally possible to do so. He will keep his word even when it hurts.

Between these two extremes of the merely inconvenient baby-sitting engagement and the financially disastrous business agreement, there are numerous instances in which all of us make commitments that from time to time may prove costly to keep. At times such as these we especially need, by God's grace, to manifest the fruit of the Spirit that is faithfulness.

## UNSWERVING LOYALTY

The faithful person is not only honest and dependable, but also loyal. As an issue, loyalty arises most often in connection with our friends. The word has come to have a connotation of sticking with someone through thick and thin. There is perhaps no greater description of loyalty than Solomon's words, "A friend loves at all times, and a brother is born for adversity" (Proverbs 17:17).

There is no such person as a "fair-weather friend." If a person's loyalty doesn't insure his faithfulness to another in times of stress, then he really isn't a friend. He is simply using the other person to satisfy some of his own social needs.

King Saul's son, Jonathan, provides probably the best illustration of loyalty in the Bible. His loyal friendship with David almost cost him his life at the hands of his own father. Amazingly, Jonathan realized that his loyalty to David would, in the end, cost him the throne of Israel. Whether it be in honesty or dependability or loyalty, faithfulness is frequently a costly virtue. Only the Holy Spirit can enable us to pay that price.

There is a kind of loyalty that we must avoid, however: a so-called "blind loyalty." This kind refuses to admit the mistakes or faults of a friend, and it is actually a disservice. Proverbs tells us, "The kisses of an enemy may be profuse, but faithful are the wounds of a friend" (Proverbs 27:6). Only the truly faithful friend cares enough about you or me to undertake the often thankless task of pointing out where we are wrong. None of us enjoys being confronted with our faults or sins or mistakes, so we often make it difficult for our friends to do so. As a result, most of us are more concerned about speaking agreeableness to each other than about speaking the truth. This is *not* loyalty. Loyalty speaks the truth in faithfulness, but it also speaks it in love. Loyalty says, "I care enough about you that I will not allow you to continue unchecked in your wrong action or sinful attitude that will ultimately be harmful to you."

## MEETING GOD'S REQUIREMENT

As with the other graces of Christian character, the first step in growing in faithfulness is to acknowledge the biblical standard. Faithfulness entails absolute honesty, utter dependability, and unswerving loyalty. It is to be like Daniel: neither corrupt nor negligent. Develop convictions consistent with this standard based on the word of God. Plan to memorize one or more verses on the topic of faithfulness, either from the references cited in this chapter, or from others that may have come to your mind.

Second, evaluate your life with the aid of the Holy Spirit and perhaps a spouse or close friend. Do you seek to be scrupulously honest? Can others depend on you even when it is costly? Will you stick by your friend when he is in difficulty, and will you confront him in love when he is wrong? Don't be satisfied with generalities. Try to think of specific instances that either affirm your faithfulness or show you where you need to grow.

Where you see a specific need for faithfulness, make that both a matter of prayer for the aid of the Holy Spirit and the object of some concrete actions on your part. Remember that your working and His working are coextensive. You cannot become a faithful person merely by trying. There is a divine dimension. But it is also true that you will not become a faithful person without trying. Jesus said to the church in Smyrna, "Be faithful, even to the point of death" (Revelation 2:10). This is something we must do, even though it is at the same time the fruit of the Spirit.

Consider the reward for faithfulness. In the parable of the talents, the master replied, "Well done, good and faithful servant! You have been faithful with a few things; I will put you in charge of many things. Come and share your master's happiness!" (Matthew 25:21). It may be argued that the faithfulness here is in relation to God, rather than to one another, as we have been discussing in this chapter. That is indeed true. But faithfulness to God *includes* faithfulness to one another. That is the ultimate point of each of the Scripture passages we have considered. It is God who requires that we be faithful in all of our earthly relationships. So only if we seek to grow in the grace of faithfulness toward one another, will we have any hope of hearing Him say, "Well done, good and faithful servant."

---

NOTES

1. *Webster's New Collegiate Dictionary* (Springfield, Mass.: G. & C. Merriam, 1974).
2. As quoted in *Character of the Christian*, book 4 of the STUDIES IN CHRISTIAN LIVING series, 1st ed. (Colorado Springs: NavPress, 1964), page 26.
3. Jerry White, *Honesty Morality & Conscience* (Colorado Springs: NavPress, 1978, 1996), page 53. I highly recommend this book for further study on the topic of honesty.
4. Sanderson, *The Fruit of the Spirit*, page 117.

# 13
# Peace

*If it is possible, as far as it depends on you,
live at peace with everyone.*

Romans 12:18

Untold millions of dollars are spent annually in search of peace. Every year thousands of people seeking personal or family peace flock to professional counselors. Diplomats fly around the world pursuing peace between nations. Our court systems are jammed with cases arising from a breakdown of peace between individuals or corporations.

Christians are not exempt from this turmoil of a sinful world. We, too, experience the anxiety of disquieting circumstances and the anguish of broken relationships.

But peace should be a hallmark of the godly person, first because it is a Godlike trait: God is called the God of peace several times in the New Testament. He took the initiative to establish peace with rebellious men, and He is the author of both personal peace as well as peace among men. Peace should be part of our character also because God has promised us His peace, because He has commanded us to

155

let peace rule in our lives and relationships, and because peace is a fruit of the Spirit and therefore an evidence of His working in our lives.

A close look at Scripture reveals that peace is actually threefold:

- ❖ peace with God
- ❖ peace within ourselves
- ❖ peace with other people.

These are not three parallel but unrelated types of peace; rather, they are three different expressions of one peace—the peace that God gives, which is called the fruit of the Spirit. These different facets complement and reinforce one another, producing an overall character trait. Each aspect has unique characteristics that contribute in varying ways to the life of a man or woman of peace.

## PEACE WITH GOD

The basis of our peace with God is our justification by faith in Jesus Christ. Scripture says, "Therefore, since we have been justified through faith, we have peace with God through our Lord Jesus Christ" (Romans 5:1). This is the point at which all peace begins. We cannot have peace within or peace with other people until we first have peace with God.

Prior to our salvation, because we were born in sin, our relationship to God was characterized by alienation and enmity (Colossians 1:21). We were objects of His wrath, in a state of rebellion against Him. Even though the religious stupor in which we lived and the particular circumstances which surrounded us may have given us a false sense of peace, in reality we were "like the tossing sea, which cannot rest, whose waves cast up mire and mud," because, as God has said, "There is no peace for the wicked" (Isaiah 57:20-21).

Upon entering a personal relationship with God through faith in Jesus Christ, however, all this changes. Instead of being opposed to us, God is now for us. Instead of leaving us to the mercy of circumstances, He promises to work in all of them for our good (Romans 8:28). Proverbs 16 tells us that He even promises to make our enemies live at peace with us.

Peace with God, then, is the foundation of peace within ourselves and peace with other people. This foundation does not guarantee, of course, that these other aspects of peace occur automatically. We must pursue what makes for peace, both within and without, in dependence upon the Holy Spirit, realizing that the fruit of peace is His fruit, not ours.

## PERSONAL PEACE

One of the petty offenses for which we arrest people is disturbing the peace. Even though a Christian has experienced peace *with* God, there are certain "disturbers of the peace" that keep him from experiencing the peace *of* God. Like the noisy or quarrelsome offenses against society, these disturbers are often petty in nature. The more calamitous events in our lives usually force us to turn to the Lord with all our hearts, and, in so doing, we experience His grace and peace. But the more ordinary adversities of life rob us of peace because we have a tendency to try to deal with these events ourselves. We worry, fret, and scheme over distressing circumstances, and we envy or resent other people who appear to get a better deal in life, or who mistreat us in some way.

As Jesus finished talking to His disciples on the evening of His betrayal, He concluded with these words: "I have told you these things, so that in me you may have peace. In this world you will have trouble. But take heart! I have overcome the world" (John 16:33). In this assurance of peace Jesus made two promises.

His first promise was that we will have trouble in the world. The same circumstances that rob us of our joy also rob us of our peace. The common denominator of all these circumstances is uncertainty. A loved one is ill, and the diagnosis is uncertain. Or our car breaks down while on a trip; will we have enough money to pay for repairs and perhaps extra meals and lodging? How will we get to our destination in time? Our luggage fails to arrive with us on an airline flight. Will we ever see it again? What will we do until it is returned to us? These and countless other circumstances continue to prove that Jesus was indeed correct when He promised us that we will have trouble in the world.

But the second promise that Jesus made was just as correct. He has overcome the world. Ephesians 1:22 tells us that "God placed all things under his feet and appointed him to be the head over everything for the church"; that is, Jesus has been appointed head over everything *on behalf* of the church. He has power over all the universe, and He exercises it on our behalf and for our good. In Matthew 10:29-31, Jesus tells us that not even a sparrow can fall to the ground apart from the will of our Father. And even the very hairs of our head are all numbered. No detail is too small or minute that it escapes the Father's eye and attention. And now Jesus in His ascended glory exercises that same watchful care on our behalf.

So why do we worry? Because we do not believe. We are not really convinced that the same Jesus who can keep a sparrow in the air knows where our lost luggage is, or how we are going to pay that auto repair bill, or how we can get to our destination on time. Or if we believe that He *can* deliver us through our difficulties, we doubt if He *will*. We let Satan sow seeds of doubt in our minds about His love and care for us.

Two passages of Scripture will prove most helpful to us

in coming to Him to find peace. The first is Philippians 4:6-7: "Do not be anxious about anything, but in everything, by prayer and petition, with thanksgiving, present your requests to God. And the peace of God, which transcends all understanding, will guard your hearts and your minds in Christ Jesus." The great antidote to anxiety is to come to God in prayer. We are to pray about *everything*. Nothing is too big for Him to handle, and nothing is too small to escape His attention.

Paul also declares that we are to come to God with thanksgiving. We should thank Him for His past faithfulness in delivering us from troubles (remembrance of past mercies is a great stimulus to present faith). We should thank Him for the fact that He is in control of every single circumstance of our lives, and that nothing can touch us that He does not allow. We should thank Him that in His infinite wisdom He is able to work in this circumstance for our good, and that because of His love, He would not have allowed it if it were not for our good. Finally, we can thank Him that He will not allow us to be tempted (either a seduction to evil, or a trial of our faith; both ideas are included in the word) beyond what we can bear (1 Corinthians 10:13).

The result promised to us when we come to God in prayer with thanksgiving is not deliverance, but the peace of God. One of the reasons we don't find this peace is because all too often we will not settle for anything other than deliverance *from* the trouble. But God, through Paul, promises us peace, a peace that is unexplainable. It transcends all understanding. And, says Paul, it will guard our hearts and minds against the anxiety to which you and I are so prone.

Now if you are like me, you are probably thinking, "That all sounds very nice, and I agree with you intellectually right now. But when I am in the midst of a trying situation, I really don't experience that peace. What's wrong?"

I suggest two steps to take when in this kind of dilemma. First, examine your motives—you may want deliverance instead of peace. Are you looking for the wrong answer? Second, look to the Holy Spirit to bring you that peace. Remember, peace is the fruit of the Spirit. It is His work to produce peace within you. Your responsibility is to come in prayer, asking for the peace, and looking to Him for it.

I doubt that any Christian is more vulnerable to worry and fretfulness than I am. I sympathize with others who are also prone to anxiety. I am well aware that it is only by the power of the Holy Spirit that we can experience His peace. But God tells us in His word that His peace is available, and we must not be content until we experience it. We must persevere in prayer until He answers.

In addition to Philippians 4:6-7, a second passage of Scripture that can help us deal with anxiety is 1 Peter 5:7-9: "Cast all your anxiety on him because he cares for you." In the next verse Peter tells us to be alert to the devil, who prowls around looking for someone to devour. One of the many ways in which the devil tries to devour us is related to the meaning of his name. The Greek word for devil means "accuser," or "slanderer." As the prince of slanderers, he accuses man before God, but he also slanders God to man. One of the thoughts that often enters our minds when we are undergoing some trial is, "If God really loved me He would not have allowed this to happen to me." Or, "If God loved me, He would provide a way out of this trying situation."

Such thoughts come from the devil; failure to recognize this origin causes two problems. First, we assume those thoughts originate within our own hearts, so we add a sense of guilt for thinking harsh thoughts about God to our already anxious mind. Now we have both anxiety and guilt to contend with, compounding our problem. Second, we fight the wrong battle. Instead of resisting the devil, we try to deal with our own wicked hearts. Although there are plenty of times when we do have to deal with our own wicked hearts, this is not one of them: this is a time to resist the devil. We have a very clear command, coupled with a promise: "Resist the devil, and he will flee from you" (James 4:7).

This is the Bible's solution to a lack of peace within our-selves: Take our anxieties to God in thankful prayer, and resist the devil when he slanders God to us. Only when we have experienced peace *with* God, through bringing our anxieties to Him, are we able to deal with the third aspect of peace: peace with other people. Inner conflict and turmoil often result in conflict with others, so we must achieve inner peace to effectively pursue peace with others.

PEACE WITH MEN
When Paul listed peace as one of nine traits of the fruit of the Spirit, he was probably thinking primarily of peace with other people. He had already warned the Galatians against "biting and devouring each other" (Galatians 5:15). And in his list of the acts of the sinful nature, immediately preced-ing his list of the fruit of the Spirit, those actions that are totally opposite to peace are predominant: hatred, discord, jealousy, fits of rage, selfish ambition, dissensions, factions, and envy. As he began to list traits of godly character that the Galatians needed to keep foremost in mind, peace with one another must have been near the top of his list.

The importance of this aspect of peace is amply evident from major references to it in the New Testament. Here are just a few:

Blessed are the peacemakers. (Matthew 5:9)

As far as it depends on you, live at peace with every-one. (Romans 12:18)

Make every effort to do what leads to peace.
(Romans 14:19)

Let the peace of Christ rule in your hearts, since as
members of one body you were called to peace.
(Colossians 3:15)

Make every effort to live in peace with all men.
(Hebrews 12:14)

Whoever would love life and see good days . . . must
seek peace and pursue it. (1 Peter 3:10-11)

Three times in these references we are exhorted to
"make every effort" toward, or "pursue," peace. The Greek
word used here also means "persecute," conveying the idea
of intense effort or vigilance in tracking down something in
order to harass and torment. In a positive sense, it means
single-minded pursuit: to leave no stone unturned in our
efforts, to lay ourselves out and to humble ourselves, if need
be, in order to achieve the goal of peace with others.

The pursuit of peace does not include an easygoing,
peace-at-any-price kind of attitude; it does not include capit-
ulating to wrong or injustice just for the sake of maintaining
appearances. That kind of behavior often leads instead to
strife within ourselves. The conflicts that are disturbing our
peace with others must be courageously but graciously faced
and dealt with. Pursuing peace does not mean running away
from the causes of discord.

Let's consider some practical, biblical steps we can take
to pursue peace in conflicts with other believers:

First, *We must remember that we are fellow members
of the same body*. Paul says, "The body is a unit, though it is
made up of many parts; and though all its parts are many,

they form one body. So it is with Christ" (1 Corinthians 12:12). Farther on in the same chapter he says the goal is "so that there should be no division in the body, but that its parts should have equal concern for each other" (verse 25). It is incredible that different parts of the same body could be at war among themselves! I am convinced that there would be much less disharmony and conflict among believers if we constantly kept in mind that we are members of the same body.

Paul puts it even more strongly in Romans 12:5: "each member belongs to all the others." Not only are we members of the same body, but we *belong* to one another. That person with whom you have difficulty maintaining peace belongs to you, and you belong to him. What a contradiction to the unity of the body when there is discord among its members.

Not only must we remember that we are fellow members of one body, *We must also keep in mind that it is Christ's body of which we are members*. It is *His* glory—and the honor of *His* church—that is at stake in our relationships with one another. Few things are as dishonoring to the cause of Christ as Christians quarreling among themselves. Yet we expel people from our fellowship for adultery, while we tolerate discord between ourselves and other believers. We have failed to understand and obey the biblical imperative to "make every effort to do what leads to peace."

Third, *We must recognize that the cause of discord often lies wholly or partly with us*. We must seek a genuine spirit of humility about our own responsibility rather than entirely blaming the other person. On occasion, I have been an observer to discord between believers in which both parties wholly blamed the other for the conflict. Neither was willing to accept any responsibility for a misunderstanding.

As we pursue peace we must be prepared to face up to and acknowledge to the other party any wrong attitude, action, or words on our part.

Finally, *We must take the initiative to restore peace.* Jesus taught that it makes no difference whether you have wronged your brother or he has wronged you. Either way, *you* are always responsible to initiate efforts toward peace (see Matthew 5:23-24 and 18:15). If we are serious about intently pursuing peace, we won't be concerned about which of us is the offending party. We will have one goal: to restore peace in a godly manner. Unresolved conflict between believers is sin and must be treated as such; otherwise, it will spread throughout the body like cancer until it requires radical spiritual surgery. Far better to deal with it when it is easily contained.

There may be times, however, when you have pursued peace to no avail. The Bible recognizes that possibility (Romans 12:18), but be sure you have done all you can to restore peace.

The "going to your brother" of Matthew 5 and Matthew 18 relates to conflict among believers; pursuing peace with unbelievers requires a somewhat different approach. Obviously, we are not members of one body. We do not share the work of the Holy Spirit in enabling us to restore peace. How, then, should we handle conflict with unbelievers?

First, *If we have offended an unbeliever, it is our responsibility to take steps to restore peace.* Sometimes this is more humbling than going to a believer to acknowledge a wrong; the unbeliever is not as apt to respond in a gracious and forgiving manner. But humbling or not, we must do this if we are to maintain a Christian testimony.

What should we do, however, when the unbeliever wrongs us? When there is no common bond, no fellowship to be restored, no mutual presence of the Holy Spirit to aid in restoration, then we tend to think in terms of revenge—if not in action, at least in our thoughts.

I believe Romans 12:17-21 provides the answer. As we look at this passage we see that first, *We are to do everything we possibly can to maintain peace*, as far as it depends on us.

Second, *We are in no way to seek revenge*. We are not to repay evil for evil; we are to leave the matter of justice in the hands of God. So often when we have been wronged, or think we have been wronged, we imagine getting even with the other person. We don't *intend* to take revenge, but we actually do it in our minds. Such an attitude is clearly contrary to Scripture. Verse 19 says that it is God's prerogative to mete out justice; His judgment alone is always according to the truth. He alone knows all the facts and all the motives behind them.

As we are willing to leave justice with God, we have His assurance that He will repay. God is a God of infinite justice; no wrong inflicted on us ever goes unnoticed by Him. Although we may never be aware of the repayment, we do have God's promise of it.

Of course, our goal with regard to an offending unbeliever should not be a desire for revenge, either God's revenge or ours. The purpose of God's assurance of justice here is not to satisfy our own sense of justice, but to remove it as a consideration from our minds. God in effect is saying, "Don't concern yourself with justice. Leave that to me. You concern yourself with something else: winning over the offending unbeliever." We can win him over, or at least make an effort to do so, by repaying evil with good. However we may understand the expression "heap burning coals on his head" (verse 20), it seems clear that our intent should be to win him over.

Because peace is a fruit of the Spirit, we are dependent upon the Spirit's work in our lives to produce the desire and the means to pursue peace. But we are also responsible to use the means He has given us and to take all practical steps to attain both peace within and peace with others.

Commit to memory such passages of Scripture as Philippians 4:6-7, 1 Peter 5:7, Romans 12:18, or any others you find especially helpful. Begin to meditate upon them and ask the Holy Spirit to bring them to your mind on the next occasion in which you especially need to follow their teaching. Remember that practicing godliness involves spiritual exercise—meditating upon and applying God's word under the direction of our teacher, the Holy Spirit.

# 14

# Patience

❧

*Clothe yourselves with . . . patience. Bear with each*
*other and forgive whatever grievances you may*
*have against one another.*

Colossians 3:12-13

❧

Christian character is like a single garment woven from
threads of varying colors and shades. From a distance
the garment appears to be a single color, but closer examination reveals that it takes a combination of different col-
ored threads to produce the overall effect. The casual
observer is not too concerned with those various threads; he
notices and appreciates the garment's overall effect. But the
creator of that cloth has to consider each thread individually,
ensuring that the right shades and colors correctly follow
the pattern of the design.

Some of the traits of godly character appear to blend
together much as different shades of thread in a garment or
colors in a rainbow. Patience, for example, closely resembles
joy and peace in its effect upon our lives. The word *patience*,
as we use it in everyday speech, actually stands for several
different words in the New Testament, and is used to

describe a godly reaction to a variety of situations. These different words and usages blend together to produce an overall quality.

The truly patient Christian must display godly patience in all of the various circumstances requiring it. Just as the designer and weaver of a beautiful cloth must consider each thread individually, so the Christian who desires to grow in patience must give attention to each facet of this quality as it applies to his life.

## SUFFERING MISTREATMENT

One aspect of patience involves enduring abuse. The biblical response to suffering at the hands of others is called *longsuffering* in the *King James Version*, and that rendering perhaps best describes its meaning. This aspect of patience is the ability to suffer a long time under the mistreatment of others without growing resentful or bitter. The occasions for exercising this quality are numerous; they vary from malicious wrongs all the way to seemingly innocent practical jokes. They include ridicule, scorn, insults, and undeserved rebukes, as well as outright persecution. The Christian who is the victim of office politics or organizational power plays must react with long-suffering. The believing husband or wife who is rejected or mistreated by an unbelieving spouse needs this kind of patience.

The apostle Paul especially stressed the need for long-suffering in the life of a godly person. He mentions it in his first letter to the Corinthians, in his list of qualities that characterize love. He includes it as one of the nine traits which he calls the fruit of the Spirit in Galatians. When he describes to the Ephesians a life worthy of God's calling, he includes the trait of long-suffering. He also includes it when he gives the Colossians a list of godly qualities with which Christians should clothe themselves. He stresses it to the Thessalonians, and commends his own life to the Corinthians and to Timothy partly because patience is one of his character traits.

How can we grow in this aspect of patience, that suffers long under the ill-treatment of others? First, we must consider the *justice* of God. In his instructions to slaves who needed to be patient under the unjust treatment of harsh masters, Peter tells them to follow the example of Christ: "When they hurled their insults at him, he did not retaliate; when he suffered, he made no threats. Instead, he entrusted himself to him who judges justly" (1 Peter 2:23). Note that the opposite of retaliation is to entrust ourselves to God, who judges justly. God's justice is absolute, and, as Paul reminds us in Romans 12:19, He promises us, "I will repay."

One of the thoughts that most disturbs a suffering Christian who has not learned patience is this issue of justice. He is concerned that his tormentor will escape justice, that he will not receive the punishment he deserves. The patient Christian who suffers leaves this issue in the hands of God. He is confident that God will render justice, though he knows that this may not occur until the time of our Lord's return (2 Thessalonians 1:6-7). Instead of hoping and waiting for an opportunity for revenge, he prays for God's forgiveness of his tormentors, just as Jesus and the martyr Stephen prayed for their executioners.

To develop patience in the face of mistreatment by others, we must also develop a conviction about the *faithfulness* of God to work on our behalf. Peter tells us that "those who suffer according to God's will should commit themselves to their faithful Creator and continue to do good" (1 Peter 4:19). We should entrust ourselves to God's justice and commit ourselves to His faithfulness. God will deal not only in justice (and we pray, in mercy) with our tormentor, but also in faithfulness with us.

Joseph exemplified such a commitment to the faithfulness of God. After he had been abused by his brothers, he was able to say to them, "You intended to harm me, but God intended it for good to accomplish what is now being done, the saving of many lives" (Genesis 50:20). God can and does take the deliberately harmful acts of others and turn them into acts for good, both for us and for others. The person who is patient under mistreatment by others is the person who has developed such a confidence in the wisdom, power, and faithfulness of God that he willingly entrusts his circumstances into His hands.

RESPONDING TO PROVOCATION

The aspect of patience that is called long-suffering is also used to describe the response of the godly person to provocation by others. I use the word *provocation* to denote those actions of others that tend to arouse our anger or wrath—that cause us to lose our temper. Unlike mistreatment by others, which is often out of our control, provocation finds us in a position of power to do something about it. It may come in the form of defiance of our authority—a parent, teacher, or supervisor on a job—or it may be a deliberate goading or nagging of us. Whatever form the action takes, it is often deliberate, and we are in a position to retaliate or punish swiftly and harshly.

When we exercise patience under provocation we are emulating God Himself. In Exodus 34:6-7, God describes Himself as "slow to anger . . . forgiving wickedness, rebellion and sin." Daily, God bears with great patience the provocation of sinful, rebellious men who despise His authority and ignore or show contempt for His law. It is to these very people that Paul addresses the question, "Do you show contempt for the riches of his kindness, tolerance and patience?" (Romans 2:4). They despise not only His authority, but His patience. And yet God continues to show the *riches* of His patience to those who least deserve it.

The key to patience under provocation is to seek to develop God's own trait of being "slow to anger." James tells us to be "slow to become angry" (James 1:19). Paul says that one characteristic of love is that it is not "easily angered" (1 Corinthians 13:5).

The best way to develop this slowness to anger is to reflect frequently on the patience of God toward us. The parable of the unmerciful servant (Matthew 18:21-35) is designed to help us recognize our own need of patience toward others by recognizing the patience of God toward us. In this parable, the unmerciful servant was deeply indebted to his master—according to the *New International Version*, by several million dollars. The king of the parable obviously represents God, while the deeply indebted servant represents each of us in our relationship to God as sinners. As the parable develops, the first servant is completely forgiven of his huge debt. But just after he leaves the presence of his master, he finds a fellow servant who owes him only a few dollars, and impatiently demands payment—even having the man thrown into prison.

We are like the unmerciful servant when we lose our patience under provocation. We ignore God's extreme patience with us. We discipline our children out of anger, while God disciplines us out of love. We are eager to punish the person who provokes us, while God is eager to forgive. We are eager to exercise our authority, while God is eager to exercise His love.

This kind of patience does not ignore the provocations of others; it simply seeks to respond to them in a godly manner. It enables us to control our tempers when we are provoked and to seek to deal with the person and his provocation in a way that tends to heal relationships rather than aggravate problems. It seeks the ultimate good of the other individual, rather than the immediate satisfaction of our own aroused emotions.

The person whose temperament is conducive to losing his temper must especially work at patience under provocation. Rather than excusing himself by saying, "that's just the way I am," he must acknowledge his quick temper as a sinful habit before God. He should meditate extensively upon such verses as Exodus 34:6, 1 Corinthians 13:5, and James 1:19. He must also pray earnestly that God the Holy Spirit will change him inwardly. He should apologize to the person who is the object of his outburst *each time* he loses his temper. (This helps him develop humility and a sense of his own sinfulness before God.) Finally, he must not become discouraged when he fails. He needs to realize that his problem is as much a sinful habit as it is a result of temperament. Habits are not easily broken, and there will be failure. But, in the words of Proverbs 24:16 (TEV), "No matter how often an honest man falls, he always gets up again. . . ."

## TOLERATING SHORTCOMINGS

It is likely that most of us have occasion to show patience toward the faults and failures of others more often than we do toward mistreatment or provocation from others. People are always behaving in ways that, though not directed against us, affect us and irritate or disappoint us. It may be the driver ahead of us who is driving too slowly, or the friend who is late for an appointment, or the neighbor who is inconsiderate. More often than not it is the unconscious action of some family member whose irritating habit is magnified because of close daily association. The kind of patience it takes to overlook these circumstances is probably demanded of us most often within our own families or Christian fellowships.

Impatience with the shortcomings of others often has its roots in pride. John Sanderson observes, "Hardly a day passes but one hears sneering remarks about the stupidity, the awkwardness, the ineptitude of others."[1] Such remarks stem from a feeling that we are smarter or more capable than those with whom we are impatient. Even if that is actually true, Paul tells us in 1 Corinthians 4:7 that whatever abilities we possess have been given to us by God, so we have no reason to feel that we are any better than anyone else.

The patient reaction to the faults and failures of others is probably best described by the word *forbearance*, as it is used in Ephesians 4:2 and Colossians 3:13 (KJV). Literally, the word can mean "to put up with" and can be used in a negative sense of grudging endurance of another's faults. That is obviously *not* the sense in which Paul uses the word. Rather, he uses forbearance in the sense of gracious tolerance of another's faults. Since forbearance is not a common word in the daily vocabulary of most people, the word *tolerance* is probably best used to describe this aspect of patience.

Forbearance or tolerance in the Scriptures is associated with love, the unity of the believers, and the forgiveness of Christ. In Ephesians 4:2-3 Paul says, "Be completely humble and gentle; be patient, *bearing with one another in love*. Make every effort to keep the unity of the Spirit through the bond of peace." Peter tells us that "love covers over a multitude of sins"; love for the other person causes us to overlook or tolerate his shortcomings.

I recall an instance when a friend of mine forgot an appointment we had together. Rather than being peeved, I simply shrugged it off. Later I tried to determine why I had had such a tolerant reaction to his failure. I concluded it was because I deeply loved and appreciated this person, and the principle that Peter stated—"love covers over a multitude of sins"—was at work.

Paul says we are to bear with one another in order to preserve the "unity of the Spirit"—the unity applied by the Spirit to the body of Christ. We are to *make every effort* to maintain this unity. We are to consider the unity of the body far more important than the petty irritants or disappointments of others. Again, as in maintaining peace, Romans 12:5 is very helpful: "each member belongs to all the others." When I am tempted to become irritated with my brother in Christ, remembering that he belongs to me, and that I belong to him, helps quell that budding sense of exasperation.

In Colossians 3:13 Paul equates forbearance with forgiveness: "Bear with each other and forgive whatever grievances you may have against one another." The thought of grievances or complaints used in this verse seems to connote the idea of fault-finding with petty actions rather than concern over more serious problems. Instead of letting those actions irritate us, we are to use them as an opportunity to forgive as the Lord forgave us.

The principle of forgiving as the Lord forgave us is taught in the parable of the unmerciful servant. The main point of that parable lies in the tremendous contrast between the two debts: several million dollars versus a few dollars. Jesus also makes a point of the timing of the two encounters: the unmerciful servant, fresh from the forgiving presence of his master, turns around and harshly demands immediate payment from his debtor.

How well this parable depicts us when we are impatient with others! Every day God patiently bears with us, and every day we are tempted to become impatient with our friends, neighbors, and loved ones. And our faults and failures before God are so much more serious than the petty actions of others that tend to irritate us! God calls us to graciously bear with the weaknesses of others, tolerating them and forgiving them even as He has forgiven us.

Such scriptural forbearance does not forbid correcting another's faults or confronting someone about an irritating habit. Rather, Jesus teaches us that such correction should be done with the right attitude. We are not to seek to remove the speck of sawdust—that irritating habit or fault—from our brother's eye until we have first removed the plank from our own eye. The plank in our eye can be any wrong attitude toward our brother that is a reaction to his fault or weakness. It may be irritation, pride, or a critical or disdainful attitude. Whatever our wrong attitude may be, we must first deal with it, making sure our desire to correct or confront is not from a spirit of impatience, but from a spirit of love and concern for the welfare of the other person.

WAITING ON GOD

Another area in which most of us need to learn patience is in the outworking of God's timetable in our lives. Perhaps we have been praying for many years for the salvation of a loved one, for the resolution of some problem we face, or for the fulfillment of some long-awaited desire. Abraham's long wait for the birth of his son, Isaac, is the classic biblical illustration of the need for patience to await God's timing. Like Abraham, many of us have attempted to speed up God's timetable or to substitute another solution as Sarah and Abraham did with Ishmael, only to end up with sorrow instead of fulfillment.

Saul is another example of one who would not wait for the fulfillment of God's timetable, and for this he lost his kingdom. Both Abraham and Saul grew impatient because of unbelief in the faithfulness of God and an unwillingness to wait on Him. God, in His sovereign grace, gave Abraham another chance and so he became the father of those who believe.

In contrast to Saul, David waited for the Lord to fulfill

His plan for him. He consistently refused to take matters into his own hands, instead saying,

> I waited patiently for the Lord;
>   he turned to me and heard my cry.
> He lifted me out of the slimy pit,
>   out of the mud and mire;
> he set my feet on a rock
>   and gave me a firm place to stand. (Psalm 40:1-2)

James addresses the problem of waiting by referring first to the patience of the farmer who waits for his crop, then to the patience of the prophets who all died without seeing the fulfillment of most of their prophecies, and finally to the patience of Job, who in the end did experience the Lord's deliverance. The ultimate event for which we all wait, of course, is the Lord's coming. With the apostle John, we cry in our hearts, "Come, Lord Jesus" (Revelation 22:20).

The cure for impatience with the fulfillment of God's timetable is to believe His promises, obey His will, and leave the results to Him. So often when God's timetable stretches into years we become discouraged and give up. I think of a desire of mine that I thought God would soon fulfill. When several years went by, I virtually gave up, but in the seventh year, God answered that prayer. I think of another answer to prayer that has occurred just recently. I had been praying for that request for so many years that when the answer finally came, I felt it was too good to be true. I think of still another God-given desire that I prayed over for some thirteen years before God answered. But when He did, the answer came in abundant measure.

Yet in spite of these long-awaited answers to prayers, I still struggle with impatience over God's timetable. I still want to give up or try to work something out on my own. I need to take to heart this admonition of the writer of Hebrews: "We do not want you to become lazy, but to imitate those who through faith and patience inherit what has been promised" (6:12). If you struggle, as I do, with the patience of waiting, that might be a good verse for you to memorize and meditate over in the months ahead.

PERSEVERING THROUGH ADVERSITY

Whereas long-suffering should be our patient reaction to *people* who mistreat or provoke us, endurance and perseverance should be our patient reaction to *circumstances* that try us. *Endurance* is the ability to stand up under adversity; *perseverance* is the ability to progress in spite of it. These two English words are translations of the same Greek word and simply represent two different views of the same quality: a godly response to adversity.

The source of adversity may be the ill-treatment of other people, as when Joseph's brothers sold him into slavery, or when Saul persecuted David, or when the Jews rejected and crucified the Lord Jesus. At other times our trials are a result of Satan's attacks, as in Job's case. Still another source of adversity is the direct disciplinary hand of God in our lives.

Whatever the source of our adverse circumstances, the key to endurance and patience is to believe that God is ultimately in control, working out events for our good. Romans 15:4 says, "For everything that was written in the past was written to teach us, so that through endurance and the encouragement of the Scriptures we might have hope." The stories of Abraham, Jacob, Joseph, David, and Job were written so that we might have the privilege of seeing God at work, controlling their circumstances for their good and His glory. These examples should encourage us to believe that God controls our circumstances as well, even though we do not always recognize this control. For many years it has helped me to realize that God never explained to Job why his trials had occurred. You and I are taken behind the scenes and shown the battle between God and Satan. But Job never knew. He simply came to the place where he accepted whatever God allowed. Most often, we do not see the purpose of trials. But through the encouragement of the Scriptures we should hope, and through hope we should persevere.

Endurance and perseverance are frequently associated with hope in the Scriptures. In each of four instances in which Paul speaks of perseverance or endurance in Romans, it is in the context of hope. He commends the Thessalonian believers for their endurance inspired by hope. And the entire treatment of endurance and perseverance by the writer of Hebrews closely links endurance and perseverance with hope (see especially chapters 10–12). Hebrews 11, the great chapter on faith, is a part of this lengthy challenge to endurance and perseverance; it begins by defining faith as "being sure of what we hope for and certain of what we do not see."

The object of this hope, of course, is our ultimate glorification with Christ in eternity. The life we live on this earth is simply a pursuit of this hope. The author of Hebrews likens it to a distance race which must be run with perseverance. Our Christian experience is not a sprint that is soon over; it is a distance race that lasts a lifetime. It requires perseverance, because the reward—the object of our hope—is in the distant future.

Endurance and perseverance are also frequently associated with suffering in the Bible. We may not like this connection, because we may shrink from the suffering, but we must come to terms with it. Endurance can be produced only under stress, whether physical or spiritual. In Romans, Paul says suffering produces perseverance. James says trials that test our faith develop perseverance. Endurance and perseverance are qualities we would all like to possess, but we are loath to go through the process that produces them. That is why God is so faithful to allow or to bring trials into our lives, even though we shrink from them.

So we see that God uses the encouragement of the Scriptures, the hope of our ultimate salvation in glory, and the trials that He either sends or allows to produce endurance and perseverance. He also works directly in our hearts. In Romans 15:5, Paul tells us that God gives endurance and encouragement. We know from verse 4 that God uses the Scriptures, but He must also work directly, making those Scriptures meaningful and personally applicable to us. When Paul prayed that the Colossians would have great endurance and patience, he was counting upon God to work directly in their hearts. We cannot explain this direct ministry in the heart of the believer, but that does not make it any less valid. The Bible constantly affirms this direct ministry of the Spirit of God (for example, see Romans 8:26-27, 2 Corinthians 1:3-4, and Ephesians 3:16-19).

The fruit of patience in all its aspects—long-suffering, forbearance, endurance, and perseverance—is a fruit that is most intimately associated with our devotion to God. All character traits of godliness grow out of and have their foundation in our devotion to God, but the fruit of patience must grow out of that relationship in a particular way. Only as we fear God will we submit to the trials He sends or allows. And only as we deeply apprehend His love for us in Christ will we find the courage to bear up under them. Trials always change our relationship with God. Either they drive us to Him, or they drive us away from Him. The extent of our fear of Him and our awareness of His love for us determine in which direction we will move.

---

NOTE
1. Sanderson, *The Fruit of the Spirit*, page 90.

# 15
# Gentleness

*The fruit of the Spirit is . . . gentleness.*
Galatians 5:22-23

*Clothe yourselves with . . . gentleness.*
Colossians 3:12

We pray for patience, we pray for love, we pray for purity and self-control. But who of us ever prays for the grace of gentleness? Writing in the year 1839, George Bethune said, "Perhaps no grace is less prayed for, or less cultivated than gentleness. Indeed it is considered rather as belonging to natural disposition or external manners, than as a Christian virtue; and seldom do we reflect that not to be gentle is sin."[1]

The Christian attitude toward gentleness does not seem to have changed in the more than 140 years since Bethune penned those words. I once asked a coworker in our own ministry if he was aware of anyone who was praying for or seeking to cultivate gentleness. He thought for a moment, and said no. This is not to say that the grace of gentleness is entirely absent from the Christian community; but perhaps we don't value it as highly as God values it.

Gentleness is somewhat difficult to define, because it is

often confused with meekness, which is another Christian virtue that we should pursue. Billy Graham defines gentleness as "mildness in dealing with others . . . it displays a sensitive regard for others and is careful never to be unfeeling for the rights of others."[2] Gentleness is an active trait, describing the manner in which we should treat others. Meekness is a passive trait, describing the proper Christian response when others mistreat us.

Gentleness is illustrated by the way we would handle a carton of exquisite crystal glasses; it is the recognition that the human personality is valuable but fragile, and must be handled with care.

Both gentleness and meekness are born of power, not weakness. There is a pseudo-gentleness that is effeminate, and there is a pseudo-meekness that is cowardly. But a Christian is to be gentle and meek because those are Godlike virtues. Isaiah 40 is a chapter that describes both the power and the tenderness of God:

> See, the Sovereign Lord comes with power. . . .
> (verse 10)

> Surely the nations are like a drop in a bucket; they are regarded as dust on the scales; he weighs the islands as though they were fine dust. (verse 15)

> "To whom will you compare me? Or who is my equal?" says the Holy One.
> Lift your eyes and look to the heavens:
> Who created all these?
> He who brings out the starry host one by one,
> and calls them each by name.
> Because of his great power and mighty strength,
> not one of them is missing. (verses 25-26)

Tucked in the middle of this description of God's power are these words:

> He tends his flock like a shepherd:
>     He gathers the lambs in his arms
> and carries them close to his heart;
>     he gently leads those that have young. (verse 11)

The same passage that stresses the infiniteness of God's power also beautifully portrays His gentleness. What better illustrates gentleness than a shepherd carrying his lambs close to his heart? Yet the Holy Spirit uses this word picture, framed with illustrations of sovereign power, to describe God. We should never be afraid, therefore, that the gentleness of the Spirit means weakness of character. It takes strength, God's strength, to be truly gentle.

An interesting and enlightening variation between translations of a phrase in Psalm 18:35 helps define true gentleness. The *New American Standard Bible* and the *King James Version* translate David's declaration, "Thy *gentleness* makes me great." The *New International Version* renders it, "You *stoop down* to make me great." Gentleness is stooping down to help someone. God continually stoops down to help us, and He wants us to do the same—to be sensitive to the rights and feelings of others.

THE GENTLENESS OF CHRIST
Paul appealed to the Corinthian Christians "by the meekness and gentleness of Christ" (2 Corinthians 10:1). How does the New Testament describe the gentleness of Christ?

A familiar passage provides a picture of Christ's gentleness:

> Come to me, all you who are weary and burdened,
> and I will give you rest. Take my yoke upon you and

learn from me, for I am gentle and humble in heart, and you will find rest for your souls. For my yoke is easy and my burden is light. (Matthew 11:28-29)

William Hendriksen says that the Syriac New Testament translates the word *gentle* as "restful"; accordingly Jesus' expression is, "Come to me . . . and I will *rest* you . . . for I am *restful* . . . and you shall find *rest* for yourselves."[3] Christ's whole demeanor was such that people were often restful in His presence. This effect is another outworking of the grace of gentleness. People are at rest, or at ease, around the Christian who is truly gentle.

Matthew 12:20 gives us another picture of the gentleness with which Christ treats us: "A bruised reed he will not break, and a smoldering wick he will not snuff out, till he leads justice to victory." The bruised reed and the smoldering wick refer to people who are hurting, spiritually weak, or of little faith. Jesus deals gently with such people. He does not condemn them for their weakness; He does not come down with a "heavy hand"; rather, He deals with them gently until their true need is exposed and they are open to Him for help. How beautifully His encounter with the Samaritan woman illustrates His gentleness. Firmly, yet gently, Jesus continued to probe her need until she recognized it herself and turned to Him to meet it.

In the very act of his appeal to the Corinthians by "the meekness and gentleness of Christ," Paul illustrated that gentleness for us. We could paraphrase his remarks as, "Acting as Christ would act in this situation I appeal to you. I do not demand; I do not insist, but I *appeal* to you." Paul could have berated the Corinthians for allowing into their fellowship those who sought to undermine his apostolic authority, but he didn't; instead, he chose to exercise the Spirit-produced fruit of gentleness.

When Paul wrote to the Philippians, "Your attitude should be the same as that of Christ Jesus," he was specifically referring to Christ's humility; but we can apply this command to *all* of Christ's character traits. As His followers, we should cultivate the same gentleness that characterized His life.

## TREATING OTHERS GENTLY

A profile of gentleness as it should appear in our lives will first include actively seeking to make others feel at ease, or "restful," in our presence. We should not be so strongly opinionated or dogmatic that others are afraid to express their opinions in our presence. Instead, we should be sensitive to others' opinions and ideas. We should also avoid displaying our commitment to Christian discipleship in such a way as to make others feel guilty, taking care not to break the bruised reed of the hurting Christian or snuff out the smoldering wick of the immature Christian.

Second, gentleness will demonstrate respect for the personal dignity of the other person. Where necessary, it will seek to change a wrong opinion or attitude by persuasion and kindness, not by domination or intimidation. It will studiously avoid coercion by threatening, either directly or indirectly (as Paul, for example, avoided it in his appeal to the Corinthians).

Gentleness will also avoid blunt speech and an abrupt manner, instead seeking to answer everyone with sensitivity and respect, ready to show consideration toward all. The gentle Christian does not feel he has the liberty to "say what I think and let the chips fall where they may." Instead he is sensitive to the reactions of others to his words, and considerate of how others may feel about what he says. When he finds it necessary to wound with his words, he also seeks to bind up those wounds with words of consolation and encouragement.

The gentle Christian will not feel threatened by opposition or resent those who oppose him. Instead, he will seek to gently instruct, looking to God to dissolve the opposition, just as Paul taught Timothy to do in chapter 2 of his second letter.

Finally, the gentle Christian will not degrade or belittle or gossip about the brother who falls into some sin. Instead he will grieve for him and pray for his repentance. If it is appropriate for him to become personally involved with the erring brother, he will seek to restore him gently, as Paul instructs us in Galatians 6, aware that he himself is also subject to temptation.

The Christian who truly seeks to obey God through gentle character will actively pursue gentleness, striving to clothe himself with it (see Colossians 3:12 and 1 Timothy 6:11). He will place this godly virtue high on his list of spiritual traits and look to God the Holy Spirit to produce this fruit in his life.

## TREATING OTHERS CONSIDERATELY

There is a trait closely related to gentleness that should also characterize the godly Christian who is seeking to manifest the fruit of the Spirit in his life. I have chosen to call it *considerateness*, although according to the commentators, the scriptural term requires several English words to bring out the fullness of its meaning. It appears in Philippians 4:5: "Let your *gentleness* be evident to all." In the *New International Version* it is always translated as *gentleness* or *considerateness* (see Philippians 4:5, 1 Timothy 3:3, Titus 3:2, and James 3:17). The *New American Standard Bible* also uses *gentleness* or *considerateness*, except in Philippians 4:5, where it uses the term *forbearing spirit*.

William Hendriksen says a number of synonyms are necessary to show the broad meaning of this word: yieldedness, reasonableness, big-heartedness, geniality, considerateness.[4] James Adamson uses the word *humane* in his commentary on James and says it describes "the man who is fair, considerate and generous rather than rigid and exacting in his relations with others. . . . It is contrasted with 'strict justice' and is used of judges who do not press the letter of the law. . . . It is also used of people who listen to reason."[5] W. E. Vine says it is "the trait that enables us to look humanely and reasonably at the facts of a case . . . not insisting on the letter of the law."[6]

The Pharisees, rigid in their absolute adherence to tradition, perfectly demonstrated the opposite of considerateness. They were always asking, "Is it lawful?" They never asked, "Is it kind or reasonable?" Jesus was always getting into trouble with the Pharisees because He constantly broke away from their rigid traditions and, in many cases, exposed their utter absurdity.

The considerate Christian listens to reason and is fair-minded and humane. Instead of insisting on the letter of the law, he asks, "What is the right thing to do in this situation?" This kind of thinking should not be confused, however, with the humanistic philosophy that says, "If it feels right, do it." That philosophy is entirely self-centered and focuses on one's carnal desires. Considerateness, on the other hand, focuses on the other individual and asks, "What is best for him?"

Paul's admonition in Philippians 4:5 provides the proper motivation for a considerate attitude. "Let your gentleness (or considerateness) be evident to all. The Lord is near." We might rephrase it, "The Lord is standing at my shoulder, waiting to see how I will handle the various relationships I have with people today. Will I be rigid and exacting in my demands of them? Or will I be gentle and considerate, seeking to understand the pressures and insecurities they face and making allowances accordingly?" We are to show consideration to all—

the store clerk, the bus driver, family members, nonChristians as well as Christians.

I fear that all too often we Christians may be less humane and considerate than nonbelievers. We think we are standing on principle when in reality we may be only insisting on our opinion. How do others see us? Do we appear to be rigid, unyielding, and inflexible, or do we come across as genial, reasonable, and humane in our relationships with other people? The Pharisees of Jesus' day had encrusted God's commands with their own traditions. Let us be careful to avoid doing the same thing.

The trait of considerateness is one of the characteristics of heavenly wisdom (see James 3:17). If we want to be wise in God's eyes, we must cultivate this trait of reasonableness and geniality.

## SEEKING A GENTLE SPIRIT

I suspect that of all the character traits of godliness in this study, gentleness will be the least appealing to many male readers. For some reason we seem to have difficulty believing that manliness and gentleness can be part of the same personality. Men often want to see gentleness in their mothers and wives, but not in themselves. The macho image of the nonChristian male world has a tendency to rub off, even on us. But the apostle Paul uses the example of a mother's gentleness to describe his own character. He was able to say to the Thessalonian believers, "We were gentle among you, like a mother caring for her little children." A friend of mine, an ex-Marine, often signs his letters, "Keep tough and tender"—tough on ourselves and tender with others. That is the spirit of gentleness.

What are some steps we can take to develop a gentle spirit? First we must decide that this is a trait we really do want to develop. We have to decide that we want to be mild and sensitive in our dealings with others, that we are willing to live without a rigid structure of black-and-white rules. We have to decide if we really want to *care* about people.

Second, we can ask those who know us best and will be honest how we come across to other people. Are we dogmatic and opinionated, blunt and abrupt? Do we seek to intimidate or dominate others by the sheer force of our personality? Do people feel ill at ease in our presence because they think we are silently judging their weaknesses and correcting their faults? If any of these traits are characteristic of us, we must face them honestly and humbly.

As we face our overall need, we should also ask the Holy Spirit to make us aware of specific situations in which we fail to act with gentleness or considerateness. It is not enough to concede in a vague sort of way that we may be lacking in this godly virtue. We need to identify specific instances in which we fall short. Only then will we be driven to pray fervently for the grace of gentleness. And, as always, we ought to memorize one or more passages of Scripture on this topic. I suggest you quickly scan back over this chapter and select at least one Scripture reference to memorize for future meditation. Then put this need on your private prayer list, and pray that God will so work in your life that by His power you will demonstrate the fruit of gentleness.

---

NOTES
1. Bethune, *The Fruit of the Spirit*, page 100.
2. Billy Graham, *The Holy Spirit* (Waco, Tex.: Word Books, 1978), pages 205-206.
3. William Hendriksen, *The Gospel of Matthew* (Grand Rapids, Mich.: Baker Book House, 1973), page 504.
4. William Hendriksen, *Exposition of Philippians* (Grand Rapids, Mich.: Baker Book House, 1962), page 193.
5. James Adamson, "The Epistle of James," *The New International Commentary on the New Testament* (Grand Rapids, Mich.: Eerdmans, 1976), page 155.
6. W. E. Vine, *An Expository Dictionary of New Testament Words*, page 474.

# 16
# Kindness
# and Goodness

～

*Therefore, as we have opportunity,*
*let us do good to all people,*
*especially to those who belong*
*to the family of believers.*

Galatians 6:10

～

Kindness and goodness are so closely related that they are often used interchangeably. These two traits finish a natural progression in godly character: patience denotes a godly response to ill-treatment; gentleness defines a godly demeanor toward people at all times; kindness and goodness involve an active desire to recognize and meet the needs of others.

*Kindness is a sincere desire for the happiness of others; goodness is the activity calculated to advance that happiness.* Kindness is the inner disposition, created by the Holy Spirit, that causes us to be sensitive to the needs of others, whether physical, emotional, or spiritual. Goodness is kindness in action—words and deeds. Because of this close relationship, we often use the two words interchangeably.

I tend to think of kindness in terms of our awareness of those around us and the thoughtfulness that we can express to them, almost incidentally. Kindness may be as simple as a smile to a store clerk, a thank-you to a waitress, an encouraging word to an elderly person, or a word of recognition to a small child. None of these expressions is costly in time or money. But they do require a sincere interest in the happiness of those around us. Apart from God's grace, most of us naturally tend to be concerned about *our* responsibilities, *our* problems, *our* plans. But the person who has grown in the grace of kindness has expanded his thinking outside of himself and his interests and has developed a genuine interest in the happiness and well-being of those around him.

Goodness, on the other hand, involves deliberate deeds that are helpful to others. Although the Bible uses the word *good* to refer to what is upright, honorable, and noble about our ethical or moral character, it also uses it to describe actions that are not only good in themselves, but beneficial to others.

Bethune well observes, "The best practical definition of goodness is given in the life and character of Jesus Christ: 'Jesus of Nazareth, who went about doing good.' [Acts 10:38] So far as we resemble Jesus, in his devotion to the welfare of men, do we possess the grace of goodness."[1] Do we aspire to be Christlike? Then we must be continually sensitive to how we might meet the needs of those around us.

GOD'S UNFAILING KINDNESS

We need to constantly keep in mind that our goal in practicing godliness is to grow in both our devotion to God and our likeness to Him in character and conduct. The New Testament has much to say about the kindness of God. The first mention is in Luke 6: Jesus says that God "is kind to the ungrateful and wicked." Next we find that God's kindness leads sinners toward repentance (Romans 2:4). In Ephesians 2:7, in the context of our utter lostness and sin, Paul speaks of the incomparable riches of God's grace, expressed in His kindness to us in Christ Jesus. He draws a similar contrast in Titus 3: after describing our lost condition, he declares, "But when the kindness and love of God our Savior appeared, he saved us. . . ." It seems the Bible goes out of its way to portray the kindness of God in stark contrast to man's total undeservedness.

What lesson can we draw from these accounts of the kindness of God? He is kind to all men—the ungrateful, the wicked, the utterly lost and hopeless, the rebellious—without distinction. If we are to become Godlike, we, too, must be kind to all men.

Our natural inclination is to show kindness only to those for whom we have some natural affinity—family, friends, likable neighbors. But God shows kindness to those who are most despicable—the ungrateful and wicked. Have you ever tried to be kind to someone who was ungrateful? Unless God's grace was working in your heart in a significant way, your reaction to his ingratitude may well have been, "I'll never do anything for him again!" But God doesn't turn His back on the ungrateful. And so Jesus says to us, "But love your enemies, do good to them, and lend to them without expecting to get anything back" (Luke 6:35).

We need to develop a kind disposition, to be sensitive to others and truly desire their happiness. But sensitivity alone is not enough: the grace of goodness impels us to take action to meet those needs.

CREATED TO DO GOOD
Most of us are familiar with Ephesians 2:8-9, which teaches that salvation is by grace, through faith, and not by works. But we should be just as familiar with the next verse: "For we are God's workmanship, created in Christ Jesus to do good works, which God prepared in advance for us to do."

This is an amazing statement. Not only are we created in Christ Jesus—born anew for the purpose of doing good works—but we are created to do good works that God *prepared in advance for us to do*. Before we came to know Christ, and, according to Psalm 139:16, before we were even born, God prepared certain good works for us to do.

The *New American Standard Bible* provides a more literal translation of verse 10: "For we are His workmanship, created in Christ Jesus for good works, which God prepared beforehand, that we should walk in them." The word *walk* suggests our common, everyday experience, not the unusual and heroic. We all have a tendency to rise to the special occasions of our lives, but God has created us to do our good works in the midst of the humdrum of daily living. Bethune quotes an earlier writer as saying, "much of the happiness of the world depends upon what are termed little things; and it is rare that God honors us with heroic and famous distinctions in doing good."[2]

Paul aptly illustrates the ordinariness of most good deeds in 1 Timothy 5:9-10. He says that in order for a widow to qualify for church assistance, she must be "well known for her *good deeds*, such as bringing up children, showing hospitality, washing the feet of the saints, helping those in trouble and devoting herself to all kinds of *good deeds*." None of these items on Paul's list is especially exciting or glamorous. They are simply opportunities to do good in the course of daily living. Although this particular passage applies specifically to women, the principle applies equally to men. Most of our opportunities for good deeds will arise out of the course of our daily lives. The challenge to us is to be alert for these opportunities and to see them not as interruptions or inconveniences, but as occasions for doing the good works God has planned for us.

DOING GOOD AT WORK •

Perhaps one of the most obvious areas in which God has prepared good works for us to do is our life's calling or vocation. The good works God has prepared for us individually are consistent with the abilities He has given us and the circumstances in which He has placed us. When there is something wrong with my car, and a qualified mechanic fixes it, that is a good deed, in my thinking. If he did it as a part of his calling before God and as a service to his fellowman, it is also a good deed in God's sight, even though he was paid for his work.

Most honorable vocations exist to meet the needs of people. God has ordained His world so that people with various abilities meet various needs. We should think of our vocation, therefore, not as a necessary evil to pay the bills, nor even as an opportunity to become rich, but as the primary path of our Christian walk wherein God has planned good deeds for us to do. Most of us spend half or more of our waking hours at our vocations. If we fail to find opportunities to do good works there, we are throwing away half of our lives as far as fulfilling God's purpose for us here on earth. If we feel our particular job does not allow us to genuinely meet the needs of people, we ought to prayerfully consider a change.

But let me be very clear at this point. I am talking about meeting the *ordinary* needs of people—for clothing, transportation, education, health care, and so on. I am not talking about changing jobs to go into so-called full-time Christian work. If God has called you to that, wonderful! But that is not the only arena of life in which God prepares good works for us.

Evaluate your work situation; if you are a student, consider the work you are thinking of pursuing. Does it lend itself to doing the good deeds God has planned for you?

What about your attitude toward your job? Do you view the job as an opportunity to do many of the good deeds God has planned for you by meeting the needs of people, or do you view it as a necessary evil to earn the money you need? If we are to grow in the grace of goodness we must have the right attitude about our vocation.

Many women, of course, do not work outside the home and may wonder how this section on vocation applies to them. For those of you in this situation, homemaking is your vocation, and a rich arena in which to do those good deeds God has called you to do. Few things are more difficult than making a home and rearing children. The dishes, the diapers, the washing, the waxing, the cooking and cleaning may at times seem insignificant and distasteful; yet few, if any, vocations render greater benefits to those they serve than godly homemaking. You also may have greater opportunity for good deeds outside the home, such as ministering to the sick and lonely, providing hospitality, preparing meals for others, or caring for someone else's children. Review 1 Timothy 5:10 to see how Paul expected homemakers to be involved in good deeds beyond their own families.

DOING GOOD AT HOME
In Galatians 6:10, Paul tells us to "do good to all people, especially to those who belong to the family of believers." Our good deeds are to be scattered upon all men, Christian and nonChristian. We are to follow the example of our heavenly Father, who "causes his sun to rise on the evil and the good, and sends rain on the righteous and the unrighteous" (Matthew 5:45).

Nevertheless, there is in Paul's instruction a priority of responsibility: first believers, then nonbelievers. I believe we can infer from this order a similar priority involving our families. We are to do good to all men, especially members of our own families. Paul told Timothy, "If anyone does not provide for his relatives, and especially for his immediate family, he has denied the faith and is worse than an unbeliever" (1 Timothy 5:8). Good deeds should begin at home. If we are out doing good deeds for others while neglecting the needs of our spouse, our parents, or our children, we are not practicing the grace of goodness.

I recently heard of a course on biblical marriage in which one of the lessons is entitled, "Who Takes Out the Garbage?" That may be a humorous title to grab our attention, but the author is on to something. Mundane household duties are sore points in many homes, even Christian homes. But for the Christian growing in the grace of goodness, the distasteful and despised duties of the home provide the opportunity of doing good deeds for those he loves most.

One of the rich heritages of The Navigators, the organization I work for, is the emphasis on serving others which our founder Dawson Trotman built into the very fabric of the work from its earliest days. As a result, Navigator discipleship training always includes serving others. But when I have had opportunity to address young people on this subject, I encourage them to begin at home. It is a lot easier to clean up after a weekend conference than to clean out Dad's garage back home. Somehow it seems more spiritual to baby-sit some other lady's children for free than to help Mom with the dishes after Sunday dinner.

Husbands, most of us have a lot of growing to do in this area of good deeds at home. There are a lot of little things we can do *in* the house, as well as *around* it, to be more sensitive in meeting our wives' needs. Who *does* take out the garbage at your house? The best teaching is by example. If we would train our children to do good deeds (and they *must* be trained—they do not learn it naturally), then we must be examples to them. I wonder how many boys growing up in Christian homes ever have the privilege of seeing their dad do the dishes or mop the kitchen floor? Let us do good to all, but especially to our own family.

## DOING GOOD TO ALL PEOPLE

Good deeds in our vocations and in our homes are important, but there is still a big world out there for each of us, with numerous opportunities for doing good. Thus far I have emphasized meeting the physical needs of people; but being a disposition to promote the happiness of others, goodness certainly directs much of its energies to the spiritual and eternal needs of others. Here again, God has prepared good works for each of us, consistent with our gifts and circumstances. We need to pray, "Lord, what will You have me to do?" and then we should *do* it.

Although we do need to observe Paul's priority in Galatians 6 for "the family of believers," let us not overlook the "all people" referred to in the same verse. Because opportunities for doing good are virtually unlimited, we must be sensitive to God's Holy Spirit as He selects opportunities for us.

One kind of behavior we must guard against is the impulsive and often superficial response to the needs of others. On this point Bethune very wisely remarks,

> True goodness is not merely impulsive, but rational and considerate—It will therefore pause, and be at some trouble to inquire what service, and how best may it be rendered. . . . Goodness should be willing to give time, and thought, and patience, and even labor; not mere money and kind words and compassionate looks.[3]

196

True goodness is self-sacrificing, not only of money but of time. Like the Macedonian Christians who gave "even beyond their ability" (2 Corinthians 8:3), the Christian who wants to do good for others will often have to give time he does not have. Often this is an act of faith just as much as giving money we think we cannot afford. We will always be too busy to help others, unless we truly grasp the importance God puts on our doing good deeds for others.

One of the less obvious but more critical needs that many (shall I say most?) people have is for someone to listen to them. They don't need our advice as much as our attention. A friend of mine went through a personal tragedy. I couldn't think of anything to say, so I hesitated to contact him. Finally I called and invited him to lunch. For an hour I sat and listened—no advice, just listened. The only time I talked was to draw him out. One thing he said stuck in my mind: "It really meant a lot to me when you called last night." We hadn't even gotten together yet. Just the phone call and the invitation to lunch encouraged him; just realizing that someone cared meant a lot to him.

I believe most people, Christians as well as nonChristians, are so starved for the genuine interest of one other person that a little bit of concern from someone who cares goes a mighty long way. One of the most plaintive statements in the Bible is David's cry in Psalm 142:4, "No one cares for my soul" (NASB). Do you know someone who possibly feels that way? If so, you have an opportunity to do good to that person by saying, "I just want you to know I care."

True goodness is not only self-sacrificing, it is also untiring. It does not "become weary in doing good" (Galatians 6:9). It is one thing to do good in a few, or even in a number of, isolated instances; it is quite another to face cheerfully the prospect of doing some particular deed of goodness day in and day out for an interminable period of time, particularly if those deeds are taken for granted by the recipients. But true goodness does not look to the recipients, nor even to the results, of its deeds for its reward. It looks to God alone, and, finding His smile of approval, it gains the needed strength to carry on.

Perhaps one of the most sobering statements in the Bible is found in Hebrews 12:14: "without holiness no one will see the Lord." It is not my profession, but my holiness that proves the validity of my Christian experience and my possession of eternal life. But Jesus' account of the judgment day recorded in Matthew 25 is just as sobering. There the test is good deeds: feeding the hungry, giving water to the thirsty, clothing the needy, showing hospitality to the stranger, attending to the sick, and visiting those in prison. Jesus is teaching in that passage not that doing good deeds earns our admittance to heaven, but that they are necessary and vital evidences that we are bound for heaven. Bethune explains,

> And so in the judgment day, the inquiry will be made not into our opinions or professions alone, but into our deeds, as proving the correctness of our faith and the sincerity of our professions. Never can we know that we are in the right way, except we walk in the footsteps of Him, who did good in all his life and death. He came from heaven to do good on earth, that we in doing good might tread the path to heaven.[4]

Without holiness no one will see the Lord. The essence of Matthew 25:31-46 is that without goodness no one will see the Lord. Both of these thoughts are very sobering to the one who takes seriously the words of Scripture.

## WATCHING FOR OPPORTUNITIES

One objective in studying godly character traits is to become more conscious of the vital importance of some of the perhaps lesser-known qualities. Have you ever reflected, for example, upon how important good deeds are to Jesus, as He indicates in Matthew 25:31-46? What better stimulation to good deeds can we have than to meditate on that passage of Scripture from time to time? Or you might prayerfully consider the truth of Ephesians 2:10, asking God to make clear to you some of the good works that He has prepared for you to do.

Consider your gifts, your talents, your vocation, and your circumstances as a special trust from God with which to serve Him by serving others. As Peter says, "Each one should use whatever gift he has received to serve others, faithfully administering God's grace in its various forms" (1 Peter 4:10). Remember that you are responsible not for doing all the good that needs to be done in the world, but for doing what God has planned for you.

Remember also that most opportunities for doing good come across the ordinary path of our day. Don't look for the spectacular; few people ever have the opportunity to pull a victim from the wreckage of a flaming automobile. *All* of us have the opportunity to administer the kind or encouraging word, to do the little, perhaps unseen, deed that makes life more pleasant for someone else.

Accept the cost of good deeds in time, thought, and effort. But remember that opportunities for doing good are not interruptions in God's plan for us, but part of that plan. We always have time to do what God wants us to do.

Acknowledge your need of His divine grace to enlarge your soul and enable you to look beyond yourself to the concerns and needs of those around you. Then come to His throne with confidence to receive the grace you need to grow in the fruit of kindness and goodness. May it be said of each of us as it was of Dorcas, that we are "always doing good and helping the poor" (Acts 9:36).

---

NOTES
1. Bethune, *The Fruit of the Spirit*, page 117.
2. Bethune, page 126.
3. Bethune, pages 127-128.
4. Bethune, page 132.

# 17
# Love

*. . . And over all these virtues put on love,
which binds them all together in perfect unity.*

Colossians 3:14

When Paul lists those godly traits he calls the fruit of the Spirit, he puts love first — very likely to emphasize its importance. Love is the overall grace from which all the others grow; I have reserved it for last in these studies, because, as Paul indicates in Colossians 3:14, love binds all the other virtues together in perfect unity.

Devotion to God is the only motivation acceptable to God for the development and exercise of Christian character (see chapter 5). But devotion to God finds its outward expression in loving one another. Or, to state it another way, our devotion to God is validated by our love for other people. As the apostle John puts it, "For anyone who does not love his brother, whom he has seen, cannot love God, whom he has not seen. And he has given us this command: Whoever loves God must also love his brother" (1 John 4:20-21).

We cannot truly love God without loving one another.

To recognize that there is someone I do not love is to say to God, "I do not love you enough to love that person." This is not to deny the reality of spiritual struggle in loving a particular person, because it often exists. I am referring to the attitude of not even wanting to love the person, of being content to allow a lack of love for someone to reside in my heart unchecked and unchallenged.

Jesus linked loving God to loving man in Matthew 22:37-40, when He was asked about the greatest commandment in the Law. George Bethune observes of this passage, "The command to man to 'love God with all his heart, and with all his mind, and with all his strength,' is followed by a command to 'love his neighbor as himself,' which could not be, unless love to our neighbor is included in love to God; for how else can we give all our heart to God, and love ourselves and our neighbor too?"[1]

Devotion to God is the ultimate motivation for Christian character, but it is also true that love for our brother is the more proximate motivation for the exercise of Christian graces among one another. If we rephrased the virtues of love in 1 Corinthians 13 in terms of motivational statements, they might sound something like this:

- ❖ I am patient with you because I love you and want to forgive you.
- ❖ I am kind to you because I love you and want to help you.
- ❖ I do not envy your possessions or your gifts because I love you and want you to have the best.
- ❖ I do not boast about my attainments because I love you and want to hear about yours.
- ❖ I am not proud because I love you and want to esteem you before myself.
- ❖ I am not rude because I love you and care about your feelings.

❖ I am not self-seeking because I love you and want to
  meet your needs.
❖ I am not easily angered by you because I love you
  and want to overlook your offenses.
❖ I do not keep a record of your wrongs because I love
  you, and "love covers a multitude of sins."

Expressing love in this manner, as a motivational factor,
helps us see what Paul had in mind when he said that love
binds together all the virtues of Christian character. Love is
not so much a character trait as the inner disposition of the
soul that produces them all. Bethune says love is "a holy,
abiding and vigorous spirit, which rules the whole man, ever
directing him to the humble and loving fulfillment of all his
duties to God and man."[2] But although love may be more a
motivational force than an actual display of Christian virtue,
it *always* results in actions on our part. Love inclines us and
directs us to be kind, to forgive, to give of ourselves to one
another. Therefore, Peter says to us, "Above all, love each
other deeply" (1 Peter 4:8).

GOD IS LOVE
We have already noted in chapter 10 that the apostle John
makes two statements concerning the essential nature of
God: "God is light" and "God is love." Love is not defined
here as an action, nor even as a character trait, but as an
essential part of God's nature. As Bethune notes, "God was
love long before he had made any creatures to be the objects
of his love, even from all eternity."[3]

God is infinitely glorious in all His attributes, but the
Bible seems to give preeminence to His holiness and to His
goodness or love. In Exodus 33 there is an instructive relationship between God's goodness and God's glory. In
response to Moses' request, "Now show me your glory," God

replies, "I will cause all my goodness to pass in front of you, and I will proclaim my name, the Lord, in your presence" (verses 18-19). Yet in verse 22 God says, "When my glory passes by. . . ." It appears from the correlation of verses 18 and 22 that God equates His glory with His goodness. And how does God describe His goodness? Exodus 34:6-7 says, "And he passed in front of Moses, proclaiming, 'The Lord, the Lord, the compassionate and gracious God, slow to anger, abounding in love and faithfulness, maintaining love to thousands, and forgiving wickedness, rebellion and sin.'"

The children of Israel seemed to recognize God's goodness as the expression of His glory. At the dedication of Solomon's temple, according to 2 Chronicles 7:2, the glory of the Lord so filled the temple that the priests could not enter. Then verse 3 tells us,

> When all the Israelites saw the fire coming down and
> the glory of the Lord above the temple, they knelt on
> the pavement with their faces to the ground, and
> they worshiped and gave thanks to the Lord, saying,
> "He is good; his love endures forever."

Notice the Israelites' response when they saw God's glory: "He is good." God's goodness is the preeminent expression of His glory. If we desire to be Godlike and to glorify God in our lives, therefore, we must make the cultivation and exercise of love in our hearts an urgent priority. There are three overall prayer requests I make for myself and for others for whom I pray: that I and they would grow in holiness, humility, and love. Of these three, however, love has priority, for if I love God I will seek to be holy, and if I love other people I will seek to be humble, putting their interests ahead of mine.

If love to God and to our neighbor should be our highest priority, then it is important for us to know how love expresses itself. First Corinthians 13 is, of course, the most familiar description of love. And the list of qualities covered in that passage have, for the most part, already been addressed in previous chapters of this book. There are two other Scripture passages, however, that seem to sum up the essence of love into two overall traits that will be easily remembered. These passages are 1 John 3:16-18 and 4:7-11.

LOVE GIVES, WHATEVER THE COST

In 1 John 3:16 John says, "This is how we know what love is: Jesus Christ laid down his life for us." The key idea here is that *love gives, even at great cost to itself*. Jesus gave His life for us. John 3:16 tells us that the Father so loved that He gave His only Son to die for us. In Jesus' incarnation and death, both the Father and the Son gave in response to our desperate plight. Nothing but the Savior's incarnation and death would suffice to rescue us. The cost was infinite, but God the Father and God the Son loved us so much they did not hesitate to pay the cost to meet our need.

John says in his epistle that we too should give even at great cost to ourselves: We should "lay down our lives for our brothers." In the context of Jesus' sacrifice, John's challenge to us seems overwhelming and impossible—the ultimate act of love. But John's application is very practical and down-to-earth: He asks that we share with our brother in need. We are to do this out of pity and compassion, however, not duty. We are to put our love into practice by meeting our brother's need—even at great cost to us.

There are tremendous needs in the world today, and we Christians ought to be involved in meeting those needs. John is very clear on this point: "If anyone has material possessions and sees his brother in need but has no pity on him, how can the love of God be in him?" Paul tells us the Macedonian Christians exhibited this kind of love: "Out of the most severe trial, their overflowing joy and their extreme poverty welled up in rich generosity. For I testify that they gave as much as they were able, and even beyond their ability" (2 Corinthians 8:2-3). They gave out of love and at great cost to themselves to meet the material needs of Christian brothers in Jerusalem, whom they had never even met. We should give to our church and to the work of missions, but we should not overlook the fact that the most well-known passage in the Bible on giving, 2 Corinthians 8–9, has to do with giving to the poor.

But material needs are not the only ones our brother has. Often he needs a listening ear, a word of encouragement, or a helping hand. But to meet those needs requires us to give of ourselves—our time, our attention, and often our heart. This can be more difficult than giving money. Paul said of Timothy, "I have no one else like him, who takes a genuine interest in your welfare" (Philippians 2:20). As he compliments Timothy, Paul adds a striking indictment of others: "For everyone looks out for his own interests, not those of Jesus Christ" (verse 21).

To meet the non-material needs of others costs getting out of ourselves, our concerns, and our interests. We cannot take a genuine interest in the welfare of others, as did Timothy, unless we are willing to become involved in their interests and their concerns. And we cannot do this unless we are willing to forego our own interests. But love willingly pays the price.

LOVE SACRIFICES TO FORGIVE

The second passage in which John instructs us in the meaning of love is 1 John 4:7-11. Immediately following his declaration that "God is love," John says,

> This is how God showed his love among us: He sent
> his one and only Son into the world that we might
> live through him. This is love: not that we loved God,

but that he loved us and sent his Son as an atoning
sacrifice for our sins. Dear friends, since God so loved
us, we also ought to love one another.

Once again John points us to God's sacrifice in sending
His Son into the world that we might live through Him. But
the central thought is that *God gave in order that He might
forgive*. He sent His Son as an atoning sacrifice for our sins.
The concept of atonement is best expressed by the marginal
reading of the *New International Version*: "the one who
would turn aside his wrath, taking away" our sins. God gave
His Son, who took away our sins by bearing in His own body
God's wrath, thus turning away that wrath from us. God's
justice required that our sin be punished, and forgiveness
was impossible as long as justice was unsatisfied. So God
gave His Son in order that He might forgive us. He forgave
at great cost to Himself.

Now John once again applies God's love to our relationships with one another. He says since God so loved us, we also
ought to love one another. Do we love one another enough to
forgive each other, with or without apologies for wrongs done
to us? So often we want to exact the last ounce of remorse and
repentance from our erring brother before we will even consider forgiving him. But God did not do this. When we were
still sinners, still His enemies, He sent His Son to die for us so
that He might forgive us. And John urges us to do likewise.

Forgiveness cost God His Son on the cross, but what
does it cost us to forgive one another? Forgiving costs us our
sense of justice. We all have this innate sense deep within
our souls, but it has been perverted by our selfish sinful
natures. We want to see "justice" done, but the justice we
envision satisfies our own interests. We must realize that justice *has* been done. God is the only rightful administrator of
justice in all of creation, and His justice has been satisfied. In

order to forgive our brother, we must be satisfied with God's justice and forego the satisfaction of our own.

I recall a personal struggle a number of years ago to love one of my brothers in Christ. One evening the Holy Spirit addressed to my mind the rather startling question, "Do you believe I love him just as he is?" I hadn't thought of that before, but I did concede that surely God must love him just as he was, faults and all. And then God pressed this question to my mind, "If I can love him, can you?" God was teaching me to love as He loves, to forgive as He forgives. And love forgives at great cost to itself; it does not demand justice or even changed behavior from its brother.

This forgiving aspect of love enables us to be patient with one another and to live at peace with one another. It enables us to deal gently with our brother, even when he sins against us. If we are to grow in the grace of love, we must be ready to forgive, even at great cost to ourselves.

LOVE REACHES OUT

Often in our teaching on love, we stress—and rightly so—that biblical love is not emotions or feelings, but attitudes and actions that seek the best interests of the other person, regardless of how we feel toward him. Vine says, for example, "Christian love . . . is not an impulse from the feelings, it does not always run with the natural inclinations, nor does it spend itself only upon those for whom some affinity is discovered."[4] An illustration from *The Pursuit of Holiness* provides an example of this kind of love:

> Suppose you were meditating on 1 Corinthians 13, the
> great love chapter. As you think about the chapter,
> you realize the importance of love and you also see
> the practical outworkings of love: Love is patient and
> kind and does not envy. You ask yourself, "Am I impa-

tient or unkind or envious toward anyone?" As you
think about this, you realize you are envious toward
Joe at work who seems to be getting all the breaks.
You confess this sin to God, being very specific to
name Joe and your sinful reaction to his good fortune.
You ask God to bless him even more and to give you a
spirit of contentment so that you will not continue to
envy Joe, but will instead love him. You might memorize 1 Corinthians 13:4 and think about it as you see
Joe at work. You even look for ways to help him. Then
you do the same thing tomorrow and the next day
and the next till finally you see God working a spirit of
love in your heart toward Joe.[5]

So love is very much a matter of actions rather than
emotions. However, although this emphasis on *acts of love*
is certainly necessary, we can sometimes give the impression
that love doesn't involve any emotion—that it is entirely an
act of the will, of one's duty, regardless of how one feels. We
can even promote the "I can love him but I can't like him"
type of attitude. The Bible does not support such an unbalanced concept of love.

In describing the Christian's love toward his brother, the
Bible uses such expressions as "Love one another deeply,
from the heart" (1 Peter 1:22) and "Be devoted to one
another in brotherly love" (Romans 12:10). Other translations choose such words as *fervently*, *fondly*, and *affection-
ately* in the same passages to describe the love Christians
ought to have for one another. Three different writers use
the expression "brotherly love" or "love as brothers," all indicating that Christian love is to be characterized by an affec-
tion that family members have—or ought to have—for one
another (see Hebrews 13:1 and 1 Peter 3:8).

All of these passages from the Bible indicate that our

emotions are involved. We are to reach out and embrace our brother with a deep fervency of spirit, in our hearts if not in actuality. Obviously such a fervency of spirit cannot substitute for loving actions, but surely it should accompany them. We dare not settle for less.

From the contents of Paul's epistles to the churches, we can safely say the two churches that caused him the most grief were Corinth and Galatia. Yet listen to the emotion in Paul's voice when he writes to the Corinthians, "For I wrote you out of great distress and anguish of heart and with many tears, not to grieve you but to let you know the depth of my love for you" (2 Corinthians 2:4). And to the Galatians he wrote, "My dear children, for whom I am again in the pains of childbirth until Christ is formed in you, how I wish I could be with you now and change my tone, because I am perplexed about you!" (4:19-20). Distress, anguish, tears, and pains of childbirth are all terms calculated to express the deep emotion of Paul's love toward these people. That their actions made them difficult to love only deepened the intensity of his love for them. And that love was not just an impersonal act of writing them letters of correction in their best interest; he reached out and embraced them even while he rebuked them.

One of the greatest moments of my Christian life occurred one day when I opened my arms and warmly embraced a brother in Christ whom I had somewhat disliked for several years. God had so dealt with me that I finally realized that to think about anyone, "I will love him, but I can't like him" was a great deal less than God's standard of love and was therefore a sinful attitude on my part.

Love is more than a mere act of the will. Going back again to Bethune's definition, love is a *vigorous* spirit that rules the whole man, ever directing him to the humble and loving fulfillment of his duties to God and man. We should do more than just *decide* to do acts of love: we should *desire* to do them. This is not to say we are to do acts of love only when we feel like doing them; it is to say we are not to content ourselves merely with acts of the will, good as those acts may be. We are to lay hold on God in prayer until He gives us that vigorous and loving spirit that delights to reach out and embrace our brother and to meet his need or forgive his sin, even if it is at great cost to ourselves.

GROWING IN LOVE

It is obvious that the love we have been considering can be produced in our hearts only by the Spirit of God. Paul wrote to the Thessalonian believers, "You yourselves have been taught by God to love each other" (1 Thessalonians 4:9). And yet just a few words later Paul says, "Yet we urge you, brothers, to [love] more and more" (verse 10). Once again, and especially as we draw to the close of these studies on godly character, we must review this principle: Godlike character is both the fruit of the Spirit as He works within us and the result of our personal efforts. We are both totally dependent upon His working within us and totally responsible for our own character development. This is an apparent contradiction to our either-or type of thinking, but it is a truth taught over and over in the Scriptures.

How then can we fulfill our responsibility to love "more and more"? Recognizing that love is an inner disposition of the soul produced only by the Holy Spirit, what can we do to fulfill our responsibility? First, as we have already seen, the Spirit of God uses His word to transform us. Therefore, if we want to grow in love, we must saturate our minds with Scriptures that describe love and show its importance to us. First Corinthians 13:1-3, for example, tells us of the emptiness of all knowledge, abilities, and zeal apart from love. First Corinthians 13:4-7 describes love in terms of specific attitudes and actions. Romans 13:8-10 describes love in terms of fulfilling the law of God in our lives. We have already looked at the two passages in 1 John in terms of giving and forgiving. Do you truly want to grow in love? Then you must begin by meditating on some of these love passages.

The second thing we must do is pray for the Holy Spirit to apply His word to our hearts and to our daily lives. Paul did not just exhort the Thessalonians to grow in love; he looked to the Lord to work in their hearts: "May the Lord make your love increase and overflow for each other and for everyone else, just as ours does for you" (1 Thessalonians 3:12). As we see instances in our lives of failing to love, we should confess them to God, asking Him to help us grow in those specific areas and be more sensitive to such occasions in the future.

Finally, we must obey. We must do those things that love dictates. We must do no harm to our neighbor (Romans 13:10); we must meet our neighbor's needs and forgive our neighbor's wrongs against us. We must put his interests before our own, and we must reach out and embrace our brother in Christ. But we must do all this in dependence upon the Holy Spirit, who works in us to will and to act according to His good purpose.

Does this all sound too methodical? Can we in fact structure love? No; nor can we structure the work of the Holy Spirit in our lives. But we can structure our responsibilities in seeking to grow in love. We can decide to meditate on Scripture—and set aside a time to do it. We can decide to pray over our need to grow in love—and set aside time to do it. We can think of people who need our time, our interest, or our money, and plan to meet those needs. We can admit our failures to love in specific situations and bring those failures to God in confession and dependence upon Him for His help in the future.

All these things we can do, and we *must* do, if we are to grow in the grace of love. But we must do them all in the utter realization that only God can cause love to grow within our souls. And we know that it is His will that we grow in love.

As we do our part, we can count on God to perform His, not because our working obligates Him to work, but because He is a gracious and loving God, and He wants us to become gracious and loving children of His.

NOTES
1. Bethune, *The Fruit of the Spirit*, page 40.
2. Bethune, page 41.
3. Bethune, page 38.
4. W. E. Vine, *An Expository Dictionary of New Testament Words*, page 693.
5. Jerry Bridges, *The Pursuit of Holiness*, pages 101-102.

# 18
# Reaching the Goal

*I have fought the good fight, I have finished the race,*
*I have kept the faith.*

2 Timothy 4:7

The practice of godliness is a discipline. It requires serious commitment and persevering effort to reach the goal. Writing to the Philippians near the end of his life from a Roman prison cell, Paul acknowledged that he had not yet reached it. He still running the race of godliness; he still wanted to know Christ more and become more like Him.

What kept Paul going as he strained toward what was ahead? What motivating factor did he count on when he wrote to Timothy, "train yourself to be godly," fully knowing that such training was an arduous task, full of difficulties and discouragements? Someone has remarked that desire without discipline breeds disappointment, but discipline without desire breeds drudgery. Was the pursuit of a godly life a drudgery to Paul? Did he expect Timothy in his discipline toward godliness simply to grit his teeth and endure the Christian life?

## PAUL'S MOTIVATION

Paul's description of his own practice of godliness, in Philippians 3:12-14, answers these questions. He was deeply motivated. There is no suggestion of either disappointment or drudgery. He was running a disciplined race, but he was running it with strong desire. What was the source of Paul's motivation, the object of his strong desire? Let's take a close look at the passage in Philippians:

> Not that I have already obtained all this, or have already been made perfect, but I press on to take hold of that for which Christ Jesus took hold of me. Brothers, I do not consider myself yet to have taken hold of it. But one thing I do: Forgetting what is behind and straining toward what is ahead, I press on toward the goal to win the prize for which God has called me heavenward in Christ Jesus.

Paul admitted that he had not obtained the goal of godliness. He had not yet been made perfect; he was still running the race. Note the intensity, though, of his running. He declares, "I press on . . . straining toward what is ahead." The word translated "press on" is the same word translated "pursue" in such passages as 1 Timothy 6:11, 2 Timothy 2:22, and 1 Peter 3:11. It is also the same word for "persecute," which means to track down and harass or torment. It is a word of great intensity. "Strain toward" brings to our minds the attitude of the runner with his eye fixed firmly on the goal, his body bent forward, every muscle and nerve in his body straining to reach the goal. Anyone who has ever seen the look of agony on the faces of runners straining for the tape can readily recognize the intensity conveyed by the verb "strain toward." Yet this intensity was Paul's experience, day in and day out. Paul never had an off season; he never slacked off in his efforts. It was a lifelong discipline. How could he sustain such intensity? Was it because of his intense personality, and thus unique to him and those of like temperament? Or was there a motivation in Paul's heart that should be the common experience of every Christian?

In verses 12 and 14, Paul speaks of two motivating factors. In verse 12 he presses on to take hold of that for which Christ Jesus took hold of him. In verse 14 he presses on to win the prize for which God had called him heavenward in Christ Jesus. The first speaks of God's *objective* for him; the second speaks of God's *reward* for him. Let us look at each of these to see how they so strongly motivated Paul.

CHRIST'S OBJECTIVE FOR US

Paul pressed on to take hold of that for which Christ took hold of him. He earnestly strove to reach Christ's objective for him. What was this objective? Titus 2:14 tells us that Christ "gave himself for us to redeem us from all wickedness and to purify for himself a people that are his very own, eager to do what is good." Christ Jesus' objective in dying for us was to redeem us *from* sin—not merely from its penalty, but from its power and dominion. The same thought is expressed in the word *purify*, which speaks of the inward cleansing from the pollution and defilement of sin.

Ephesians 5:25-27 expresses the same idea of Christ giving Himself for His church "to make her holy, cleansing her by the washing with water through the word, and to present her to himself as a radiant church, without stain or wrinkle or any other blemish, but holy and blameless." That is Christ's objective for us. That is why He died. That is the purpose for which He took hold of Paul on the Damascus road and for which He takes hold of us individually to bring us to faith in Himself. He died to save us not only from the guilt of sin, but from sin's power and pollution. He died not to make us happy, but to make us holy.

But there is still more to Christ's objective for us. Titus 2:14 also speaks of us as "a people that are his very own, eager to do what is good." A people of "his very own" refers to His Lordship in our lives: "You are not your own; you were bought at a price" (1 Corinthians 6:19-20). "Eager to do what is good" refers to the working out of the fruit of the Spirit, the traits of godly character in our lives.

This, then, is the objective for which Christ Jesus took hold of Paul, and for which He has taken hold of us: He intends to make us holy—to purify us from the pollution of sin in our lives. He intends to be Lord of our lives, and He intends that we exhibit the traits of godly character.

That was Paul's objective also. That was the goal toward which he pressed, the aim of his strenuous effort. It would have been unthinkable to Paul to pursue any other aim in life than that for which Christ Jesus had taken hold of him.

Note how God-centered Paul's motivation was. It was the keen awareness of Christ's objective for him that caused Paul to press on with such intensity. How different we so often are from Paul. All too often we are motivated by desires other than Christ's objectives for us. As I have observed earlier, we may often be motivated by a desire for "victory" or a desire to "feel good about ourselves," or a desire to conform to the lifestyle of the Christian fellowship with which we have become associated. We may even be motivated by pride, by a desire for a good reputation in the community, especially in our church or Christian group.

None of these motivations will sustain a daily "pressing on" such as that which characterized Paul's life and which should characterize ours. Some of them, such as the desire to conform and the desire for reputation, focus on goals that fall far short of Paul's goal of godly perfection. These goals can be easily met; we don't have to deal with inner corruption, only outward acts. Other goals such as a desire for "victory" or "feeling good about ourselves" are basically self-centered goals. Instead of spurring us on, they all too often discourage us because they set up within us a struggle between two self-centered desires: the desire to feel good about ourselves and the desire to indulge ourselves.

The currently popular desire to "feel good about myself" is quite distinct from genuine godly self-respect, however. The former focuses on self; the latter focuses on God. The former depends upon our own efforts or the affirmation of other people; the latter depends upon God's grace. Godly self-respect is possible when we realize that we are created in the image of God, that we are accepted by God solely on the merits of Jesus Christ, that nothing we will ever do will cause Him to love us more or love us less, and that He has a plan for our lives and will enable us through His Spirit to live out that plan. The person with godly self-respect freely admits that nothing good lives in his sinful nature. But he also knows that nothing—not even his sin or failures—can separate him from God's love. He has decided that since God has accepted him on the basis of His grace, he will accept himself on the same basis: God's grace. He therefore looks outside of himself to Christ to find his self-respect. He strives toward the goal not to win acceptance, but because he has already been accepted.

The first of Paul's motivating drives, then, was the desire to take hold of that for which Jesus Christ took hold of him. He desired perfection in godly character, though he knew he would never attain it in this life. But he knew it was for this purpose that Jesus died for him, and he longed for that purpose to be fulfilled so Jesus Christ might be satisfied. This same earnest desire should motivate each of us today.

## THE DESIRE FOR GOD'S PRIZE

Not only did Paul press on toward Christ's objective for him; he also pressed on to win the prize for which God called him heavenward in Christ Jesus. What is this prize which so motivated Paul that he strove for it with great intensity? Jac J. Müller answers, "the prize of this calling toward which he presses forward with all his might, is the everlasting, heavenly glory."[1] Paul knew his citizenship was in heaven, and he pressed on to obtain that heavenly prize. His mind was not on earthly things, but on the glory that would be his when Christ transformed his lowly body so that it would be like Christ's glorious body.

If the prize, however, is the glory of eternal life, wasn't Paul already assured of that reward? Would a man strive with Paul's intensity to win what was already his as a gift of God's grace? The Bible is quite clear that the glory of eternal life is given to us solely through the redeeming work of Jesus Christ on the cross. It is the gift of God (Romans 6:23); it is by grace through faith—not by works (Ephesians 2:8-9). Yet it is also true that this gift cannot be taken for granted. True grace always produces vigilance rather than complacency; it always produces perseverance rather than indolence. Saving faith always manifests itself by the pursual of the heavenly goal.

The same Savior who said, "I give them eternal life, and they shall never perish" (John 10:28) also said, "Strive to enter by the narrow door; for many, I tell you, will seek to enter and will not be able" (Luke 13:24, NASB). The same apostle Peter who said, "In his great mercy he has given us new birth . . . into an inheritance that can never perish" (1 Peter 1:3-4), also said, "Therefore, my brothers, be all the more eager to make your calling and election sure" (2 Peter 1:10). And Paul himself, who said nothing "will be able to separate us from the love of God that is in Christ Jesus our

Lord" (Romans 8:39), also said, "I beat my body and make it my slave so that after I have preached to others, I myself will not be disqualified for the prize" (1 Corinthians 9:27).

Commenting on Paul's strong language to the Corinthians, Charles Hodge says,

> What an argument and reproof is this! The reckless and listless Corinthians thought they could safely indulge themselves to the very verge of sin, while this devoted apostle considered himself engaged in a life struggle for his salvation. This same apostle, however, who evidently acted on the principle that the right-eous scarcely are saved, and that the kingdom of heaven suffereth violence, at other times breaks out in the most joyful assurance of salvation. . . . The one state of mind is the necessary condition of the other.[2]

This is the great antinomy of the New Testament: the apparent contradiction between grace and personal responsibility. But it is there, and we avoid it at our peril.

But Paul was not concerned about theological knots at this point. He was simply baring his soul about the deep wellsprings of personal motivation, the secret of his ceaseless drive toward the goal. And what is that inner source? It is the glory of heaven.

Over and over again the Bible holds forth the glory of heaven as a motivation for Christian perseverance (see, for example, Romans 5:1-5, 2 Corinthians 5:1-5, Hebrews 12:22-29, and 1 Peter 4:12-13). One of the old masters of the Puritan era, Thomas Manton, said of this motivation,

> What is the reason Paul was so earnest that a little grace would not content him, but he was striving for more so earnestly and zealously? He was called to

enjoy a high prize, a glorious reward. There is excellent glory set before us; this race is not for trifles. Christians are the more cold and careless in the spiritual life because they do not oftener think of heaven.[3]

How do we respond to the motivational drives of the apostle Paul? Does the love of Christ so compel us that we also press on to take hold of that goal of godly perfection for which Christ Jesus took hold of us? Does the glory of heaven and the prospect of that prize draw us forward so that we too strain toward what is ahead? We have considered many of the character traits of the godly person. Here, though, are two over-arching traits that clearly distinguish the godly person. His attention is focused on Christ's objective for him, and his eye is fixed on heaven. He is God-centered in his devotion, and he strives to be Godlike in his character.

In Philippians 3:12-14, Paul describes himself as still running the race. In 2 Timothy 4:7, he speaks as one who has now finished the race: "I have fought the good fight, I have finished the race, I have kept the faith." Dear reader, when you and I come to the end of life's journey, will we, too, be able to utter those words? Only if we have obeyed Paul's command in 1 Timothy 4:7-8 to Timothy and to us: "Train yourself to be godly," and if we have kept before us the companion promise, "Godliness has value for all things, holding promise for both the present life and the life to come."

NOTES

1. Müller, "The Epistles of Paul to the Philippians and to Philemon," *The New International Commentary on the New Testament*, page 124.

2. Hodge, *An Exposition of the First Epistle to the Corinthians* (Edinburgh, Scotland: The Banner of Truth Trust, 1959), page 169.

3. Thomas Manton, *The Complete Works of Thomas Manton*, Vol. 16 (Worthington, Penn.: Maranatha Publications, n.d.), page 178.

# About the Author

JERRY BRIDGES is an author and Bible teacher. He has authored several books, including *The Discipline of Grace* and *Trusting God* (both NavPress). Jerry is currently a part of the Navigator collegiate ministry group where he is involved in staff training and serves as a resource to campus ministries. Jerry and his wife, Jane, have two grown children and three grandchildren.